The Politics of Chinese Language and Culture

The Politics of Chinese Language and Culture combines the concepts and methods of cultural studies with a thorough knowledge of China, in a wide-ranging and accessible introduction to contemporary Chinese language and culture.

The authors apply ideas from semiotics, critical linguistics and discourse theory to the teaching and learning of the Chinese language and culture, and build up a repertoire of ways of reading China through many kinds of cultural texts. Such texts include traditional and contemporary fiction, literary criticism, journalism, film and popular culture, comics and the customs of everyday life. The book explains some of the mysteries of the Chinese language in its written code and grammar, showing how and why it is often ambiguous, and the ideological and discursive functions it serves. It also examines the intricacies of Chinese identities and sexualities in well-known classics and unusual political tracts.

This new text challenges the traditional approaches to Chinese Studies and will also prompt Cultural Studies students to question their own cultural assumptions. It will be essential reading for students who wish to find an intellectually exciting and relevant conceptual framework for Chinese Studies.

Bob Hodge is Foundation Professor in Humanities at the University of Western Sydney, Hawkesbury. **Kam Louie** is Professor of Chinese Studies and Head of the Department of Asian Languages and Studies at the University of Queensland.

Culture and communication in Asia
Edited by David Birch
Deakin University, Australia

Trajectories
Inter-Asia Cultural Studies
Edited by Kuan-Hsing Chen

Constructing 'Post-Colonial' India
National Character and the Doon School
Sanjay Srivastava

Culture, Politics and Television in Hong Kong
Eric Ma

The Politics of Chinese Language and Culture

The art of reading dragons

Bob Hodge and Kam Louie

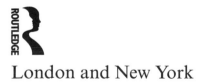

London and New York

First published 1998
by Routledge
11 New Fetter Lane, London EC4P 4EE

Simultaneously published in the USA and Canada
by Routledge
29 West 35th Street, New York, NY 10001

Typeset in Times by RefineCatch Limited, Bungay, Suffolk
Printed and bound in Great Britain by
Biddles Ltd, Guildford and King's Lynn

British Library Cataloguing in Publication Data
A catalogue record for this book is available
from the British Library

Library of Congress Cataloging in Publication Data
A catalogue record for this book is available
from the Library of Congress

ISBN 0-415-17265-9 (hbk)
ISBN 0-415-17266-7 (pbk)

To
Anna, John, Jen
Chris and Alex

Contents

Figures

Series Editor's Foreword

Critical scholarship in cultural and communication studies world wide has resulted in an increased awareness of the need to reconsider some of the more traditional research practices and theoretical/analytic domains of arts, humanities and social science disciplines, towards a recognition of the differing imperatives of what critical studies of culture and communication might look like in an Asian context. The demands for research materials, undergraduate textbooks and postgraduate monographs grow and expand with this increased critical awareness, while developments across the world continue to recognise the need to situate work in communication and cultural studies on and in Asia within a more global framework.

This series is designed to contribute to those demands and recognition. It is aimed at looking in detail at cultural and communication studies from critical perspectives which take into account different 'Asian' imperatives. In particular, it focuses on work written by scholars either living in or working on the region, who have specific interests in opening up new agendas for what constitutes critical communication and cultural studies within and about Asia. The overall aims of the series are to present new work, new paradigms, new theoretical positions, and new analytic practices of what might often be traditional and well established communication and cultural activities and discourses.

The theoretical direction of the series is principally targeted at establishing these new agendas and by critically reflecting upon the appropriateness, or otherwise, of theories and methodologies already well established, or developing, in cultural and communication studies across the world. Having said this, however, the series is not aimed at producing a monolithic blueprint for what constitutes critical cultural and communication studies in or about Asia. Nor is there a specific agenda for what the series might consider to be an appropriate critical cultural and communication studies for Asia.

The series is not, therefore, designed to create an orthodoxy for 'Asian' communication and cultural studies, but to open up new ways of thinking and rethinking contemporary cultural and communication practice and analysis in the arts, humanities and social sciences. The series is aimed to counter, as much as possible, those essentialising processes of colonialisation, marginalisation, and erasure, which have taken place in the past by the unproblematised imposition of western theory upon cultures, societies, and practices within, and on behalf of, Asia.

Many of the books in this series may not necessarily fit comfortably into traditional disciplines and paradigms of Asian studies of cultural and communication studies, and nor are they intended to. The main aim of the series is for all of its books to argue for a diversification and opening up of existing theoretical positions and specific discourses across a wide range of texts, practices and cultures. All of the books in the series will be positioned to argue persuasively for the development of studies in culture and communication which are able to frame critical commentary through theoretical and analytic practices informed first and foremost by a concern with Asian cultures and discourse.

The series has as its fundamental premise a position which argues that analysts can no longer operate as neutral, disinterested, observers of some 'reality' which supposedly pre-exists the discourses that they are analysing. To be critical necessarily means to be self-reflexive. In that sense, then, the series is designed to position cultural and communication studies in and about Asia as critical disciplines which require, within their own practices, an approach to developing some sort of praxis that enables the work that we do as analysts to significantly contribute to political, social, and cultural discourses and awareness, at both the local, regional, and global levels.

Series Editor: David Birch, Deakin University, Australia

Editorial Advisors
Ien Ang, Murdoch University, Australia
Tony Bennett, Griffith University, Australia
Chen Kuan Hsing, National Tsing Hwa University, Taiwan
Jae-Woong Choe, Korea University, Korea
Chua Beng Huat, National University of Singapore, Singapore
Lawrence Grossberg, University of North Carolina, Chapel Hill, USA
Sneja Gunew, University of Victoria, Canada
Annette Hamilton, Macquarie University, Australia
Ariel Heryanto, Universitas Kristen Satya Wacana, Indonesia
Masao Miyoshi, University of California, San Diego, USA
Yoshinobu Ota, University of Kyushu, Japan
Gyanendra Pandey, University of Delhi, India
Ubonrat Siriyuvasak, Chulalongkorn University, Thailand
Panuti Sudjiman, University of Indonesia, Indonesia
Trinh T. Minh-ha, University of California, Berkeley, USA
Yao Souchou, Institute of Southeast Asian Studies, Singapore
Robert Young, Wadham College, Oxford, UK

Preface

This book has been a delight to write. It is the result of a ten-year conversation between the authors, and it incorporates many aspects of our independent research in Chinese Culture and Cultural Studies. Both of us felt that our respective disciplines had much territory which needed to be explored. In the ten years since the book was first conceived, there has indeed been a great widening of terrain in both disciplines and we have had to change our own focus and writing a number of times. The process of sharing and reworking our ideas has been an exciting one. We hope that the readers of this book will share some of this excitement and that the book will act as a stimulus for re-reading different cultures.

We began our project at Murdoch University. Bob has since moved to the University of Western Sydney while Kam moved to the University of Queensland. To colleagues at all three universities, we would like to express our thanks for their ideas and support. We have benefited from the help and advice of Louise Edwards, Gabriela Coronado, Zhu Daomin, Yewjin Fang, Rachelle Allen, David Goodman, Tim Wright, Katrina Schlunke and Jane Williamson-Fien. Louise in particular has been a constant source of insights and challenges which have benefited the work in countless ways. David Birch as Series Editor believed in our work and supported it all the way; and Victoria Smith from Routledge gave invaluable guidance and tactful help. To them all, we express our sincere thanks. We are also grateful to the University of Queensland for a grant which enabled us to get together on a number of occasions to continue our collaborative work.

During our academic careers, our fascination with cultures and ideas has meant that we were able to spend much less time with our children than we would have liked. Dedicating this book to them is but a small token of our abiding affection and love.

1 How to read dragons

The politics of understanding Chinese culture

This book represents the results of a dialogue between Chinese Studies and Cultural Studies to generate new meanings about the two disciplines. China today is vast, complex, dynamic and heterogeneous. Its boundaries, physical and cultural, are unstable, organised by categories that are collapsing into each other, reforming, reconfiguring themselves. Economic, technological and social developments that collectively have been called postmodernism have produced cultural forms in a global culture that is so different from the culture of late capitalism that some have claimed that the previous categories of analysis are no longer applicable. 'China' is eagerly leaping into this global world of postmodern culture, while still negotiating the claims of traditional Chinese values and a state socialist system. New technologies are being introduced which may have unpredictable effects on the central discursive forms of contemporary China.

Two hundred years ago Napoleon reputedly called China 'the sleeping dragon', in awe at its potential power. Now the 'dragon' is well and truly awake. The Asian region is politically and economically the most dynamic part of the contemporary world system. Within this region, China and Chinese culture and society cumulatively represent perhaps the greatest single challenge to Western assumptions of political, cultural and economic superiority. China contains approximately one quarter of the population of the world, and is an indispensable player in the new world system. Mainland China is the largest political unit that has ever existed, and its language and culture are an intrinsic part of that political achievement, one of the most amazing achievements of human culture. And then there is the 'diaspora', 55 million overseas Chinese, a larger population than Great Britain with a GNP of $450 billion in 1994, 25 per cent more than the whole of mainland China (Seagrave 1995: 15). Chinese language and culture reach beyond the mainland, and overseas Chinese communities are influential throughout the Asia-Pacific region. Across the boundaries in maps which define the political entity that is 'China', the diversity of life within China and the diaspora is changing so rapidly that it would be futile to try to fix its meaning definitively.

At the same time notions of Chineseness are rapidly becoming more fuzzy, as cultural and national identities are called into question. Allen Chun expressed one response in the title of a recent article, 'Fuck Chineseness: On the Ambiguities of Ethnicity as Culture as Identity' (1996: 111). The readers we seek, the 'new generation' we refer to, are as heterogeneous as this new China in background, identity and purpose. Some may have Chinese origins, recent or remote. Others may be non-Chinese but fascinated with China, committed to live and work in some way that involves close contact with Chinese people and Chinese culture. Many others may be positioned less clearly between China and the West, seeking precisely to extricate themselves from a conditioning that places such absolute boundaries around ideas and identities of 'East' and 'West', aspiring after more comprehensive forms of knowledge of themselves and their culture that will be more open and critical, less racist and Eurocentric.

In carrying out this task we draw on an exciting new set of approaches to the study of language and culture that have recently emerged in the West. Sometimes these are brought together and labelled 'Cultural Studies' but they also exist independently, as a tendency that has in various ways touched and transformed every discipline in the Humanities and Social Sciences. The ideas in this loose confederation of disciplines do not comprise a single new discipline which can be simply applied to this new set of problems, the 'problem of China', to produce a definitive new knowledge of China. On the contrary, the task of understanding China, 'reading the dragon', is a major challenge for all disciplinary knowledges in the West. The assumptions and ideas in current Western-style Cultural Studies are not exempt from this challenge. They too have a history, formed in an intellectual environment that has been Euro-centric in countless subtle ways. 'Cultural Studies' needs to be open to the challenge of understanding China if it is to understand itself.

Dragons at the gate: Sinology and the study of Chinese culture

There is a new awareness of the importance of China in the West. The signs seem good: an end to the dark ages of Western ignorance of China, as rapid a change as anyone could hope for. Presidents and Prime Ministers make pilgrimages to Beijing, and China is respected as a major political and economic force, reported in all the main media. The study of Chinese in schools and universities has increased dramatically over the past two decades in the USA and Australia, though not so much in the UK, supported by governments who see the urgency of the need.

This book is written out of the conviction that all this is not nearly enough, in scale or quality. To understand this huge phenomenon is not something that can be handed over to a few specialists. It is everyone's business. Our goal, utopian though it may sound, is to make this kind of understanding, in different forms and at different levels, available to everyone in every contemporary English-speaking nation, as a basic right of citizenship. What is needed is not just a doubling or trebling of the numbers who study Chinese and China, but a quantum leap in numbers, a Gestalt shift in approach.

The core problem here is the continuing hold of traditional methods of studying China. There are more departments of Chinese or Asian Studies, with more undergraduates studying in them, more students in schools learning Chinese and other Asian languages, but the numbers involved are still totally inadequate, and the assumptions behind most of these programmes are profoundly limiting. They set up a curriculum that is often narrowly language or literature-based, demanding and exclusive. In the past, when this was the only way that Chinese could have any presence in universities, this form of curriculum was the best way of maintaining some level of interest in China and Chinese. Today, it is precisely these assumptions that are holding Chinese Studies back from being the broad, flexible and inclusive form of studies that would be even more viable and attractive if only it could find its place.

In the past, Western 'experts' on China were mainly Europeans trained in the 'Sinological' tradition. Sinology (from *Sinae*, the Chinese, *logos*, the study of) in the nineteenth century was an elitist pursuit, run by the few Westerners who understood enough of the language to seem qualified to pronounce with authority what the mysterious mind of the East really thought. Their assumptions and practices developed over a long period in specific political contexts, situated in host societies with long and deeply embedded histories of xenophobia and ignorance about all things Chinese. Governments in the West have continued in the main to establish and instruct Asian language departments with the express purpose of meeting 'the demands of commerce and diplomacy' (Barrett 1989: 119). As a result, academic Sinologists have often felt pressured to be more 'practical' while by inclination they prefer to be more esoterically scholarly. In reality, Sinologists were a very small minority of the population, and they were situated in environments which were not conducive to interacting with ordinary Chinese people on an everyday basis. Their understanding of the language and culture therefore tended to concentrate on the classical past. Although some of them, such as the first Oxford Professor of Chinese, James Legge, were excellent scholars, in practice they often had to rely on ethnic Chinese experts such as Wang Tao in their work.

Given their background, European Sinologists who dominated departments in Western universities between 1850 and 1980 tended to value above all linguistic competence in older forms of the language. They provided the kind of understanding of China that their societies and times demanded and felt was sufficient. They felt no need to make this knowledge widely available. In their view, only a small elite could or should know it, in order to carry the tradition to a new elite. All this historical and ideological baggage is unhelpful and possibly harmful to Chinese Studies outside China if it is to become a major presence in the curriculum, as part of a sea-change in Western societies. Old-style Chinese Studies multiplied by ten or a hundred would not meet the new needs, and old-style Chinese Studies would strongly resist any such expansion, on ideological and pedagogical grounds.

In contrast, we want knowledge about China to circulate as freely and widely as possible. The 'China' we seek to understand is not a single oppressive object out there, remote in time and space, protected by layer upon layer of specialist knowledge. We are interested in how meanings are generated in and about China in many sites, functioning as part of its language and culture in the broadest sense. We try to insert these processes in a wider politics as the key to their understanding, the reason for their importance.

To illustrate what is at stake for a politics and practice of reading in our strategy for 'reading dragons', we will contrast two ways of reading: 'Sinological' and 'cultural studies'. First, there is a warning built into the inverted commas around the two approaches. Tidy-minded readers might want us to define what we mean by these two terms before we then go on to apply them. We want to work in the other direction, starting with definitions which are fuzzy and inclusive but which allow the exploration of concrete instances to begin, allowing the full complexity and heterogeneity of the terms to emerge slowly as the work continues.

We begin by looking at two images of dragons. The first is embroidered on a silk robe from the Qing dynasty of the nineteenth century, currently displayed in the Gulbenkian Museum of Oriental Arts in Durham, England. The second comes from a mug, made in China and bought in Sydney, Australia, for $A2.50 in 1993.

The first kind of image is at home in museums or the private collections of rich connoisseurs: precious, rare, exotic, hand-made in a foreign court over 100 years ago, apparently untouched by the taint of modern life or Western influence. From a Sinological point of view, this object can be seen to carry the mysterious essence of the real China; it is beautiful in itself and yet quaint and mysterious to ignorant Westerners, in need of expert (Sinological) interpretation. The circle in the centre, for instance, is the disk traditionally associated with dragons. Scholars dispute whether it represents a pearl, the moon, the earth or cosmos, but the masses would hardly know or bother. This dragon has five claws, again a coded meaning, signifying that it is an imperial dragon (and hence, from this point of view, more truly Chinese). Commoners' dragons had only four claws. The pleasure of this kind of textual interpretation is limited to scholars, who can have the vicarious pleasure of living in an exotic world of emperors and their courts, in which the centre was privileged, and its domination over all systems of meaning was complete. Nostalgia for the imperial regime is part of the meaning that Sinologists clung to and which they sought to preserve, under the pretext that they were preserving the essence of China itself.

In contrast, the image reproduced on the mug is mass-produced, cheap, designed as much for export as for home consumption, a familiar and functional shape for anyone who buys it in the West. At the time of writing it is difficult to estimate how many mugs of tea or coffee this one has contained, on how many pleasurable occasions, embedded in the informal practices and routines of everyday life. Of course, a Sinologist might say, this mug tells us less than nothing about China, now or in the past.

Figure 1.1 Dragon embroidered on a silk robe from the Qing dynasty, currently displayed in the Gulbenkian Museum of Oriental Arts in Durham, England

But the mug's design draws as much on tradition as the embroidered dragon. There is no easily available 'authentic version' to demonstrate the superiority of the imperial design. Attentive eyes can see the energy of the two dragons on the mug, the clouds they fly amongst and the waves they hover above. The disc is easier to identify than the one in the embroidery, with its smiling face on a shape like a new moon, trailing strange clouds. This mug represents two dragons, not one as on the robe. This is a common iconographical form with dragons, where two of them play with or fight over the 'pearl', like *yin* and *yang* in the dualist universe of traditional China. The Qing dynasty did not invent the meaning of dragons, they appropriated a meaning whose origins are lost in the deep past, part of a common heritage of Chinese people.

All this meaning is a bonus. At $A2.50 this mug was bargain enough. It and many others like it have entered houses and homes in Western countries, bearing an unobtrusive, rich set of meanings that are not kept in a few museums, visited only by dedicated visitors or school parties, but freely circulating and in general use. In order to understand either image, it's true, you need background, both specific and generic. The French sociologist

Figure 1.2 Mug costing $A2.50, made in China, illustrated with two dragons playing
with 'dragon pearl'

Pierre Bourdieu (1984) found that people need a kind of 'cultural capital',
which he argued is distributed along class lines, in order to be able to appreciate and enjoy museums. The same is true for Chinese mugs. This 'capital' is
not a set of specific facts about China or dragons, but a generic orientation,
which can be developed equally well with everyday and accessible objects.
Not every school class can go to Durham's Gulbenkian Museum of Oriental
Art, but all children can take a closer look at mugs and other things that they
have bought cheaply in local markets, or watch a Chinese New Year parade.
China has left the museums of the West and taken to the market place.

Not every commodity from China bears such traces of Chineseness, but
global trade has made China part of everyday life and culture in the West.
Western consumer goods have similarly found a place in Chinese life. This
mug is a signifier of that new global reality, as well as a bearer of signs of
Chinese culture and tradition. Neither meaning is closed or unambiguous, or
politically innocent. Both have a latent politics. What we call the Sinological

reading of the mug despises the contemporary, the commercial, defending the interests of a now irrelevant empire, thereby sustaining the status of their modern Western supporters. It is a politics of cultural separatism. A pluralistic reading such as we have sketched is politically inclusive. It situates the reading of the object in the life of the two societies and in their interaction. The openness of the reading it encourages is an invitation to cross-cultural collaboration, a move towards mutual understanding.

The semiotics of Chinese culture

Perhaps the single most powerful and enabling assumption in the various developments that make up the field of Cultural Studies is its redefinition of 'language', making it an object so comprehensive that it comes to cover almost the same ground as culture itself. Language of course has always been recognised as important in understanding different cultures, but in the 'linguistic turn' that Cultural Studies has taken, it becomes possible to say that culture itself is a language or set of languages, made up of different kinds of text, circulating under various constraints.

Such a claim is only credible because of the redefinition of language that goes under the name of *semiotics*, particularly in the form of semiotics known as social semiotics. Social semiotics as developed in Hodge and Kress (1988), provides the basic framework for the rest of this book, so we will take some time here to explain some of its key terms and principles. But readers should not suppose that this is a new and separate sub-discipline within Cultural Studies. It's more like a particular route through the same territory, with well-marked roads leading off it to other sites of interest in the same broad domain. It has particular advantages for our purposes in this book, which is concerned with the interrelations of Chinese language, culture and politics. Social semiotics extends the concept of language further than most other approaches in Cultural Studies, and provides powerful methods of analysing details of language and texts, including aspects of grammar and syntax, which immediately present as problems to non-Chinese in their first encounter with the language and culture.

Semiotics itself is basically a simple concept. It refers to the study of all sign systems, all the media and means by which humans and other animals communicate or have communicated with each other. Verbal languages like English or Chinese are semiotic systems that have been extensively studied. Other sign systems that are crucial in social life have not been so systematically studied, although members of a culture need to acquire the full range of sign systems in order to cope with the various demands made on them by others. We call all these systems 'languages', which together make up the repertoire of ways by which people make sense of themselves and the actions and objects they are immersed in: their culture.

There is one seemingly large problem with this approach: the word 'language' itself. This is part of the English language, referring basically to the spoken and written forms. We don't want to rewrite English, even if we could. So we continue to use the word in its usual sense, as well as in its extended semiotic sense. We write of 'language and culture', which ought to be non-sense for us, if language and culture cover more or less the same territory. But we do not see this as a problem in practice. The context makes it clear how we are using the word. It is only a problem in theory, in a theory we don't agree with, which aims at a purity of meaning which is not the normal condition of language.

In spite of its obviousness, the core idea of semiotics as applied to Western culture initially met with resistance in Western academic circles. The Western curriculum in the humanities and social sciences is highly word-centred. Most academics are trained as experts in words and the use of verbal resources. Relatively small departments of art history existed for the study of visual texts, and the mass media were difficult to ignore completely, but basically the experts on the word who dominated the curriculum felt no need to go outside verbal language. Semiotics was a challenge to the basis of their expertise.

Chinese culture challenges these assumptions. Even classical Sinology is more semiotic than Western disciplines because Chinese culture is more overtly semiotic than the Western system of codes. Painting and writing are interrelated in Chinese culture. The word for 'write' 写 (*xie*), for instance, can also mean 'to paint'; 'painting from life' is *xiesheng* 写生 and 'free-hand brushwork in painting' is *xieyi* 写意. Texts combine words and pictures more typically than is the case in Western culture. Thus, Chinese paintings inevitably incorporate the artists' calligraphy as part of the creative process. Chinese culture is strongly visual and semiotically promiscuous, and the study of Chinese needs to be semiotically broader than the study of European languages has been.

Our example of the two dragons illustrates something of the scope of social semiotics. A mug and a robe can be readable texts as much as books or paintings. What we read in this way is not simply a set of meanings encoded in different media, but social meanings which circulate through various con-texts and uses. These social meanings are not only local meanings confined to a particular text but generic, constructing images of nation and class. They also produce kinds of 'subject', kinds of readers and users of these texts who are positioned by particular kinds of reading. The mug is not simply a picture of a dragon, it is a commodity that is used and read in different ways in different contexts. The embroidered dragon functioned behind the walls of the 'Forbidden City' in the nineteenth century with different meanings and effects from its present resting place, behind a glass wall in a provincial museum in England, where it produces readers who feel knowledgeable, included in an elite, and others who feel excluded, ignorant.

The value of this approach is that everything potentially carries meanings about the culture and social forms: the full set of codes, popular and elite, visual and verbal, and the full set of practices through which everyday life is lived and has its meanings. So we look at various practices and customs, greeting rituals and classroom protocols, ways of eating, dressing, walking and talking, at comics and films, posters and paintings and photographs, as a small sample of the infinite set of texts through which meaning is encountered and negotiated in and about China today.

A social semiotic approach is always alert to the ways that power acts through and on semiotic codes and practices. The connection is so close that a given language would not have the forms it has if it did not serve particular social and political functions, and those functions in their current form would not be able to exist outside the available semiotic resources (codes and practices). This generalisation is as profoundly true of Chinese as of English, French and all other semiotic systems. But the way this works is not simple or predictable, across languages or even within them.

China for instance is not a simple, homogeneous nation, and the Chinese language has a complex political relationship to the notion of 'China'. Within China there is not just one language, but a multiplicity of languages, ranging from Tibetan and Mongolian to the majority Han language. Even in the Han language, the spoken form has hundreds of different varieties, many of them as different as Spanish is from Italian. The official language, 'Mandarin' or *putonghua*, serves the same political function as English once did in the British Isles, to integrate the nation, or as English did for the old 'British Empire'. Like English across the empire, even *putonghua*, the standard language, is spoken in different ways in different parts of mainland China, which have immediate political readings and effects. And then there are Taiwan and Hong Kong, with their form of the standard language existing alongside other forms of Chinese or other languages, and the similarities and differences are currently of intense and explicitly political interest.

Language and power have always had a problematic relationship in the understanding of China. For most of the last 2000 years China has been a major power, an empire, and this fact has had a pervasive effect on its forms of language and culture. During the past century China has undergone a revolutionary process, and that is another important fact. The revolution has been a complex process, incorporating numerous counter-revolutions, and the process is still not over. Both the exercise of empire and the struggles for and against wholesale revolution have had to take place in terms of the givens of language and culture, which have made their own contribution to how power has been practised or challenged.

At the same time, Chinese language and culture (in some areas and aspects more obviously or more vigorously than others) are constantly being remade by a populace in the process of living through these states and all their vicissitudes. There have been various ideologically motivated attempts to reform aspects of the language, and equally ideological efforts to resist and derail the reform process. Alongside these public processes, language and culture evolve and change for reasons that may not ever be articulated. Society and culture, language and politics are inseparable components of a shifting, unstable complex. This is the smallest unit of study; not language or culture on their own but a single transdisciplinary object, society-culture-language-politics-history.

Discourse and power in China

In European Cultural Studies, a major influence has been the French theorist Michel Foucault, many of whose ideas on discourse and power are illuminating about Chinese culture and society. Of discourse he writes: 'I am supposing that in every society the production of discourse is at once controlled, selected, organised and distributed according to a certain number of procedures, whose role is to avert its powers and its dangers, to cope with chance events, to evade its ponderous, awesome materiality' (1976: 216). Discourse in these terms is concerned equally with knowledge and power, with the interweaving of effects of knowledge and power in discourse. Foucault was especially interested in what he called 'new technologies of the exercise of power' (1980: 124) which he saw as marking the boundary in Europe between the feudal period and modern techniques and technologies. In feudal societies, he argued, power 'functioned essentially through signs and levies'. The seventeenth century in Europe, especially as exemplified by the French monarchy, saw the dominance of a 'regime of spectacle' which was followed by an ever more elaborate 'regime of surveillance', continued with increasing elaboration and ingenuity into the contemporary period.

It is not our intention to apply these ideas in detail to the case of China, beyond noting that imperial China was a strongly centralised system which operated in many ways through a regime of spectacle, while socialist China is equally strongly centralised, more so than any Western nation, but operates through discursive mechanisms. The specific intricacies, permutations and elaborations in the operations of discourse and power in China over the past one hundred years are too interesting and important to be treated as a mere footnote to the history of Europe. For Foucault, the operations of power are never simple and obvious, even in systems which seem to concentrate power exclusively at a highly visible centre. Even under a monarchy in its most confident phase, power was subject to dispersals, to different rarefactions and concentrations; it was not something that was collected at the centre and redistributed. This is likely to be true of power in imperial China and also to power as wielded by the party during the Cultural Revolution period, when to outsiders it appeared most monolithic and overwhelming.

However, there are important differences between the various regimes of power, and in particular in their *discursive regimes*: that is, the systems for managing and policing discourse (who produces or evaluates what will count as true or valid knowledge and what will not, and the conditions of such truth), and how these different kinds of system operate with different systems of power, and this provides the background for analysis of particular instances of semiosis. For instance, imperial China used spectacle to construct a persuasive image of central power, in which images of dragons on imperial robes played their part. Social life in the period of the Cultural Revolution is an extreme instance of society regulated by continuous surveillance, in which everyone watched everyone else to ensure, among other things, a total absence of dragons. Both regimes required the support of verbal discourse in different forms, circulating amongst the elite and in the mass media, in posters, in debates and 'confessions'. In Chapter 5 we look in more detail at the major discursive regimes in Chinese political life and their contemporary formations and deformations, as these contribute to a wider comparative understanding of discourse and power.

'Discourse' in the sense used by Foucault and his followers is a powerful concept, so powerful that some theorists in Cultural Studies have suggested it should simply replace two other terms, 'language' and 'ideology', which once covered much the same territory now claimed by 'discourse'. Initially the idea may sound attractive to newcomers to Cultural Studies, who often complain about an excess of 'jargon'. One term instead of three sounds like it would make life easier. 'Discourse' is currently the most fashionable of the three, so it seems the obvious choice.

In this book we do not go down this road. These three terms do overlap, as different ways of understanding and thinking about the relations between meaning and power; but each one foregrounds different aspects of this complex common object in different ways. Because of their differences they allow different connections to be made, and different things become more thinkable in terms of each. The mathematics of the three-into-one solution is less straightforward than it looks. If you have one term to understand instead of three it looks as though you only have one-third of the work in learning terminology. But from another point of view this one term now has to do the work previously done by three. Each of the three is complex, and their combination into one term gives that term too much work to do. In these conditions, 'discourse' would become horrendously complex, or it would slip into a simpler concept which would lose much of its original complexity. In practice both happen all the time. It's what happened with 'language' and 'ideology' over their history. In terminology, three words are often better than one.

'Discourse' comes from the Latin *dis-currere*, literally 'to run backwards or forwards'. Its value is its emphasis on process and interaction, either a text or set of texts produced by interaction or the rules which allow that to happen. In Foucault's work, 'discourse' usually refers to a set of regularities organised in relation to one of two kinds of elements: a field of objects (e.g. 'racist discourse', 'sinologism') or an institution or agent of discourse (e.g. 'medical discourse', 'academic discourse'). 'Language' is related to the Latin *lingua*, a tongue, human speech with its grammar, vocabulary and sound systems which involve a massive learning task for all language learners, plus all the mysterious knowledges which make communication possible.

These knowledges include rules of discourse and sedimented maps of the social world, but the implicitly political affiliations of these contextual knowledges can be concealed under the seemingly neutral term 'language'. That's where the term 'ideology' is still useful. It was put into circulation by Karl Marx over a hundred years ago. Marx himself used it in a number of different ways, and later writers have added to the confusion. The word's etymological meaning is 'system of ideas', but Marx gave it a political inflection: systems of ideas that are motivated by specific political or class interests. 'Discourses' in Foucault's sense are implicated in relations and processes of power, and Foucault's ideas on discourse developed out of his reflection on the category of 'ideology'. But 'ideology' is still a useful term to add to the other two. For instance, it's helpful to be able to talk about the ideology that underpins the writing system, as we do in Chapter 3, or ideology in the system of grammar, as we do in Chapter 4.

Sinologism and the discursive construction of China

Discourse in Foucault's sense operates as part of a mechanism for social control in other spheres of public life. Sinology in the West is a classic instance of a discursive regime in this sense, in its role as a site for controlling who can speak with authority about China, what can be known and what is constituted, by the rules of this discursive formation, as forever unknowable, unspeakable, about China. In fact it is illuminating to use Foucault's ideas in this area also, to look at the processes that have constructed China in and for the West.

Here we can start from the work of Edward Said, who used Foucault's ideas on discourse to examine what he called 'Orientalism' (1978). Said was concerned to show how 'the East' was carefully constructed by Western discourses, popular as well as academic, in a way that ultimately served the political and economic interests of the Western colonising powers in the Asian region, in the 'Middle East' and throughout Asia, following the major expansion of European interests from the nineteenth century. Important to his conception was the fact that knowledge of the Oriental 'Other' was the preserve of the coloniser, or more precisely, the Occidental expert, who alone could survive contamination from immersion in the culture of the Other and transmit its meanings to the dominant society. The expert alone could speak on behalf of the Other, who could not be trusted to understand or speak in his (her) own voice.

Sinology showed many classic features of what Said called 'Orientalism'. However, for a number of reasons it is useful to propose a distinct branch of 'orientalism' which we will call 'Sinologism'. 'Sinologism' has some distinct features compared to other forms of orientalism, so that even today, some scholars insist that there is 'no orientalism in Chinese studies' (Hägerdal 1996: 31). This is hardly surprising as cultures in 'the East' and 'Middle East' are so diverse. In particular, China like Japan was not invaded and colonised, so that the forms of its appropriation in discourse were importantly different. And Sinologism can also be usefully distinguished from Sinology. Sinology is the name of an academic discipline, and as a name it has almost disappeared.

There are not many university departments with that name, and few academics who identify themselves as 'sinologists'. But Sinologism as a discourse, as a set of knowledges and assumptions about the study of China, is still alive and well, permeating popular forms as well as academic knowledges as it has always done. The specific features of Sinologism as a particular sub-species of Said's 'Orientalism' increase our understanding of the processes of orientalism itself, helping us to see better the interrelations of knowledge and power within academic disciplines themselves, challenging the old claim that academic knowledges were objective and free from social, ideological or political considerations.

In the case of Chinese, it's important to recognise that the China constructed by Sinologism was not simply a Western invention. The key assumptions of Sinologism are partial truths, which makes it especially important to address them and disentangle them from the forms in which they are packaged in classic Sinology. Sinologism takes major tendencies within Chinese culture and turns them into absolute values, essential truths about Chineseness or 'sinicity': an ideology above dispute, not a set of provisional, contested hypotheses and generalisations in need themselves of further examination and enquiry.

In every case the premises of Sinologism are in opposition to equally powerful tendencies within Chinese culture. These opposing tendencies are not the result of some Western plot, but part of the total dynamics of Chinese society, which are the real context in which to situate Sinologism. Sinologism is not just an effect of power from Western academic discourses, it is also an effect of political processes within China. China is not now and never has been a simple traditional and patriarchal society, as projected by Sinologism. But by the same token, it is unlikely ever to break completely with the powerfully conservative traditions that have been so much a part of its long history.

Sinologism is based on a number of premises. Primary among them is the belief in the necessary and inherent difficulty of the Chinese language, as the sole route into any worthwhile understanding of China. The spoken Chinese language here is understood to be *putonghua,* Mandarin, the standard language which is in practice a second language for many Chinese even within the People's Republic of China (PRC). It is a foreign language for many others, with a written form that has been simplified in the PRC but without approaching the goal of universal literacy amongst mainland Chinese.

It is undoubtedly the case that the Chinese language is difficult to learn; or more precisely, that its written form is difficult to master. This is true for Chinese people, too. This difficulty of the written script is a primary fact about Chinese, one of the keys to its ideological function, within China as well as for overseas Chinese and foreigners. But it is not a simple fact, to be accepted without question. Throughout this century there have been concerted efforts to reform the language and simplify its written form, but these have all failed. We can see something of the deeper causes of this failure in contradictions that exist in the two main justifications used to resist reforms: that the traditional script represents the Chineseness of Chinese, and that it is efficient in representing the difficult spoken language. In fact, as we will argue, it does effectively transmit a cohesive ideology of Chineseness, but it does so at a huge cost in practical efficiency. Far from disambiguating Chinese, it allows ambiguity as an endemic and highly functional aspect of written discourse. The Chinese language, especially the Chinese written code, is indeed one of the most fascinating constructions of the human mind, as Sinologism claims, but we can only appreciate the nature of its achievement through a socially and politically informed understanding of how it works.

The relative difficulty of the Chinese language is used to great advantage by Sinologists in creating the myth of a unique Chinese 'essence', 'sinicity', which can only be properly understood if you are Chinese (from the educated classes) or if you have a very special talent for decoding the culture (that is, a good training in Sinology). Until very recently, very few non-Chinese had mastered the language, so that this talent was the exclusive realm of only a select few (who were of course the judges of what counted as mastery of the language, from a Western point of view). This concern with sinicity has also been a concern amongst Chinese themselves throughout the twentieth century. Critics and defenders of traditional Chinese culture such as the iconoclastic writer Lu Xun (1881–1936) and the neo-Confucianist philosopher Liang Shuming (1893–1988) were fascinated by the idea of a 'Chinese essence' which is found only in China. This essence was defined in different ways, from the pathetically escapist 'Ah Q spirit' condemned by Lu Xun (1957a: 102–54) to the glorious Confucian 'Golden Mean' lauded by Liang Shuming (1922).

As more and more Western anthropologists, sociologists, historians, political scientists, etc. work and research in China, Taiwan and Hong Kong, the Chinese essence is evaporating. Furthermore, the number of Chinese scholars resident in the outside world has increased steadily in the last few decades. While a number have continued to cling to the idea of a Chinese essence, many have also embraced a more cosmopolitan outlook, and their attitudes are influencing their compatriots back home. However, within university Chinese departments themselves, Sinologist tendencies are still strong.

When China opened its doors to foreign tourists and business people in the 1980s, what the Western visitor found was a country without much nightlife and a drab daylife. Where was the splendour discovered by Marco Polo or the mysterious and sinister China of the Fu Manchu years? It had to be created. Chinese writers and film makers were happy to oblige. Exotic and erotic images inundate the pages of novels and cinema and television screens. As Louise Edwards indicates, translators and critics of Chinese departments were quick to select and interpret these weird and wonderful phenomena as essential aspects of Chinese culture (Edwards 1995). The twisted and contorted images were said to be non-mainstream, such as southern Chinese or Communist Chinese, but Chinese nevertheless.

These interpreters are not wrong. In a country like China, with a history of several thousand years, a population of over a billion, and an ethnic diversity of over fifty racial groups even by official reckoning, there are bound to be many fantastic and incredible practices. But these practices are exotic to most Chinese too. Indeed, as Louisa Schein has shown, the Han Chinese have also been actively 'orientalising' their own ethnic minorities (Schein 1997). The danger for students of Chinese and culture is that the exotic provides symbols and signifiers for the 'real' Chinese culture. As we will show, the search for the Chinese essence continues, a search which points to the language as well as tradition, in both its Confucian and unorthodox strands. We do not pretend to know the true nature of the 'real' China, but we do know the signs are often wrong in the directions they point to, with messages that are often ambiguous, while the signified is neither mysterious nor pure.

Chinese sexuality provides another perhaps even more stark example of discursive controls operating through Sinologism which we want to contest in our own attempts at understanding Chinese culture. Sinologism constructs traditional Chinese society as patriarchal, repressing women and sexuality in public and private life, in all forms of representation and discourse. Clearly, this was indeed the case. The traditional family and its values have been reproduced with massive consistency across major political and social changes, as Sinologism claims, and this is a phenomenon not to be discounted. But that achievement has to be seen as highly complex. To take the position of women, for instance: on the one hand the position of women in traditional China was notoriously difficult, but there has been a kind of gender revolution in China, too, and traditional language and culture contained some positive models and valuations of women. So China, past and present, is both patriarchal and yet full of positive models for gender relations. Even the classic image of the dragon participates in this ambiguity. As a creative spirit associated with water, fertility and the moon it has feminine gender, but in imperial China it was associated with highly masculine forms of power.

A similar paradox concerns forms of sexuality. The traditional patriarchal ideology, in China as in the West, was sexually repressive and heterosexist. It controlled the sexuality of men and women, and then denied the existence as well as the validity of sexual behaviours and feelings outside the dominant pattern. Sinologism takes the fact that expressions of dissident sexuality were so carefully controlled in traditional society as proof that the actions and thoughts of Chinese people, conscious and subconscious, were equally controlled. It is a massive act of denial. The reasoning, if we spell it out, is something like this. Because Chinese did not write easily about forbidden forms of sexuality, they did not feel or act on these emotions. The subconscious did not exist anywhere until Freud wrote about it at the beginning of the twentieth century. And, as he was an Austrian Jew, his ideas do not apply to Chinese society.

Sinologism offers a persuasive version of the history of China which is still alive in the contemporary West, circulating in popular media. It sees a golden age in imperial China; an un-Chinese experiment in the communist rule under Mao, epitomised by the Cultural Revolution; and a combination of traditional ethics and acceptance of the virtues of capitalism in contemporary China. But traditional values survived even during the Cultural Revolution, for social, cultural and linguistic reasons that need to be understood, and they were never homogeneous, never universal.

One paradox of Sinologism is that its dominance in the West up to the 1970s owed much to the effects of Communist rule in the PRC. Chinese policies towards the West (continuing attitudes that run deep in China's history) restricted the access of non-ethnic Chinese to the language and the momentous political and cultural events of modern China. Academic Sinologists were a scarce commodity. The new open-door policies of the Chinese towards the West have had major effects on the politics of knowledge in the academy, with significant changes to the position of Sinologism. In that context, the balance of power within academia has been further altered by the new floods of political, economic and educational emigrants from China, Taiwan and Hong Kong and the receptive West that has welcomed them. The arrival in the West of many bright young China scholars coincided with the rapid growth of Chinese Studies in recent years.

In spite of the predominance of senior Sinologists at the top in Chinese departments, the discourse of Sinologism is under threat in modern Chinese Studies. This small phalanx of traditional scholars are under pressure from younger scholars, many of them with better language skills than their professors, acquired because of easier access to China, many of them ethnic Chinese with first-hand experience of China, able to migrate to the West in the new market situation. In the last few decades the diaspora has played a vital role in enriching Chinese Studies. Scholars such as Leo Ou-fan Lee, Rey Chow and Tang Xiaobing often have all the understanding of language and culture of the old Sinologists, and more, because they were brought up speaking the language, and at the same time they are among the first to try out the new methods of study. The pages of journals such as *Positions* and *Modern Chinese Literature* now provide a forum for these ideas to begin the task of building a new form of Chinese Studies.

As the demand for Chinese increases, driven by the huge expansion in commercial and cultural contacts between China and the West, the majority of staff in Chinese Studies departments will come from sources not so deeply formed by Sinologism. Old-style Sinologists, already conservative and given to pessimistic analyses of contemporary society, will have good reason to feel beleaguered, resisting the new trends with all the power they can muster, till age takes its toll and they have to retire, leaving the world to those they see as barbarians: exactly the scenario they most feared. Yet from another perspective the outcome is the fulfilment of what they worked for all their lives: a better knowledge of China, spreading into every nook and cranny of the Western curriculum and the Western mind, flowing back to China itself.

New options for the study of China

Sinologists of the old school are no longer the only sources of knowledge about China in the West. In more recent times, China and Asia have become too important to be left to antiquarian scholars. Economists, political scientists, sociologists – the 'Asian Studies' scholars – have come forward to interpret trends and events that demanded explanation. Much of this has been culturally under-informed or Eurocentric, although, increasingly, crude Eurocentrism and the lack of linguistic skills are recognised as a problem on practical grounds alone. Sometimes these courses remain in their 'home' department, but they are often gathered together in what are called 'Asian Studies' departments, in which the many differences between the societies, cultures and histories of the Asian region are reduced to a common disciplinary factor. Increasingly, courses in both Chinese and Asian Studies are filled with students with a pragmatic wish to understand China, as a place to work in or trade with or, just as important, with a vaguer but powerful desire to understand themselves and their own culture, its limits and possibilities, through opening themselves to the unpredictable difference of another.

The position is rather different in departments or sections which teach new forms of 'Cultural Studies'. The last two decades have seen a dramatic growth in Cultural Studies, sometimes separately, more often as part of a disciplinary department such as English, History, Sociology or Anthropology. This tradition has the sophisticated account of language, power and cultural process which was lacking in old-style Sinology, which is still under-developed in the individual disciplines such as politics and economics. But an increasingly mainstream Cultural Studies has largely passed over any attempt at a substantive understanding of Chinese political and cultural forms and processes in all their specificity and complexity. Unfortunately, because of this lack of knowledge of China, Cultural Studies experts, with the best of intentions, do sometimes make errors of judgement when they venture into interpreting Chinese things. One example is Julia Kristeva's overly enthusiastic analysis of the position of Chinese women after a brief trip to China during the 'Gang of Four' days (Kristeva 1977).

Early forms of Cultural Studies were strongly influenced by Marxism, and tended to be naively Eurocentric, in spite of their radical sympathies. Current forms of Cultural Studies have been affected and shaped by critiques from feminism, postmodernism, post-structuralism and post-colonialism. Particularly important here has been the critique of Eurocentric (and masculinist) forms of knowledge from feminists like Spivak and Trinh Minh Ha. As a result of these critiques Cultural Studies is now broader, less fixed. It ought to be available as a source of critical transdisciplinary theories and methods for studying Chinese culture. This indeed is the assumption on which we have based this book.

We believe that the case of China represents an important new challenge in the development of Cultural Studies. How could a general theory of cultural forms and processes be content to proceed in ignorance of cultural phenomena in one quarter of the world's population today? The study of China represents a chance to interrogate again the fundamental assumptions of Cultural Studies, identify its continuing ethnocentrism, refine its terms and generalisations. This is an exciting and basic task for Cultural Studies. A study of China from a comparative point of view is educative for everyone, from the West as well as from parts of China. But a danger still remains. Cultural Studies has shown some expansionist tendencies within Western academia. It could so easily become yet another instrument for colonising the non-Western others, a more sophisticated and updated form of Sinology. We hope not, but we and others have to be permanently alert to prevent it happening. The price of interdisciplinarity is eternal vigilance.

Reading China from the West: the problem of interpretation

Some powerful and sophisticated ideas have emerged in Cultural Studies about the nature and processes of interpretation, yet along with this has gone a new awareness of the difficulties in interpretation itself. On the one hand, various writers have pointed out how open and creative the process of interpretation can be. Discursive regimes typically set strict limits to what can be said, and what can be understood to be in a text, but readers can circumvent these limits. In fact, the more exacting are the limits on what can be said, the more necessary it is for readers to develop ways around those limits, to get at what they think is the unsaid of a text.

But reading and interpretation have a complex politics, depending on who is doing it to whom. For those who feel excluded from the dominant discursive process, over-interpretation or aberrant readings can be a guerrilla act, a way around the discursive defences of the dominant group. But the same strategy can act like corrupt police, 'planting' evidence on innocent discourses, 'finding' meanings in them which the interpreter wanted to find. Or maybe the discourse was not entirely innocent. Interpretive practices that can be called *symptomatic readings* can uncover suppressed truths or insinuate new meanings, or both. They are a double-edged weapon, source of the most liberating and also the most dangerous interpretations in Cultural Studies.

Psychoanalytic approaches are one such approach, attempting to find the 'cultural unconscious' of a society hidden in various texts. Psychoanalysis can be ethnocentric, projecting the unconscious of the analyst on to a different culture, which may have different patterns of prohibition and desire. Psychoanalysis and Orientalism make an especially dangerous mix when applied to another culture, because the concept of the Other has a potent role in psychic organisation. But it is also the case that sexuality and desire are policed in every culture, entering into public discourse only under certain strict conditions. A blanket rejection of psychoanalytic approaches has its own politics, because its effect is an alignment with the forces and interests that manage sexuality.

The case of China is particularly interesting in this context, because in many respects the dominant discursive regime requires a reading mode that in other contexts would be called paranoiac. Despite the onslaught of consumerism in the 1990s, official discourse, in the press and in the rest of the public domain, is still highly controlled compared to the 'free' press of Western democracies. An official version of the past, present and future is constantly circulated with massive redundancy. Yet precisely because of this degree of discursive control, various practices of symptomatic reading have developed as a survival strategy for many Chinese citizens who scan the newspapers and wall posters to determine what has really happened or what is likely to happen. These symptomatic reading practices have been incorporated into the dominant discursive strategy in a rule-governed way, so that some readers will pick up clues that are there and get the meanings that are intended, by ignoring the bulk of a text. Other readers may guess more than they are meant to, guessing right or wrong and not always knowing which is which. Others may refuse to risk a symptomatic reading, and stay with the surface text.

The discursive regime that has greatest visibility is characterised by two dominant forms. One form is the closed form, such as the slogan or decree or editorial, in which ambiguity seems to be removed, so that there is no doubt about what attitude is right, or what must be done. The other is the open form, represented most clearly by artistic texts, in which the compression of language or form allows scope for multiple interpretation.

These two forms appear to have opposite characteristics. The closed form seems highly reductive, expelling everything from the surface of the text except the decree, the judgement, the command. The *chengyu* form (set phrases usually of four characters) is a typical instance of this. The open form is highly allusive, using its minimalist form to suggest much more than has been said, leaving the way open to apparently infinite interpretation. Classic forms of art and poetry are like this, though the slogan seems unaesthetically political, while the poem seems aesthetic but apolitical. And there are also poems that are political but not noticeably aesthetic.

Both forms draw on the same property of the written language, the ambiguity that is the consequence of compression. The closed form typically functions to close an argument, to give official weight to one side rather than the other, but the debate is usually still alive, inside the party or outside. Otherwise there would be no need for the slogan. And since the slogan aspires to a comprehensive, taken-for-granted status, it typically subsumes the opposing argument in some way. A high level of ambiguity is a major semiotic resource of Chinese. Its discursive regimes are built around it, and the ambiguity remains because it is so functional.

This means that such texts are always in need of some commentary, incomplete without it. As a result a large set of genres of commentary text has evolved, each of which controls and limits the meaning of referent texts, fixing how they should be read and what they mean. But while individual commentary texts normally identify the one meaning of the text, and there can be a massive redundancy in commentary texts which attempt to fix the meaning of a core text or problematic event, there are also many discrepancies between them. In these discrepancies and gaps lie one kind of unsaid or unsayable. But commentaries often bring the unsaid into the partial light of day, and in practice the argument of the commentary does not make full sense unless it is read against a background knowledge of the issues in dispute, the opposing point of view that is travestied and demolished. And under cover of the multiple meanings and multiple commentaries, meanings can be silently renegotiated by those currently in power, after new alignments have taken place or new compromises accepted.

The Chinese situation, then, is one in which discursive regimes function in such a way that both texts and commentaries require supplementary symptomatic readings. The culture at every level is full of secrets that are meant to be half known, suppressed but effectively circulating. Controls act effectively and strictly on the content of what is said or done and on what is done with it, but not so strongly on the meanings that it can have, so that meanings flourish on the margins of texts or in the gaps. Considerable resources are devoted by agents of the state to these processes of discursive control, so that the underside of multiple meanings normally does not appear prominently, and may seem to be socially marginalised and of no importance. But periodically those controls lapse, and what was repressed explodes into social action. This has been a pattern for 2000 years of Chinese history: periods of apparent calm and general consensus, disrupted by revolts or uprisings. Modern-day China has not been immune from this process, and nor have other Chinese communities such as Taiwan.

Postmodern China and a new curriculum

As we have said, our aim in this book is to make it easier for a new generation of students in the West to understand China as it is and as it is becoming. Our approach has been deliberately heterogeneous, and our book is meant to be able to connect with and mediate between a range of different practices which are normally regarded as irreconcilably opposed. In Chinese Studies departments in the West, for instance, a new generation of students is beginning to emerge who want new things from their study of Chinese. For them the concepts of social semiotics and discourse analysis will extend ideas of 'language' and 'reading' to cover a wider range of cultural texts and forms of knowledge. Many who spend a lot of time in Chinese communities are no longer enchanted with the narrow concerns of Sinologism. Their knowledge of China is already gained from perceptions of life around them. They recognise the importance of written material, but are aware that there is a wide range of alternative texts which have the potential to make sense of Chinese culture: slogans, posters, art, calligraphy, comics and films. They can travel to China more easily than in the past, but just as important, China can come to them in many forms, through Chinese relatives, neighbours and friends; videos they can buy or rent; television programmes via satellite from China, Hong Kong, Taiwan and Singapore; visits to local Chinatowns or Chinese temples; Chinese food eaten perhaps with Chinese friends; a myriad series of encounters with myriad versions of 'China'.

But there is no need to choose between 'texts' of this kind, many of which we will analyse in this book, and the literary works that are still commonly used in university Chinese departments as a key to understanding China. To make the point the next chapter begins with an analysis of one of the best stories written in the 1980s, Ah Cheng's 'Chess King'. Instead of developing an 'aesthetic appreciation' of this work as literature, however, we develop the notion of 'reading style' as a fundamental set of semiotic practices in Chinese society, looking especially at the practices around greeting rituals and formal encounters. It contrasts the forms and rules described in textbooks for overseas Chinese and foreigners learning Chinese with the much more complex and open-ended set of rules that govern such exchanges in Chinese life. Textbooks often begin with the expression '*ni hao*' ('how are you?') and some take this expression as their title (Fredlein and Fredlein 1995), but this seemingly common greeting is a very recent phenomenon, and it signifies Western good manners and modernity. Such culture-bound patterns which are rarely made explicit in language learning are discussed in some depth in Chapter 2.

This chapter also looks at some other codes which are important in Chinese social semiotics, again using Ah Cheng as a semiotic guide: calligraphy as an important source of information about the self; accent and dialect as signifiers of class and regional identity; and literary and artistic styles as potent ways of negotiating ideological affiliations in the uncertain environment of modern China. This approach to Chinese Studies brings traditional Sinological concerns with language and literature squarely into the mainstream of social semiotics. Equally important, it provides students who have not mastered the written language with an understanding of the interactions which they may have with Chinese people, showing why such interactions may differ dramatically from those in elementary language textbooks. Ah Cheng's insight into the subtleties of interactive practices in contemporary China is far in advance of these textbooks. His work can communicate this to attentive readers who read him in translation, while more than repaying the efforts of those who labour to read his text in the original. The dichotomy between Chinese-speaking readers and non-Chinese is dangerously misleading. The two kinds of reader could share the same classroom to their mutual benefit.

This leads directly to the other choice that we refuse to make, on the issue of language which in the past has acted as an absolute barrier between Chinese 'specialists' and the rest, making the understanding of China an all-or-nothing matter that depends entirely on mastery of the language. We agree entirely that learning the language is very important. In fact, we hope that as a result of studying our book, many more students will want to undertake that challenging task, and those doing so will do it better, more effectively, with greater commitment and deeper understanding. Chapter 3 centres on the core activity for most students (both Chinese and foreign) in the language classroom: learning Chinese characters. The repetitive work of rote learning hundreds of characters seems anathema to young people used to the post-modern pace of today's world, but we show how much is at stake in this practice. Each time a Chinese character is written the traditional values encoded within it are activated. The ideological processing which goes with the simple act of having to learn and then keep writing the script means that the script is highly efficient as a carrier of Chinese tradition. This important kind of meaning normally remains invisible for both the conscientious language learner, who is told not to waste time on such idle speculations, and the outsider who never reflects on the practice at all.

In a similar vein, Chapter 4 gives an ideological reading of the main features of Chinese grammar, using critical linguistics as a framework. It looks at basic sentence patterns as ideological primes, at classification systems and processes and the ideological functions that they serve, at the range of ways in which different versions and valuations of events are constructed and changed, and at the strategies for claiming or disclaiming truth and authority for different images or utterances. It deals with issues that are fundamental for anyone who seeks to understand Chinese, in a way that does not exclude readers who cannot read Chinese. This approach goes against the assumptions of Sinologism: that language is an either–or issue that absolutely divides the curriculum and separates students into sheep and goats, as though learning about the rest of the culture is a 'soft option' that will irreversibly weaken the moral fibre of students and make them lose the will to learn the One True Way of understanding, the language. Or, to bring academic politics into it, the only sound instruction in Chinese language and culture is what takes place in 'purely Chinese' classes taught by and for Chinese specialists, while Cultural Studies is allowed to retain its monopoly on 'Theory' so long as it is not applied to Chinese.

We believe in the value of a promiscuous plethora of kinds of course in this area, situated at many points within and between departments of Chinese Studies and Cultural Studies (English, History, Politics, Economics) with different levels of linguistic attainment and interests, different combinations of expertise in Chinese and Cultural Studies in teachers and taught. With such a mix we believe it is likely that many more will become motivated to go deeper into the study of Chinese language. For others, the contextualising knowledges they will gain are worthwhile in their own right, not just as a preparation to knowledge of the language. And even those students who for their own reasons already want to learn the language will do so far more productively from learning these powerful enabling knowledges about language, discourse and culture of which many of their predecessors remained dangerously ignorant, however many characters they may have acquired by rote. Our point is simple: language and discourse, cultural and contextual knowledges are so inseparable that any one on its own is dangerously incomplete. Every cultural animal operates in practice with partial knowledges. What everyone needs, more than more bits of information (another character, another rule about correct forms of greeting) is a strategy for coping with this kind of indeterminacy.

By using a Cultural Studies approach to the study of Chinese language, culture and society, we hope to open this exciting area to a new generation of students and scholars in Asian Studies. We want this book to be a stimulating introduction to the richness and complexity of Chinese culture and society and, moreover, one that challenges stereotypes and prejudices common in Sinologism. We will demonstrate that our analytic tools will be useful for interpreting China even as she is changing rapidly, recognising the flexibility that tradition can show, and the variety of ways of being Chinese that can coexist in the contemporary world: multiple Chinas as seen through postmodern perspectives, as well as contemporary mainland China seen from a modernist point of view.

But the various approaches that are subsumed under the heading of Cultural Studies are also in need of redefining their focus. Both Chinese Studies and Cultural Studies stand to gain from the increasing fuzziness of cultural and disciplinary boundaries. The study of Chinese culture should not be a mere adjunct to Western Cultural Studies. This book, we hope, will make clear why Chinese Cultural Studies should become mainstream for all students of the Humanities in the West. The Chinese world is so complex and changing so rapidly that all available tools must be utilised to keep pace. The speed of globalisation with its information superhighways and multinational corporations has meant that the integration of China into the world is occurring faster and more vigorously than was imagined only a few years ago. Cultural Studies is quickly reorientating itself as a consequence of the international climate. Students from an English-language Cultural Studies department, already studying courses with a Cultural Studies emphasis, should be open to the challenge of examining how these concepts and categories work with a major non-European language and culture. As Sinologism fades into the past and as China and the Chinese become an integral part of a global political, economic and cultural complex, the ghettoising of 'area studies' and the Eurocentrism of Western curricula alike must come to an end.

2 Reading style
Interacting the Chinese way

In English-speaking cultures, 'style' is often treated as an aesthetic category rather than as a social one. It's about appearances, surfaces, what makes a work of art or literature beautiful or distinctive, how people do things, what they wear and how they look while doing (or wearing) them. It's not about substance, reality, the essence of a text or a person. Nonetheless, it is of paramount importance for students of Chinese culture to be able to read accurately the personal or cultural style of not only characters they read about, but real people they may meet in China. By analysing different written materials ranging from language textbooks to recent literary works, this chapter will highlight the relationship between cultural sensitivity and reading style correctly. It will illustrate the principle that language cannot be studied without an appreciation of the various styles involved.

From a social semiotic point of view, the appearances and surfaces that make up 'style' are highly semiotic, and intrinsically social. The sociologist Ervin Goffman studied the processes involved in what he called 'the presentation of self in everyday life' (1959). He saw encounters between individuals as typically fraught, requiring continual care and attention by all participants, drawing on a body of semiotic knowledge that is vast and often largely unconscious, except when it breaks through to the surface in situations where the risks are greater, the uncertainties more threatening. In his view, social individuals learn to construct and maintain their social self through what he calls 'face work', using 'impression management' to guide how others perceive the self, trying to read and manipulate the 'selves' offered by significant others, reading the readings of others, second-guessing them and trying to preempt them in an on-going silent struggle.

Goffman's work was done in post-war North America, and his particular observations are specific to that culture. But no one doubts that the same general principles apply to Chinese culture, because the Chinese themselves are so conscious of the process. Goffman took the term 'face' from his understanding of Asian cultural practices. 'Style' in Chinese culture has similar pervasive importance as a complex and ambiguous signifier of social meanings.

In current as in traditional practices of teaching Chinese language, 'style', whether it be spoken or written, is usually treated as an important category. However, it is often seen as asocial, concerned with universal qualities of beauty and elegance, not qualities that maintain specific systems of inter- action and control. Associated with this concept of 'style' goes a set of attitudes to literature and its role in language learning. In China's traditional system of education the teaching of literary classics played a key role, espe- cially in the upper reaches of the system, without offering an explicit account of how this body of knowledge contributed to a general understanding of the language or the culture. But where this system could hardly envisage anything other than literary classics in the curriculum for the elite, the modern func- tional approach to language can hardly see why traditional literature should have a place at all in a practical curriculum for the contemporary world.

Both these positions seriously misrepresent the functions of literature and the meaning of style. Far from being an asocial aesthetic category, style like grammar is a continuously important carrier of major social meanings with direct social effects. 'Style' and the practices it organises and sustains occupy a large amount of time in the educational process, as an intrinsic component of the ideological system that includes the writing system and the grammar. Each reinforces the other, and each carries essentially the same ideological complexes, with the same set of contradictions working on behalf of the same set of interests.

In this chapter, we want to problematise the boundary in the curriculum between literature and culture, language and use. We will look at texts for language learners as works of fiction, heavy-handed and simplistic perhaps, but best-sellers on the scale of Agatha Christie or Harold Robbins. We will also read some works of fiction as indispensable guides to the social semiotics of style in Chinese: focusing particularly on two highly acclaimed short stories by the young writer Ah Cheng, whose stories provide suggestive insights into style as social practice, and the role that judgements on style play in everyday social life (Louie 1989: 76–90).

The imponderable risks of saying 'hello'

Goffman payed a lot of attention to greeting rituals, for good reason. The greeting ritual marks the boundary of an interaction, and establishes or re- establishes the taken-for-granted roles of all participants. With people who know each other well, such as people in the same workplace or school, the first interaction in a day still has work to do, and is normally longer and more extended than interactions later in the day. The first meeting between two individuals, especially if much hangs on its outcome, is far more fraught, its risks governed in every culture by carefully controlled moves which must simultaneously constrain the behaviours of all concerned yet allow space for differentiated meanings to occur – for claims to power to be communicated and accepted, or solidarity to be initiated.

The encounter across the boundaries of language and culture is even more open to risk, since this is the exchange that establishes the new meanings of self and other, the self that will exist in this new relationship, and the other whose meaning derives from and sustains the relationship. So, unsurprisingly, this aspect of style is incorporated early and prominently in modern courses on Chinese for foreign learners: styles of greeting in situations of first encounter. We will look at a number of popular textbooks on introductory Chinese to see how this exchange is treated.

Of all the textbooks in use, *Practical Chinese Reader,* published by the Beijing Languages Institute, is one of the most popular. In the first lesson 'we' (the reader, constructed as foreign) meet Palanka, her blonde hair streaming in the wind, who greets Gubo (also blonde but male) alighting from a train: '*Ni hao*' 你好 ('hello', literally 'you good'). Gubo responds '*Ni hao*', and the lesson ends (Liu Xun *et al.* 1981: 1–2). A complicated character edition of this popular series is now used in Taiwan as well. In the first lesson in *Elementary Chinese Reader*, another popular Beijing textbook, it is A who says '*Ni hao*' and B who responds, under a drawing of a young Western male shaking hands with a young Chinese male (Li Peiyuan *et al.* 1980: 13). Before the appearance of these two readers, the most widely used Chinese language textbook for foreigners was probably the set by DeFrancis, who also begins Lesson 1 with a 'Greeting Friends' dialogue, though he introduces a more formal, polite form of greeting (DeFrancis 1976: 3). More recently, a Chinese textbook produced in Australia even has the simple title *Ni Hao: An Introduction to Chinese*, showing how the expression now signifies 'Chinese for foreign learners' (Fredlein and Fredlein 1995).

Foreign language learners commonly have a keen interest in these greeting formulae, since they will have an immediate practical use for them in going to these countries and in negotiating relationships with the people of these countries. However, very few of these textbooks explain what precisely is going on in these interactions, what meanings are encoded in the various moves, and what are the rules of game outside the specific phrases that are given them to learn. In practice, introductions are always fraught encounters in all societies (for example, Goffman 1967). They are the interface between two systems of interaction, the moment of risk in which a new relationship, positive or negative, is to be established, a relationship which will involve types of power as well as types of solidarity. In every society various rituals develop whose function is to defuse some of the anxieties and control some of the more dangerously antisocial impulses. But some element of risk, some degree of openness to a range of contradictory signals, is also essential for real interaction to occur and for the relationship to establish its form. Politeness in its extreme form, in Chinese as in English, may be reassuring but is in fact an evasion of relationship masquerading as an ideal positivity. The rules of politeness, then, are likely to encode an ideological meaning and social practices that are ultimately neither universal social truths nor even socially useful, after a certain point.

Foreign students following the adventures of Palanka and Gubo in

Practical Chinese Reader fairly quickly find theirs an extremely boring narrative. The encounter with the unknown of Chinese society is mediated through a conventional Western couple, whose relationship with each other is never allowed to get out of hand either. A and B of *Elementary Chinese Reader* are nameless and male, and they have no strong basis for a relationship. They too are screens raised at the outset to neutralise the feared encounter with the Chinese Other, although at least one of them is Chinese.

When the students get to China themselves, they quickly discover that not only were these naratives boring, they were also useless for most of their communication needs. And they will find, too, that what contributed to the boring nature of the narrative was the elimination of conflict from it, the removal of any possibility of transgression, with the result that the language forms they learn can never help them cope with the range of needs and situations they will encounter normally. Most Chinese language textbooks construct a world of courteous friends, helpful shopkeepers and polite bus conductors. There is no desire or fear, alienation or attraction, no death, no sex, no crime, no suffering, no conflict and definitely no politics. There is no one who says anything with which anyone could disagree, nothing therefore with which one could even really be interested or engaged. Common phrases such as 'you're talking nonsense' (*Hu shuo ba dao* 胡说八道) may possibly find their way into a textbook, but not 'you're talking shit' (*ni fangpi* 你放屁), which at times may be more appropriate.

It is for this reason that 'authentic' material such as literary texts, newspapers, comics and film can have a valuable role to play. Their narratives are not only more enjoyable, they are also more illuminating about the complex meanings in exchanges between Chinese speakers. We will examine such texts in later chapters, here we will concentrate on the writer Ah Cheng who is considered by many the most accomplished stylist of the 1980s. His depictions of human interaction are drawn with sensitivity, and there is much to be learnt about Chinese life and culture in these depictions. Furthermore, his stories are well known outside China because two of them, 'The Chess King' and 'Children King', have been made into fairly popular movies. We will illustrate our point by looking at two exchanges from his most celebrated work, 'The Chess King' 棋王, published in 1984.

The story is about a group of 'Educated Youth' who are sent to a state farm during the Cultural Revolution. It describes a period of extreme hardship, but the story is not the 'woe is me' complaint so common in the 1980s. The narrator tells of people helping each other, the tensions and excitement of chess tournaments, and celebrations of food and friendship. In particular, he describes the spiritual journey of Wang Yisheng, the 'Chess King', who through his obsession with chess manages to escape the physical hardships of that time. It also relates the friendship between Wang, the narrator and Ni Bin, who, unlike the other two, comes from a wealthy background and has more cultured tastes. The first exchange describes the first meeting between Wang Yisheng and the narrator:

My seat happened to be in the same section as his, opposite him at an angle, so I sat down and also tucked my hands into my sleeves. He transferred his gaze to me for a minute, and then suddenly a light appeared in his eyes.

'Care for a game of chess?' he asked.

He'd startled me, and I hastily waved my hands. 'I can't play!'

He looked at me disbelievingly. 'Long thin fingers like that are made for playing. I bet you can. Let's have a game, I've got a set here.'

So saying, he reached up, took down his satchel from the window hook and rummaged around inside.

(Ah Cheng 1990: 30)

An exchange along these lines could have taken place between two English speakers and its main terms come across well enough even in translation. It is this 'naturalness' or legibility which foreign learners or readers can trust, even if they may not read such passages in the original language. In this exchange, neither participant says '*ni hao*'. Far from being extraordinary, this is well within the bounds of normality for Chinese speakers. In fact the '*ni hao*' form is almost un-Chinese. It is endemic in textbooks (and therefore in the language behaviour of foreign students who have learnt from them) but not in the social life in China. Hence this form has come to have a marked meaning: 'Hello (I'm a foreigner)' or, if said by a Chinese, 'Hello (I know that you're a foreigner)'. It encodes this invisible meaning without foreigners being aware of what they have been instructed to encode into their greeting. It remains invisible whilst continuing to be relevant in constructing their place as outsiders in relationships with Chinese.

Recently it has come to be used more often by Chinese speakers, but used in this way it signifies an affiliation with foreigners, having as a subtext, 'Hello (I'm someone who has a lot to do with foreigners)' or, 'Hello (I'm someone who is from the city and fairly well brought up)'. This identification tag with foreignness will soon wear off, though, as *ni hao* becomes a general term for greetings used by all in China. As 'politeness campaigns' in which the populace is encouraged to greet each other with '*ni hao*' take effect, the term will no doubt be identified as a marker of Chineseness in the same way that the kiwi fruit, although Chinese in origin, is now identified as a trademark of New Zealand.

What happens in such encounters amongst Chinese people interacting with each other as well as with foreigners is that each one sizes the other up extensively before any interaction occurs, rapidly reading numerous messages (class, age, gender, character) via many semiotic media and, as it turned out in this case, accurately. The kind of knowledge on which this act of reading is based is as essential in social life as any verbal formula, though as words go, *ni hao* is as safe as the textbooks claim.

The first meeting between Wang Yisheng and the narrator in Ah Cheng's story starts, however, with a direct question which by Western standards would be regarded in such a situation as intrusive. Similar considerations operate in Chinese social life, and there would have been many other kinds of person who would have found so direct a question unacceptable. Even in this situation, the narrator says that it 'startled' him, indicating that it was on the limits of acceptability, and his first response was a negative, which later proved a lie (he could in fact play, though he was not in the same league as the Chess King). Wang Yisheng sweeps this aside, and the game begins; and so does a relationship which is to continue throughout the story, important to each. The risks that the Chess King took could have provoked rejection and outrage, but that does not mean that risk-taking always jeopardises relationships. If the narrator had frozen him off, the consequences may not have been disastrous, but no relationship would have been established and the story would have ended there.

Somewhat later in the story a different relationship is established, by different means. This is between Ni Bin (whose nickname is Tall Balls) and Wang, a relationship which will prove useful for Wang since Ni Bin has powerful connections. It is therefore more guarded, more constrained, and will always be less solid than that between Wang Yisheng and the narrator. But social life is made up of a range of kinds of relationship, and social competence involves being able to negotiate and read them all.

The first encounter between Ni Bin and Wang is described by Ah Cheng as follows:

> He [Ni Bin] stooped over and came in, stretching out his hand while he was still some distance away.
>
> Wang Yisheng was flustered for a moment but caught on right away: he also stretched out his hand but his face turned red. After shaking hands, Tall Balls clasped his hands together and held them loosely in front of his belly.
>
> 'I'm Ni Bin – "Ni" written with the man radical and "Bin" with the characters for civil and military. Everyone calls me Tall Balls because I've got long legs. "Balls" is a very vulgar word – please don't take offence, the level of culture here is very low. May I ask your name?'
>
> Wang Yisheng was a couple of heads shorter than Ni Bin, so he looked up to speak.
>
> 'Wang – Wang Yisheng.'
>
> (Ah Cheng 1990: 59)

We note once again that this greeting is fraught and in some respects aberrant, but far from this ruining the formation of the relationship it contributes to its success. This is because even rule-breaking carries many important messages, which can play their part in constructing a relationship. Ni Bin, for instance, offers his hand too eagerly and too early, creating embarrassment for Wang (and no doubt a sense of strain for Ni Bin, though this is not commented on by the narrator). Since Ni Bin is on his own territory and of superior social standing, this action, with its meaning of excessive deference, is confusing and 'wrong', in terms of the power relationship between the participants. Wang's confusion, however, carries a positive meaning of not at all expecting this degree of goodwill, thus restoring the relationship of superior–inferior. Again the error is a kind of risk that actually advances the relationship in a way that the correct moves would not have done.

At the core of this exchange is a greeting ritual that is very common in Chinese, and virtually untranslatable because it involves the deconstruction of the main parts of the characters in his name. What Ni Bin actually says is '*Wo jiao Ni Bin, ren er Ni, wen wu Bin*' 我叫倪斌, 人儿倪, 文武斌 literally 'I am called Ni Bin, "Ni" as in "person" and "son" and "Bin" as in "literary" and "military"'. Wang's response is to explain only Yisheng (since Wang is so common a surname), using the same conventions. This is a variation of a common greeting ritual in Chinese. After the name has been communicated in the spoken code, the person is asked to write it. This encodes a lot of social information about social identity, as well as fixing the name itself. The act of writing gives a sample of the person's calligraphy, thus communicating the meanings inscribed in that code. It gives a sensitive measure of the level of education and the attitudes to tradition, even in those who are not experts in calligraphy. The variant used by Ni Bin performs an equivalent function, indicating a reasonably high level of education (beyond that of the others present, whose level of culture he claims is very low, thereby implying that they are uneducated). So the exchange not only reveals this aspect of the social identity of each, it also constructs a bond of solidarity based on this common level.

What Ni Bin goes on to say, however, constructs another kind of solidarity, telling this newcomer his derogatory nickname. Wang Yisheng doesn't respond at this level (his nickname is 'The Chess Idiot' 棋呆子) so that the relationship remains asymmetrical, with Ni Bin retaining the initiative in spite of the unflattering meaning of his nickname, because he has had the self-confidence to establish a complex bond between the two men so rapidly.

We could give a fuller commentary on this exchange, bringing out further complexities, and indicating elements in the exchange which are usual and elements which are at the limits of acceptability. But the crucial point is that in normal social interaction in China, rule-breaking is as unobtrusively continuous and systemic and functional as the rules themselves are needed to be known. The two together constitute the system that organises social interaction, a system which is a way to negotiate contradictions successfully (successfully for different persons and different purposes) and not exclusively a system for staying out of trouble at any cost. It is the second function that alone is provided for in all the textbooks, but it is itself a contradiction. People who only wanted to stay out of trouble would stay home, and not go to China or learn Chinese. But naively walking into danger in total ignorance, causing deep offence without being aware of it, is the other equally unacceptable extreme. By supplementing the language textbooks, with their artificially controlled dialogues and pattern drills, with more lively models, literary works like Ah Cheng's 'The Chess King' can play a vital role in a language-learning programme.

The meanings of accent

Chinese is usually assumed by non-Chinese speakers to be a single unitary if difficult language and set of attitudes. But that single language is socially and historically located. Once the language taught to foreigners would have been classical Chinese beloved of Sinologists. The singular modern language that is taught now is a contemporary language, a vernacular in wide use, and there is no question that if one had only the time and energy to begin to learn one form of Chinese, that form would be Modern Standard Chinese. But contemporary Chinese is much more than this standard language, and the differences of accent, dialect, variation and style make up a significant repertoire of social meanings. These are important parts of social judgements of 'face', important signifiers of the heterogeneity that lies only millimetres below the surface of Chinese social life.

The Chinese language taught in language textbooks – the so-called 'common speech' 普通话 – is described like this in the *Practical Chinese Reader*:

> What we propose to teach in this textbook is what is known as 'the common speech', the kind of modern Chinese with 'the Beijing speech sounds as the standard sounds, the Northern dialect as the basic dialect and modern classic works written in the vernacular as its grammatical models'.
>
> (Liu Xun *et al.* 1981: 9)

This concept of a single language as modern and authentic and in universal use in China is reassuring to the language learner, but at the same time implies a particular version of China as a single united society, united precisely by the common language. However useful this view is – for language learners and people who wish to do business easily in China – it remains an ideological view, not a social truth. Foreigners and language learners cannot take on the impossible task of learning an indefinite number of regionalects and dialect variations, but they can learn to be alert to the constant presence of linguistic differences, and understand in broad terms a useable map of the major social and political meanings coded in the language community.

To illustrate this, we will again use 'The Chess King', although other texts, literary and otherwise, which use vernacular in dialogue could do as well. Wang Yisheng at one point interacts with Ni Bin, the tall, well-connected Southerner whose nickname is the uncomplimentary 'Tall Balls'. In response to Wang's greeting he replies '*man hao, man hao*' 蛮好, 蛮好, which W.J.F. Jenner translates as 'Terrific, terrific' (Ah Cheng 1985) and Bonnie S.

McDougall (Ah Cheng 1990) translates as 'Super, super'. Tall Balls' use of '*man*' here is interesting. Ordinarily, the written form 蛮 means 'barbaric', 'wild' or 'southern', though, according to the dictionary, there is also a dialectic usage in which it means 'quite' or 'rather'. The overlap between these two meanings in the one character is no accident when we consider that for centuries, the 'south' has been considered barbaric.

By drawing on the dialect's meaning for this expression, Ah Cheng is using the written code to silently comment on Tall Balls' Southern origins and terminology. In practice what Tall Balls said would have been interpreted as perfectly normal, since the expression '*man hao*' is often used and when not written, would pass unnoticed. So Ah Cheng is encoding his judgement on Tall Balls, and not simply recording what Tall Balls said. So Tall Balls is made to say, by a mistake which is conventionalised, 'barbarously good', which is either nonsense or an insult: or else he is praising Wang in excessive terms for simply saying his name. Either way we can see the strength of the linguistic prejudice, or more exactly the social prejudice acting through language. It is the existence and importance of these attitudes that are removed by the fiction of the unproblematic singleness of the Chinese 'common' language. Where these attitudes appear in books on Chinese language for beginners, it is often in a form that seems to unconsciously endorse the most extreme of prejudices. Urs Bucher, for instance, introduces his textbook *Vocabulary of Modern Chinese* with 'you would best make the first steps in Chinese with a teacher from the Peking area at your side, without ever despising the southerner for their "dialectal Mandarin" which you can try to understand later on' (Bucher 1986: 15).

Shortly after Ni Bin meets Wang Yisheng, he commits another solecism. This time, the error of speech was picked up by no less a person than the former Minister for Culture in Beijing, Wang Meng. Wang Meng, however, blamed Ah Cheng the author, and not Ni Bin the speaker in Ah Cheng's text (Wang Meng 1984: 45). Ni Bin says, 'May I ask if your father's a chess *aficionado*?' (Ah Cheng 1990: 60), or that is what we can presume he meant. However the word he uses is *jia fu* 家父, which literally means 'family father', but refers to one's own father. Wang Meng insisted that the right word should have been *lingzun* 令尊, and that judgement is undoubtedly correct, from the point of view of the standard language. But Ah Cheng here is clearly piling up the mistakes in Tall Balls' speech, significant errors that both show his character and imply Ah Cheng's judgement of it. Immediately after this Ah Cheng describes 'everyone bursting out laughing' at yet another of Tall Balls' errors of speech: this is social satire, not accurate reportage. The implied judgement this time is precisely what Wang Meng directed at Ah Cheng. Tall Balls' error showed him as someone attempting to use an elaborate, high form from the classical language of the past and getting it ridiculously wrong – rather like what is called malapropism in English.

Satires of malapropisms in English are normally an expression of snobbish superiority towards aspiring members of the lower classes. Up to a point the same is true of China, and Ah Cheng. However, there is a significant twist to Ah Cheng's sense of his target here. Ni Bin is a Southerner, but he comes from a good family, one which retains good political connections. In the story he is able to do a good turn for Wang Yisheng by promising a visiting party official a beautiful old chess set that belonged to his family. Wang is so outraged by this desecration of such a symbol of the past that he refuses to accept the favour that is offered. However, Ni Bin explains that he himself is getting enough out of the exchange, since he would be transferred back to the city, and his family didn't particularly value the chess set compared to advantage in the present.

In terms of the theme of the story this is the reverse of the cultural strategy of 'abstract inheritance' (see Louie 1986), which we will discuss at greater length in Chapter 5. This Chinese obsession, as strong today as ever, is concerned mainly with keeping strong links with cultural values and texts from the past while unobtrusively but radically transforming them. The behaviour of Ni Bin shows the indifference and ignorance of those who should uphold the past, the breaking of the inheritance. North–South rivalry has been a constant throughout Chinese history, and this rivalry is often represented in cultural terms. In recent times, because the southern coastal provinces have been most open to outside influence they have been constructed by those from the North as being slick, mercenary and superficial. It is no accident that here it is a Southerner who by his speech and values is represented as unworthy of the heritage of Chinese civilisation.

At the climax of the story, Wang Yisheng defeats an old man who is the champion chess player of the region, a man who represents the best of the past and offers Wang the hand of friendship. Wang declines, choosing instead to go with his young companions, his peers, thus symbolically aligning himself with the present against the past. And in the penultimate paragraph, as Wang is sitting in the darkened auditorium which had seen his triumph, the narrator brings him a piece from the chess set made for him by his mother, an illiterate Northern woman from the city. Wang breaks down sobbing.

> His tears began to flow and he blubbered through his sobs 'Mum, I've understood now. People have got to have something before they can really live. Mum . . .
> ['*Ma, er jintian mingbai shier le, ren hai yao you dianer dongxi, cai jiao huozhe, ma . . .* ']

There are two significant points about the language here. First there is the use of '*Ma*' 妈, mum and '*er*' 儿, son. *Ma* is the colloquial form used for mothers by their children. The use of *er* instead of *wo* 我 (I) is also a childish form of language. At this moment of high emotion, Wang is regressing to the language of what is literally his mother tongue, charged with the intense and important emotions and relationships encoded in it. In this context we can see the significance of his use of the Northern *er*, which we have pinpointed.

This marks the language as dialect, the more prestigious Northern dialect. But in this instance its use is associated with the low-status Wang, as he remembers his own lowly origins and the wisdom of his low-status mother.

This is the wisdom that he is affirming, against the cultured old man, the wisdom which triumphs through his victory. So the hierarchy of value that places North above South is inverted, but it is the low status language of his mother that Wang prizes most. A number of language textbooks (including DeFrancis) mention the Northern r-form, and its gradual disappearance in high-status Northern speakers. This disappearance may not be the coming of democratic ideas, but the opposite, if Ah Cheng's story is any guide. Ah Cheng's story is likely to be a good guide, precisely because it dramatises the complex of attitudes towards the language of living speakers, whose experience *normally* includes dialectical variations and judgements on them: something that is notably missing from the social and linguistic universe which is normally offered so simplistically to the foreign reader or language learner.

Reading calligraphy

For the student of Chinese from the West, one of the most fascinating aspects of the language is in discovering very quickly the importance attached to handwriting. Calligraphy has an importance even in contemporary China that goes well beyond the role of handwriting in European societies today. People make sweeping judgements of others on the basis of their script, and know that others will do the same to them in return. These are social judgements which classify people with great authority, and often form the core of the set of valuations that make up a person's social identity. As we indicated briefly earlier, it is common practice for two people meeting each other for the first time to ask the other to write out his or her name. This has the practical function of giving the correct written form of the name, but the performance of writing gives a large amount of social information in a highly compressed form. The messages encoded in this way are set alongside the messages encoded in personal appearance – style of dress, posture, etc. – and assimilated into the social judgements that organise subsequent interaction: Goffman's 'impression management' and construction of 'face'.

The role of handwriting in this set of semiotic systems has analogues with European practices of considerable antiquity. The key term 'style' etymologically derives from a Latin word *'stilus'*, referring to the pen that wrote on wax tablets. So the category of 'style', which has been generalised to cover many other areas of activity, originally referred to handwriting as the exemplary instance of style, established in the exemplary site for the production of social meaning: the classroom. The connection of 'style' with 'character', which is at the base of the social meaning of style, again has its roots in this situation and ideological practice. 'Character' derives from the Greek word *'charattein'*, meaning to engrave, so that the idea that people's character can be read from the way they produce characters is a potent cross-cultural pun. In English, the term 'character' in the original etymological sense is now restricted to Chinese forms of writing, as though the link retains its primal force especially in the case of Chinese.

Calligraphy gains some of its social meaning from the way that writing is taught in Chinese schools. Teaching how to write characters occupies a large amount of time in the curriculum. At primary school the method still in use decomposes the target character into a set of strokes which must be produced in the proper order within an identically sized square. The effect of this is to empty the action of meaning, so that the training comes to seem one of the body only. As a result, 'success' signifies the capacity for mindless obedience to the prescriptions of authority or, more precisely, the capacity to defer the need to understand until a later stage in the learning process. 'Success' is marked by accuracy, regularity, orderliness and speed in the production of characters.

The ideology inscribed into these practices is similar to what Foucault (1977) has described in nineteenth-century regimes of instruction in handwriting in Europe. In Foucault's account, exercises in teaching good handwriting played an important role in the disciplinary process, and the outcome – good handwriting – was a trusted signifier of a 'docile body'. It could perform this role because the link between the product (a good style), the gesture that produced it, and the disciplined body that guaranteed the gesture, was intrinsic and hence difficult to fake. In Foucault's terms it was a 'trace' (Foucault 1972: 121), the inevitable effect of habits that could only be acquired through the correct training and the correct attitude to training.

But calligraphy as prized in China has one important difference from the products of careful discipline as described by Foucault. Where correct writing signifies submission and docility, fine calligraphy signifies a mastery that includes freedom and spontaneity and force. There is a contradiction here, since the 'freedom' is not any kind of spontaneity: it is the internalisation of external constraints so deep they become in a real sense 'second nature', like bones to the body, not clothes that can be changed; or like foot-binding for women, not silks or hair styles as signifiers of femininity. So calligraphy signifies both obedience and status, the rare power of one who deserves to be a ruler or to be trusted by those who rule, who has been conditioned so that even the most spontaneous movement is formed by and for the social. It is, in short, an ideal kind of signifier to legitimate the intellectual elite which has had a key role in the government of China for many centuries, including Communist China today.

Anyone who lives in China will immediately recognise the great importance attached to handwriting, but it is much more difficult to pin down the complex meanings that are read in aspects of style, and to demonstrate the links between these sets of social judgements and others which connect outwards with other areas of social life. As a focus for an explication of this nexus of meanings and practices as they function in contemporary China we will draw on another story by Ah Cheng, 'The Idiot' (Ah Cheng 1984). An analysis of the story tells us much not only about literary styles, but about current ideas on handwriting as well. 'The Idiot' pivots around Lao Li, a man noted for his skill in calligraphy. Lao Li describes the meaning of calligraphy for someone like himself, but the story does not simply provide a forum for Lao Li and his doctrine of calligraphy. Ah Cheng sets the theme of calligraphy in a wider frame, one which implies a subtle insight into the role of calligraphy in Chinese social life.

Ah Cheng begins his story with a discussion of idiots, not calligraphy, or at least, this is how it seems. His narrator claims a fascination with idiots (*shazi* 傻子), and gives a whimsical account of his social theory of idiots. For the narrator, idiots are not interesting in themselves. On the contrary, he describes them as a constant, without meaning in themselves and therefore able to signify the meanings of others in a pure form. They have two kinds of social meaning, with reference to two categories of social agent. Firstly, the narrator uses the reactions of others to classify them in terms of community identity. Those who react with surprise or hostility must be outsiders: only those who are familiar with them know they are idiots. But more importantly, the idiots are signifiers of their own families, whose attitude to them is directly signalled by elements of their appearance.

The narrator comes up with a fourfold classification system of idiots, in terms of their cleanliness and clothing. The four categories are both a parody and a repetition of classification systems in other areas of Chinese life, whose ubiquity we have already seen. Ah Cheng's narrator makes strong claims for the traditional nature and function of his system, but in terms that indicate unmistakably a critique of some basic premises of that system. 'When these four types of idiot walk in the street, they are in reality four banners for their families ... Therefore, it is an easy matter to understand the families of idiots by standing in the streets. The answer is in the type of idiot.' (Ah Cheng 1984: 38)

In this pseudo-theory, idiots are like the banners (*qizi* 旗子) which in feudal times marked aristocratic families as they marched into battle. However, the image is ironic as Ah Cheng uses it, since the feelings aroused by idiots are exactly the opposite of pride in family. The word itself (*shazi* – *sha* 傻 [simple, foolish] plus *zi* 子 [the character for 'son']) recalls the system of inheritance along the male line, and the negative effect on this system of having a son who is an idiot, and therefore not able to inherit. So Ah Cheng is describing an antisystem which mirrors the dominant system and communicates its unintended meanings alongside the official system. It is this system that the narrator draws on, to 'read' the meaning of each new community he enters.

After this ironic opening the narrator introduces Lao Li, the calligrapher, and the theme of the role of writing in reading a person's character (p. 39):

> I greatly respect Lao Li. People in the unit all think Lao Li is sincere and honest, and he does not gossip behind people's backs. I respect Lao Li

because he writes very well in the Yan style. His writing is like him: the contours bend slightly outwards, and the shape is stocky and solid.

This observation establishes the general prestige that Lao Li acquires through his skill, and also the strong link that is believed to exist between Lao Li's style of writing and his social persona, so that his style is accepted as an accurate index of his character. In the story that follows, this link is not seriously questioned. We discover that there is more to Lao Li's existence than honesty and sincerity, but his fidelity to those qualities is still not in question.

Lao Li gives his philosophy of writing, and the passage is worth reproducing in full (p. 39):

> In fact, characters are like people. I am not saying that characters look like their writers. I am talking about face (*timian* 体面). People must have face, and characters are a banner of people. This banner should be beautiful and have dignity (*timian*). Inner strength (*guli* 骨力)? Naturally, it would be very good if you can reveal inner strength in your writing. But on a signboard, how many of the rabble that are coming and going will look at inner strength? In reality, they just want to see what pleases the eye. When you look at people in this street, what do you look at? With women, it's whether the clothing they wear pleases the eye or not. No matter how great a person's body is, if the clothing he wears does not match, he still does not please the eye. If his body is no good and he wears tight pants and he walks around the streets like a mantis, if he were transformed into a written character, could he be put on to a billboard? Writing characters is writing clothing.

Lao Li's views as stated here are slightly rambling and confused. In the narrative he is slightly drunk, but the drunkenness allows Ah Cheng to show some of the contradictions at work in his position. The central contradiction concerns the scope of the 'truth' inscribed in style. At first he claims that there is a complete identity between people and their form of writing ('characters are like people'). By the end he seems to be saying that writing style is purely external ('Writing characters is writing clothing'). But these contradictory views in fact (as is the case with idiot-watchers) simply define the two classes of observers: a rabble who see only surfaces, and an elite who respect 'inner strength' (*guli*).

The same opposition between internal and external qualities is also part of the key term *timian*. *Ti* here can be translated as style, but where the common metaphor for style in English opposes style to body or substance ('Style is the dress of Thought') the Chinese word does not imply this contrast. *Ti* can mean body or substance. It is physical matter organised into form, not the form conceived of as a distinct entity. In the compound *timian* it refers to the important social category often translated as 'face', thus connecting the quality of writing with the value of the social persona, again not contrasting this with an inner, private persona. Li compares this with a banner (*qi* 旗), the same word the narrator used of the appearance of idiots, where the word ironically recalled the role of idiots in breaking family lineages. In this context Li's use of the word has an ironic implication too, since writing style is not transmitted genetically, even though families can construct a tradition of calligraphy across the generations.

In the remainder of the story the themes of idiots, inheritance and calligraphy interweave. The narrator is asked by Lao Li to dinner, an occasion at which a suitor for Lao Li's daughter is also to be present. The narrator is invited because of his skill in judging people: he is to assess whether the suitor is suitable. But the suitor will also judge the family. As the meal unfolds Lao Li's dreadful secret is revealed. His son is an idiot: not one of the four classes outlined in the opening, but a fifth sort, kept entirely out of the public gaze. So Lao Li's honesty and sincerity masks a dishonesty about his son and his family, and his treatment of his son signifies as much about him and his values as does his famous handwriting.

In the end the occasion is not a disaster after all. The suitor is not discouraged by the accidental revelation, and towards the end of the evening he professes an interest in calligraphy and in Lao Li's views on the matter. Li gives the following speech (p. 41):

> As for writing, the most important thing is inner strength (*guli*). When people look at characters, what do they look for? They look for inner strength. If you want to learn calligraphy, learn the Yan style. It is not easy to be slick with the Yan style. You must be open and correct with the Yan style, otherwise you can't do it well. First of all find a Duobaota and a Dongfanghua to model from. When that's completed, take a look at Duke Lu's Magu and Gaoshen. And once you've obtained the inner force, take a look at Yufuren Tie, Lufu, Zhengzuowei and Fangshengchi, which are beautiful and correct, not vulgar and alluring. Then take a look at General Pei, fantastic!

As this speech begins he half contradicts his earlier statement, emphasising *guli* as essential, but this is appropriate because he is talking here to his prospective son-in-law and perhaps successor, one of the elite and not one of the rabble. But as the speech unfolds an even greater contradiction opens up, because the 'inner strength' turns out to be based entirely on imitation of models. These are classic models from the Tang dynasty, the period when the Yan style (Figure 2.1) emerged to express a sturdy oppositional set of values to the elaborate and florid Wang style (Figure 2.2).

Li's advice is not idiosyncratic. This is precisely how the art of the calligrapher is acquired. A small set of models of this kind underlies the range of seemingly free and expressive forms of good writing. Conformity to one or other of these models is part of the meaning of the individual style –

Figure 2.1 Example of sturdy Yan-style calligraphy

not a slavish conformity but a recognisable relationship encompassing respect for tradition with a sense of individuality. This dimension of the meaning of style is dependent on specific knowledge, and thus is 'read' differently by different groups in society, with calligraphists being able to read subtle blends of conformism and individuality invisible even to the literate if they lack that specialised knowledge. These others will have a further problem. So great in 'good' styles is the departure from the standard form of characters that these texts are barely legible by the untrained, who may otherwise be entirely competent in reading Chinese characters. This obscures the possibility of making particular judgements on individual examples of the art, but wraps all those who can produce and read the texts themselves in an aura of privilege and

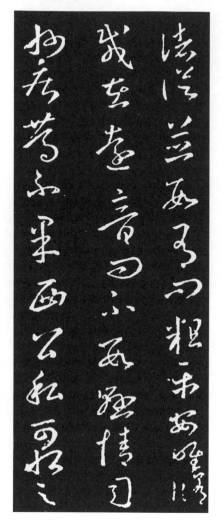

Figure 2.2 Example of more florid Wang-style calligraphy

knowledge. In short, it acts like an antilanguage to exclude outsiders and reinforce the sense of an elite, privileged knowledge. The suitor is admitted into this inner circle, and there he is told that freedom is conformity, originality is imitation and that the meaning of such a style is an identity learned from the past, not a trace from the present.

In the past, this system was extremely powerful, one of the core methods of maintaining ideological control. Emperors, for instance, displayed their calligraphy on steles which were preserved for centuries as objects of veneration. The criteria by which these were called excellent were predictably fluid. The power and prestige of emperors were not in question, so that the style did not need to confirm or express these qualities. Instead, it was able to express the individuality enabled by that power, in a seductive union of individual and social, freedom and constraint. The meanings of the style could fill out the meaning of power without cancelling its potency, thus serving to co-opt those who experienced literacy as a source of constraint into an image of unlimited freedom. Unsurprisingly these steles continue to project the same satisfying set of meanings for all those who struggle with the written language in contemporary China. Likewise political leaders in contemporary China such as Mao Zedong have publicised not only slogans but samples of their writing style, knowing that these are still highly significant carriers of ideological complexes (Kraus 1991). The relationship between handwriting and power is so strong that, even in the West, books on China are often adorned with titles written by famous scholars or public figures.

Literary style and the conquest of tradition

Having seen how styles of speech and handwriting can influence the effectiveness of social interaction and control, we will conclude this chapter with an appreciation of literary style in a language-learning programme. Literary style expresses the same range of meanings and serves the same set of functions as calligraphy. Corresponding to the role of models in calligraphy is a small set of literary models from the Chinese classics, in which poetry plays a crucial role. But the traditional on its own is not enough as a dominant meaning, for a variety of reasons. One is the need to recognise that the Chinese government has proclaimed that a Communist revolution has occurred. Equally important is flexibility, recognised in the traditional system as well, the capacity of the autonomous but well-trained individual to respond immediately and directly to new and possibly difficult circumstances. A person who writes with an admired style in contemporary China cannot simply rewrite Tang poems. Writing must be innovative as well as respecting of tradition, incorporating new experience into recognisable and familiar frames.

It is mainly for this reason that the work of Ah Cheng has been greeted with such acclaim, especially his first published work 'The Chess King'. This novella dealt with the experience of the Cultural Revolution from the point of view of an educated youth, one who participated in the move to the countryside without trauma but without great enthusiasm. Many other writers have dealt with this material. Ah Cheng's work stands out because his style has been seen as itself a potent message, a blend of traditional and new.

Most of the narrative is in a first-person style which is simple, direct, modern Chinese, close to the spoken forms of language. But because it is first person, Ah Cheng is able to shift register, incorporating colloquial forms juxtaposed to more standard forms, constructing a form of Chinese which is open to the non-standard, to varieties of difference. As we have seen in the discussion of Wang Yisheng's outburst at the end of the story, the vernacular generally coexists with the standard forms, adding concreteness and colour without challenging the primacy of the standard. The overall ideological meaning of this is an affirmation of the scope of Chinese and China itself as able to include everyday experience and language and values alongside those of the common standard.

But it is not this quality of Ah Cheng's style that has won him the most plaudits. What has impressed people is his ability to yoke together very traditional forms of language and thought with new styles and new problems. The Chess King of the title learns from an old man to adapt a Daoist philosophy to the requirements of chess, and as a result is able to play even better than the old masters themselves. The plot thus endorses the continuing relevance of basic Chinese traditions, interpreted in an adapted form, so that the new is better than and yet not hostile to the old. With this in view, it is appropriate that at key points the language of the past should appear, adapted to new contexts and problems. Ah Cheng's style shows the harmonious coexistence of old and new, and is thus a parallel way of expressing and reinforcing the message of the story.

Precisely because the ideological themes at issue in the style are also principles that are acted out in the plot, this story allows us to see and understand some of the complex social meanings of the conjunction, the 'marriage' of old and new. Ah Cheng presents people who bridge tradition and contemporary themes, in the course of a narrative that helps to explain the forces at work. For instance, the Chess King utters a comment: 'How may one abolish the dumps? Only with the art of chess' (Ah Cheng 1990: 43) (*Heyi jie bu tongkuai? Weiyou xia xiangqi* 何以解不痛快? 唯有下象棋). The narrator in conversation with him picks up this phrase, as an adaptation of two lines from Cao Cao's 'Short Song' (*Heyi jieyou, weiyou Dukang* 何以解忧, 唯有杜康 How may one abolish the dumps? Only with Du Kang.), which is almost the same except for the last two characters, which are Du Kang 杜康, the name of the legendary discoverer of alcohol. As well as being a principal military general from the Three Kingdoms period (AD 220–280), Cao Cao was a major poet of that legendary era. It is not clear, however, whether the Chess King knows the source of his wisdom, or the original version of his phrase.

The narrator describes the transformation of the phrase as 'interesting', just as an expert calligrapher might praise someone's skilful allusion to and reuse of a famous model. So the narrator is established as thoroughly familiar with the classics, superior in this respect to the Chess King. But the Chess King is able to produce a valid use of tradition without necessarily having acquired that tradition in full. What he has acquired is a more general quality of respect for the tradition and for its carriers (the old man, or rather two separate old men who are his teachers). The style and the story both imply that this, the 'spirit' of the tradition, is enough, and it needs to be complemented by freedom and independence in its use rather than a remorseless inculcation of detail.

The exchange between the narrator and the Chess King captures the essence of Ah Cheng's stylistic programme. It reaffirms the core status of the traditional wisdom as encoded in its traditional language and transmitted by the traditional methods, while recognising the insufficiency and incomprehensibility of those ideas and methods on their own. The value of the wisdom is not in question, but the method of transmitting it is; and that method, with its notions of discipline, obedience and respect, was a potent aspect of its ideological meaning and effect. Ah Cheng's 'style' is not to be seen only in his easy re-use of traditional values in language and thought. In this story and others he shows a concern with style as a distinctive strategy underlying many areas of experience.

Ever since Mencius announced that life was fundamentally concerned with 'eat, drink, man, woman', Chinese writers have dwelt on eating and drinking as important social lubricants. Banquets and sharing food with friends have become synonymous with happiness and good fortune. In some situations, it is also a way of practising good traditions. For example, in the illustration of the Hongkong Bank advertisement of June 1996 (Figure 2.3), two successful Asian businessmen sit chatting in a typical family restaurant of the type one finds in the back streets of Southeast Asia. They are clearly wealthy, as indicated by the business suits and the chauffeur polishing a black Mercedes (which presumably belongs to one of them) outside the restaurant. The text under the photograph states, 'In Asia, there are always new markets and new opportunities. And there are always new ideas, new products and new technologies. But there are also old ties and long relationships.' And to emphasise the point that traditions, friendships and simple but good food are more

Figure 2.3 Hongkong Bank advertisement contrasting tradition and modernity

important than new wealth and success, the caption on top of the photograph comments, 'Everything has changed. Except the relationship, and the barbecued duck'.

The loving detail with which the humble family café is portrayed in the advertisement is similar to Ah Cheng's treatment of eating in his stories. In 'Chess King', he goes into great depth in describing how Wang Yisheng eats his lunch, right down to the slow chewing of the grain of rice he finds on the table. Like the Hongkong Bank advertisement, however, eating with friends represents a general principle. Especially in times of want, food provides the symbol which celebrates life and the sharing of food is the bonding mechanism which cements long-lasting friendships. The snake feast in 'Chess King' must be one of the most memorable scenes in contemporary Chinese literature. As Bonnie McDougall remarks, it points to the idea that 'happiness is neither the proletarian joys of labour or of making revolution nor the decadent pleasures of the bourgeoisie, but a simple meal with friends' (McDougall 1990: 18).

This joyous hymn to the simplicity of life is almost Daoist. Thus, sharing a simple meal with friends, while seemingly concrete, points to a more general proposition about attitudes to life and tradition. It is like the game of chess itself. Ah Cheng's application of Daoism to chess in his story in practice turns out to be very unspecific, and in an interview he confessed to not knowing much about the game itself. For the purpose of writing the story he did not need to know much, as, correspondingly, readers of the story do not need to either. Daoist wisdom was originally intended to apply to all aspects of life, including the game of chess. As repeated in Ah Cheng's story it still applies more to social life and literary art than to strategies in the game itself:

> The old man said that my fault was that I was too bold. He also said that if my opponent was bold I should use softness to assimilate him, but while assimilating him at the same time create a winning strategy. Softness isn't weakness – it is taking in, gathering in, holding in. To hold and assimilate is to bring your opponent within your strategy. This strategy is up to you to create; you must do all by doing nothing. To do nothing is the Way, and it is also the invariant principle of chess.
>
> (Ah Cheng 1990: 45–6)

This is not pure Daoism: it is Daoism applied to strategy, in this case to chess but by implication to all other conflict situations. Where Daoism developed as an ethic of disengagement from active life, this is a set of tactics for a kind of war within everyday life. Cao Cao, the author of 'Short Song', whose words were adapted by Wang/Ah Cheng, was a general and a military strategist. As a writer Ah Cheng is also a strategist, but in some respects it is possible to question whose side he is on, and who is the opponent he is holding on to and transforming? As we have indicated above, food and drink are also central Confucian concerns, and Ah Cheng's emphasis on these human necessities can also be seen as Confucian humanistic concerns.

Wang/Ah Cheng's modified Daoism would fit in well with the set of strategies behind the 'presentation of the self in everyday life' that Goffman envisages. Semiotically it is intensely active, scanning the range of signs, intentional and unconscious, looking for weaknesses and points of advantage but never declaring enmity or hostility. The serenity that it projects is a deliberate trap, and underlying it is an implacable will to win that is more formidable because it is under such careful control.

Like Goffman's view of normal interaction ('impression management') this view could be seen as paranoid. Maybe so. Most Chinese people do not have the energy, skill or malevolence to be like this for long, if at all. But this sense is a useful antidote to the bland euphoria of textbooks for language learners, and their world of nice, friendly people endlessly saying 'You good' – 'You good' to each other. The problem with two-dimensional euphoria is that it leaves untouched the underlying anxieties which exist in so many social encounters, and especially strongly in encounters with important others across cultural, social and linguistic barriers. The anxiety is likely to return in the form of suspicion and paranoia, as the simple view turns out not to be adequate or safe in practice. A strategy that is designed to counteract racist stereotypes about the Other finishes up leaving them barely touched.

Harmony and balance are dominant qualities in Chinese art, as politeness and mutual respect are the dominant characteristics of codes of etiquette, but 'style' in both spheres contains many subtle ways of expressing and managing difference, conflict and anger. Outside the magic square where the rule of style holds sway, in art as in society, there are many kinds of interaction, many representations which lack style and balance and harmony, where crude power is exercised nakedly, where conflicts are resolved with brutal indifference to form. The rule of style is a form of discursive control, which removes many feelings and actions out of the scope of public discourse without, however, preventing these things from being thinkable and sayable, and ultimately acted on. It has developed forms of communication which cannot be fully trusted, which generate a suspicious reading strategy. In these situations 'reading style' does not give any direct access to truth, and always needs to be supplemented by other kinds of reading of other kinds of text which are more direct. 'Reading style' is not enough. But it is often the best place to start.

3 Writing and the ideological machine

Chinese characters and the construction of gender

The Chinese system of writing often seems like a dragon guarding the gates that lead into the Chinese mind and the texts that communicate it, dividing the world into two categories: those who can read characters, and can read what they want to and understand it in its original Chinese form, and those who can't, who are forever outsiders, dependent on translators to select and give the sense of the meanings that they need. Unlike learning a European language with its alphabetic script, the task facing those who want to learn the Chinese language in its written form is hugely difficult. They have to memorise the thousands of characters which make up the Chinese script. For people who have never learnt to read or write Chinese, the Chinese script seems fantastically difficult. In fact, the characters range from having only one stroke to some sixty-five strokes. Most characters can be broken up into two parts consisting of a radical, usually giving the semantic significance of the character, and another component which often indicates the phonetic element.

In its surveys of literacy, the government in the People's Republic of China takes 800 characters as the minimum before one is considered literate. To be considered educated, it is estimated that one has to know about 6000 characters (out of a total of some 60,000 found in dictionaries). The amount of time and effort invested in learning so many different symbols is tremendous. The characters themselves, once they are learnt, do not automatically fall into easily identifiable patterns. As any beginning student of Chinese knows, even using a dictionary can be a daunting process. Although most dictionaries use the 'radical method', where characters are classified according to the radicals, there are also dictionaries which are organised differently.

In this chapter, we want to explore just what is going on here, and why it matters for anyone wanting to understand the basic semiotic and ideological processes acting on and through the Chinese language. Our starting point is the paradox about Chinese characters. Even for native speakers of Chinese the characters are not an efficient means of communication. They represent a barrier to full literacy, yet successive efforts at language reform have been powerless to bring any substantial change. We argue that their instrumental inefficiency is outweighed by their ideological effectiveness, one important reason why they have been used for thousands of years, and why it has proved so difficult to bring in any other form of script in Chinese. We will show that the ideology encoded in the characters is based very much on traditional Chinese thinking founded on Confucianism and Daoism. This is what is at stake in arguments for the retention of characters as paramount in maintaining 'Chineseness' in the writing system. By making the ideology behind these sentiments and assumptions explicit, we believe that much of the mystery surrounding the written language will disappear. At the same time the task of learning it will become more meaningful, integrated into generalised reading strategies that any student of China can employ whether or not they know characters.

Language and ideology in Chinese

In arguing this case about how the Chinese language functions ideologically we need to say a few things about ideology and the processes of language and discourse. We will start from one influential view of the relations between language and ideology often called 'linguistic determinism', associated with the American linguist, Benjamin Whorf (1956). In this view, 'language' is taken to determine 'thought' by acting as the grid through which 'reality' is perceived and understood. Language in this view is all-powerful for a particular language community, a precondition of thought that is so all-pervasive and inescapable that it becomes invisible to its speakers, since they have no access outside language to any 'reality' outside its terms. Insofar as these structures of thought act as the ideology of the group then ideology will share the same properties of being everywhere and yet invisible.

It is indeed important for us all, whether our first language is English or Spanish or Chinese, to recognise how the terms of our language and thought, learnt as the apparently neutral means to think and communicate our supposedly individual meanings, pre-empt so many choices before we are aware of the possibility of choice. Whorf and his followers were structuralists, who assumed that language as a system was simple, coherent, and logical according to its own principles, even if those principles might be incommensurably different from one language to another. Various post-structuralists have cast serious doubt on whether any language is a single coherent system, or whether language is in fact a set of overlapping emergent systems, never homogeneous, always in a state of flux. This is the line we will be following in this book.

Instead of seeing language as a grid, an oppressively complete and homogeneous ideology acting like a set of peep-holes through which speakers peer anxiously out at reality, we see ideology as a set of forces or vectors which act through various aspects of language. 'Language' here includes semantic patterns, choices of words and phrases and syntactic forms as well as speech and writing systems. The same ideological vectors act equally through the things people talk or write about, the topics they choose, the ways they categorise and judge people, actions, contexts and things.

To illustrate what we are saying from the case of Chinese, we argue that there is a set of ideological forms in Chinese cultural life which has innumerable realisations and effects. It operates in philosophical texts and high culture and in the social practices of everyday life, in the forms of language (including the system of writing) in every text as well as in the worlds and judgements that those texts convey. It is present with such massive redundancy at so many levels, with such differing degrees of force or consciousness that no single channel is indispensable in the production of ideology. So we do not want to overstate the importance of forms of language on their own in carrying this ideological content. In practice it is best to go first to the classical philosophies upon which the culture is built for an outline of the ideological machine which generates the ideological forces acting on that culture. It is this kind of interdependence between language and ideology that we want to explore in this chapter.

But ideology is not a simple or well-understood matter either. In practice there have been many definitions of ideology (see for instance Williams 1986; Thompson 1986; and many other theorists). In this book we will follow the account of ideology argued by Hodge and Kress (1988, 1993) which insists that ideology itself is never unitary or homogeneous but operates as a complex which contains contradictions at its core.

Each ideological complex must incorporate a system of classification that assigns specific values to the various kinds of people, objects, activities and places that the ideology is designed to cover. The notion of 'classification' is usually associated with tidy, coherent and consistent schemes which organise the largest amount of material by the most economical means. 'Ideology' is often also discussed as though it is or ought to be comprehensive, coherent and consistent, constructing a single version of reality with such smooth inevitability that it seems almost like nature itself. However, Chinese language and ideology only make sense if the contrary is true, that ideology is partial, contradictory and incoherent, occurring not as a single structure but as a complex.

This occurs because ideology is designed to serve two contradictory functions: to express the power of the powerful, their difference from the non-powerful; and to assure the solidarity of the non-powerful, their identity of interests with the powerful. We will label these the P-ideology and the S-ideology respectively. The ideological complex contains, inextricably mixed, two forms of classification system to serve these two functions. This gives rise to a classification system that is constantly both suggesting and cancelling the possibility of a final subsuming order of things.

Chinese offers a particularly interesting instance of this set of processes at work because of two features which make Chinese unique. One is the role of its writing system, which we argue is more saturated with ideological functions and ideological content than any other major writing system. Secondly, this ideological complex has had a longer continuous existence than any rival system. Its extraordinary longevity and productivity are remarkable achievements in world historical terms. It is at the heart of the 3000-year-old Chinese miracle that is still capable of new twists. Perhaps its most miraculous achievement is that it has managed to seem as indispensable to various Communist regimes as it did to their imperial predecessors, and it also plays an important role in holding together the idea of China across the many different sites and systems of the Chinese diaspora. We will call this ideological complex the Chinese Ideological Machine, because it seems to operate so elegantly without apparent interventions from outside, though of course it is not a machine made of pulleys and cogs, but a generative system of meanings that only exist if people make them so.

The endless dance of opposites and the Chinese ideological machine

The revolutions in the first half of the twentieth century culminated in 1949 with the establishment of the People's Republic of China. However, the new regime continued to use the traditional written script – a script that had been denounced in the 1930s by revolutionary writers such as Qu Qiubai and Lu Xun as a major obstacle to mass literacy (see DeFrancis 1950). In the same way, the new regime also tried to adapt the traditional philosophical and moral system to new values and the fresh demands of the time. But the final outcome of this process of filtering the old traditions was, ironically, the defeat of the Cultural Revolution in 1976 and the triumph of Chinese tradition in a more outward-looking environment since that time. Traditional Chinese philosophy is still massively influential on Chinese life and thinking today (see Louie 1986). However, when its ideological function is acknowledged, it is generally only in the recognition of its 'Chineseness', as an essence which brings together all Chinese people, through its integration into patterns of socialisation in both home and school, as part of the Confucian ethos. Its classification system needs further analysis.

The French anthropologist Lévi-Strauss theorised systems of classification in a way that is illuminating when applied to the ideological structures underlying Chinese language and thought (1963, 1966). His methods of analysis were designed to interpret myths, rituals and everyday cultural practices. This method was mainly concerned with binary systems and their permutations, which followed a logic whose form he claimed was universal, though its particular manifestations varied from culture to culture. These ideas can be used with a structuralist orientation, to emphasise cultural universals and collapse the inexhaustibly rich and intricate pattern of differences between cultures. However this logic can also be seen as the source for a continual search for difference, establishing oppositions by the endlessly iterated application of a basic principle.

For example, a basic opposition between nature and culture found in all societies is repeated in the opposition between raw (natural) and cooked (altered by culture). But this new opposition does not simply repeat the earlier one, it also displaces it, allowing for combinations that can express forms of mediation and contradiction as well as opposition. For instance, food grilled over a fire is not as culturally altered as food which has been stewed, so that it can express a compound meaning, both culture and nature. Vegetables can be cooked almost to extinction, as in a certain kind of English cuisine, or more lightly cooked as in Chinese cuisine. Raw fish as in Japanese cuisine, or snake or dog as used in Chinese cuisine, are highly meaningful but strongly rejected from the point of view of traditional English food categories. Such compound meanings offer either the chance of harmonious resolution of opposites, or their dangerous and forbidden union. So meanings of this kind, in Lévi-Strauss's view, are often either highly prized or else taboo, or both, depending on the occasion.

From this point of view, taxonomies are not expected to be tidy, static sets of boxes, themselves devoid of meaning. On the contrary they are dynamic, inconsistent and open-ended, records of a dialectic process, an oscillation between the assertion and resolution of difference. The motive for this dialectic is explicable in terms of a theory of ideological complexes and their double function. The P-ideology largely expresses itself through binary oppositions constructing difference; while the S-ideology acts to blur or mask those differences. In practice, as we will see, the two forms do not necessarily act with such a neat symmetry (symmetry is itself an S-ideology effect). But it is useful to label the two forces at work in this way, precisely because it allows us to recognise the untidiness and asymmetry, instead of ruling it out as accidental and without function or significance.

Yin and *yang*, for example, have in many popular tracts on Eastern philosophy and astrology been seen as 'the basic opposing forces, negative and positive, dark and light, cold and hot, which keep the world and all of life spinning' (Palmer 1986: 32). Bailey, a linguist, saw *yin* and *yang* as 'the two sides of humanity . . . springing out of an undifferentiated *Dao* (or spring of energy). The goal of wholeness in this approach is the maintenance of . . . harmony' (Bailey 1982: 6).

The role of *yin* and *yang* in traditional philosophy is well known. Any basic book on Chinese philosophy will have a discussion on the theory of *yin* and *yang* (see for example Chan 1963: 244–50). For the *yin–yang* school these two principles were used to explain all natural phenomena. Although *yin* is explicitly linked with the female and *yang* with the male, the fact that the *yin–yang* system functions as an ideology of gender, in a way that is similar to gender systems in languages which are organised in those terms, such as ancient Latin and Greek, or modern French and Italian, is often glossed over (see for example Spender 1980: 160–2). What happens in both kinds of instance is that the world is classified in terms of a model of gender, and is thus constructed as an illustration of this model. Where this gender model is an obligatory part of the language, as in most European languages, every act of speech is a reiteration of the ideology, so automatic that it becomes an invisible, naturalised presence. When it is carried by a philosophical principle, as in the case of *yin–yang*, it functions more openly but less broadly, and much less directly implicated, in the very forms of the language itself. This makes it a more suitable kind of instance to use for examining the structures at issue, though we will then need other kinds of instance in order to demonstrate its full scope.

We will begin our examination of the connections of *yin* and *yang* with the contemporary Chinese language by looking at the dictionary entries for the two terms. (The dictionary referred to here is the *Chinese–English Dictionary* (1978), the most commonly used one for foreign students learning Chinese.)

> *Yin* (阴) (1) (In Chinese philosophy, medicine, etc.) *yin*, the feminine or negative principle in nature (2) the moon (3) overcast (4) shade (5) north of a mountain or south of a river (6) back (7) in intaglio (8) hidden; secret; sinister (9) of nether world (10) negative (ion) (11) private parts (esp. of the female)
>
> *Yang* (阳) (1) (in Chinese philosophy, medicine etc.) *yang*, the masculine or positive principle in nature (2) the sun (3) south of a hill or north of a river (4) in relief (5) open, overt (6) belonging to this world (7) positive (ion) (8) male genitals.

The respective meanings form a clear pattern whose basic form clearly derives from a philosophical foundation. The majority of the meanings given occur as binary pairs, which express and displace the primary meaning of male–female: moon–sun, north–south, hidden–open, etc. In Lévi-Strauss's notation we could describe these as having the form *yin:yang*::moon:sun etc. (i.e. the relation between *yin* and *yang* is as the relation between moon and sun). But the process is not unilinear or neutral. For the formula to work, the sun and moon must be constructed in gender terms. Conversely, the category of gender acquires some of the meanings of its transforms: femininity is moonlike, masculinity is sunlike, etc. But the meaning is not simply a matter of identifying analogues of female and male. More importantly it is a matter of establishing a relationship between the two; and it is this relationship which is the primary ideological content. However, this relationship itself takes two broad forms, which correspond to the S-ideological and the P-ideological functions respectively. In S-forms, the symmetry and inter-dependence of the relationship is what is stressed, with the *yin* and *yang* principles of equal importance (as are female and male for every act of reproduction). This is what is foregrounded in the philosophy, in the classic diagram of the principle, where each occupies exactly half a circle, and the two together make up a single whole. *Yin* leads the pair, *yang* completes the phrase.

However, the majority of the pairs listed in the dictionary are not in fact built up out of equal values. The moon is a significant heavenly body but not as large or luminous as the sun. 'Hidden' has sinister associations, unlike 'open'. These are P-forms, which use the pair to signify a relationship of unequal value. So the official philosophy of *yin–yang*, with its benign ideology of equality and respect for the feminine, coexists with another ideology of inequality and contempt for the feminine.

This can be seen even more clearly in the compounds – words formed by the combination of two or more characters – with *yin* or *yang* as the initial characters, as listed in the dictionary. There are thirty-four of these with *yin*, of which twenty-three (68 per cent) are negative, and only three (9 per cent) positive. Examples of compounds having negative connotations are *yinxian* 阴险 (sinister, insidious) and *yinyu* 阴郁 (gloomy, dismal). Of the twenty-one listed for *yang*, all are neutral or positive, only two are negative: *yangwei* 阳痿 (impotence, where *wei* means 'flaccid, paralysed', and incidentally contains a female radical as part of its structure) and *yangxu* 阳虚 (lack of *yang*, lack of virility, where *xu* means empty, void). These two confirm the overall positive value of *yang*, since they include a negation of the quality of *yang* as part of their meaning.

Two asymmetries are evident here. One is the negative value typically attributed to the female element. The other, observable in the lists of meanings as well as in the lists of compounds, is that there are more items organised by *yin* than by *yang*: twelve versus eight meanings, and thirty-four versus twenty-one compounds. In some respects the *yin* is more important than the *yang* as an ideological category. Put in another way, the system offers a richer, more developed system for denigrating the feminine than for describing or praising the masculine. This is a pattern that has also been found with terms of abuse in English, where there are many more terms of abuse for and about women than there are about men (see Schulz 1975). Yet this asymmetry in usage is masked by the elegant and judicious symmetries of the classic *yin–yang* form. The two together offer a very neat instance of an ideological complex, where P-ideologies coexist with S-ideologies, and the S-forms function to mask, but not conceal, the dominance of the P-forms.

The contradiction between S-forms and P-forms is not the only source of anomalies in the pattern of binaries. We have noted the case of *yangwei* and *yangxu,* where a term incorporates negative meanings. A more complex instance is the use of each term as its opposite when applied to 'river', so that *yin* means the south side of a river but the north side of a hill, while *yang* means the north side of a river but the south side of a hill. In this case we can see how a structure is understood in which *yin:yang*::river:hill. Here river has a negative value, and thus reverses the *yin–yang* value of north and south in the same way as did *wei* and *xu*; while hill, as a positive, masculine principle, reinforces the normal values of the two terms. This illustrates a number of important principles. One is that the gender principle encoded by *yin–yang* is a generative principle which goes beyond the set of instances listed in the dictionary. A second is that these elements can be combined in anomalous structures, whose meaning is either mediation or contradiction. We would expect one of these conjunctions to express resolution of contradictions, harmony, etc. (S-meanings), and the other to be the focus of taboo (P-meanings). In this case the north of a mountain is strongly taboo, and the north of a river is an especially auspicious location. Thus, for a balance of *yin* and *yang*, the best site would be halfway up the south side of a hill, as is in fact the case in popular Chinese geomancy.

Circles of mediation

Although a binary system can be extended indefinitely to become an infinite set, its tendency to produce symmetrical oppositions often leads to difficulties of fit, as applied to a world that is not always conveniently organised in those forms. For example, in terms of directions, as well as having elements to classify north–south, it is clearly desirable to have elements which could also classify east, west and centre. The desirability cuts both ways: it creates more refined subsets while at the same time creating more ambiguities. We now turn to the ancient system called 'five agents theory'. It is a more complex scheme which is nonetheless clearly related to and just as influential as the *yin–yang* system. Other cultures have gone through the same process of developing first a binary and then a five-fold classification system. The ancient Greek and Indian ones are the best known (see Bucknell and Stuart-Fox 1986).

According to the Song dynasty Confucian philosopher Zhou Dunyi, 'by the transformation of *yang* and its union with *yin*, the Five Agents of Water, Fire, Wood, Metal, and Earth arise' (Chan 1963: 463). To show their interrelations we will set them out in a single composite scheme, as outlined below (see p. 55):

This schema is built up by a number of taxonomic acts. First it is based on an inventory of areas to be subjected to classification: substances, seasons, flavours, organs, etc. The inventory is arbitrary and open-ended, since the principle could be applied to virtually any specific area of experience, though in making their choice of areas the five-agents theorists were naturally motivated by their own interests and purposes. Within these areas, the number of items to be included in a taxonomic subset was specified in advance as five, so that colours like blue or brown or pink are not included in this scheme. Each of the taxonomic subsets is organised along the same lines, producing the same basic pattern by application of the same principles; each is mapped on to the same scheme. So it is the common principle or principles that we need to elucidate.

As described by the original Han dynasty theorists, there is in fact a double principle organising the subsets. On the one hand each subset is built up out of a series of oppositions, but these oppositions are chained together

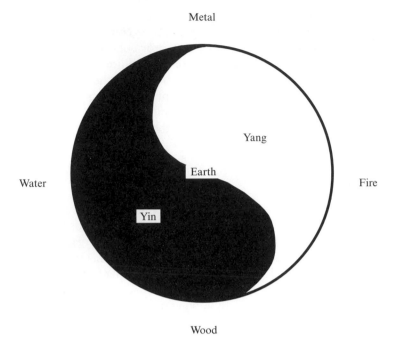

Figure 3.1 The *yin–yang* symbol and its five agents transforms

to produce a circle, so that the principle of opposition sustains a larger structure of harmonious interdependence. This illustrates once again the principle of the coexistence of S-ideology and P-ideology, with S-ideology posited as the overarching system. But on closer inspection we can see another set of organising principles at work in the construction of these taxonomies.

To illustrate, we will take the five agents themselves, the elements of wood, fire, earth, metal and water. Among these, the strongest opposition is that between fire and water. It in fact expresses the kind of irreconcilable opposition in the *yin–yang* form. In the S-form of this matrix, the two elements that have the complementary relationship are wood and metal. They can be used together, and have complementary properties and strengths. This leaves earth as an anomalous fifth entity, since it participates in different ways in both oppositions: earth is the matrix in which metal is found and out of which trees grow, and it is the element which can contain both water and fire. Spatially in this diagram it is allied with the centre, as against the cardinal points, again signifying its meaning as a mediating category.

The principle at issue, then, can be described in terms of a double operation on a basic binary pattern of oppositions, a double transformational process to construct S-forms to counterbalance the primary and underlying P-form. Using the Lévi-Straussian formula we can set them out as follows:

```
P-form          S-form
fire : water    ::   wood : metal
          earth
```

The same principle applies to the other taxonomic subsets:

Seasons   summer : winter   ::   spring : autumn
                              year

Directions   south : north   ::   east : west
                              centre

Colours   red : black   ::   green : white
                           yellow

In this analysis we note some areas where the desired tidiness is lacking. Most importantly, because it is more consistent and systemic, the continuity of S-forms makes classifications unclear and messy. To start with wood and metal, there is a problem with the gender of wood, since it is included in the *yang* qualities, but so is metal, and metal is more valuable than wood and can be seen as more 'masculine', since it is what weapons are made of. For example, in the ancient classic *Book of Changes*, metal is explicitly linked with *qian*, the male aspect of the male–female (*qian–kun*) bipolarity (see Chan 1963: 249). Thus, each of the oppositions in the S-form includes some elements of both the constitutive oppositions in the P-mode. This is unsurprising, in terms of our argument, since it is precisely their function to do so, but it leaves these categories both unstable and ambivalent.

The same ambiguity is seen in the last mediatory category, that which occupies the central position. Using the primary agents as examples again, earth clearly carries both very positive connotations (as in native earth, basis of existence) or very negative ones (dirt, the least-valued substance). Earth is apparently the inert and neutral element, the part of the *yin–yang* machinery which generates the other four agents and the site upon which they interact and return to. The double value of these central categories comes from their positioning in either P-forms or S-forms. As with *yin–yang*, we find that the seeming neatness and symmetry of the taxonomy turns out to be an ideologically motivated illusion. What we have instead is an unstable, double system whose basic principle is both endlessly repeated (in its innumerable manifestations) yet elaborately concealed.

From this analysis we can draw a number of generalisations about the two Chinese taxonomic schemes as ideological forms. First, they work with an inventory of areas of existence, which is capable of being endlessly extended. By this means they displace and conceal the principle of the system, since it is endlessly deployed and repeated, but its basic nature is not explicitly declared. At the core of the system is a small set of ideological primes, including meanings of gender and class and the relations between categories of each. The momentum of the system arises out of a dialectic between P-forms, emphasising difference and inequality, and S-forms, emphasising interrelation and symmetry. But this dialectic is not an even struggle: it would be an S-form to represent it as such. In practice there are many asymmetries, contradictions and inconsistencies, arising necessarily out of the fact that the system is realised through negotiation and struggle, involving exploitation and resistance in ways and proportions that are determined by the conditions of social existence, and not necessarily by the nature of the schemes themselves.

Conservative radicals

If this system remained in its philosophical form, as expounded in moral and philosophical treatises such as the classics of Confucianism and Daoism *Mengzi* and the *Daodejing*, it would hardly have a profound influence on the everyday thought of everyday people today. In practice, however, an evolving and often inconsistent system constituted along these lines still pervades the language itself, particularly in the system of characters which is similarly old. It is in this written form that the language clearly manifests itself as part of the texture of everyday life and thought.

The first site where we will look for this system is in the set of 200-odd 'radicals' which are found as components of a large proportion of the characters of the written language. These radicals, like the Confucian-Daoist philosophical system itself, tell much about human relations in Chinese society. Numerous books and articles have pointed out the useful and 'fun' aspects of these radicals as a way of learning and teaching the Chinese language and culture. In the popular *Strait Times* collection *Fun With Chinese Characters*, for example, comic-book style pictures illustrate how characters might best be remembered (Tan Huay Peng 1980–3). Thus, the character for 'good' 好, has three illustrations, all with a man smiling and surrounded by (1) a woman with a child, (2) a boy and a girl, and (3) a woman carrying a baby on her back. The text explains, 'Man combined 女 (girl or daughter) with 子 (child or son) to form a character for goodness and excellence. From experience he must have found his greatest good in the possession of a wife and a child or a son and a daughter. It is also good that his wife sticks to his child' (Tan 1980–3: 3). Research has also shown that these 'fun' ways of inventing stories to the radicals and characters are almost a universal aid to teaching and learning the characters (Bourke 1997). We will argue that as ideological primes, the radicals express, above all, notions of power and solidarity. To illustrate this, we will concentrate on gender relations as generated by the *yin–yang* bipolarity.

Because the radicals are normally only component parts of the characters, their ideological content can be carried in a relatively unobtrusive way, which makes them less open to inspection and critique, more able to sustain contradictory functions and ambiguous meanings. They became part of a classification system that is too diffuse and contradictory to be suspected of being a system at all, yet is so ubiquitous, automatic and obligatory that by sheer weight of repetition they still serve their coercive function effectively. As we will illustrate later, the 'woman' radical 女 is a component of many characters which connote negative values. Throughout this century, language reform committees have been alerted to this fact, and a group of women have even suggested changing all such characters by replacing 女 with the 'evil' radical 歹. But these pleas have been consistently ignored on the grounds that while the script may have originally expressed an ideological stance, it is now beyond ideology.

We believe the opposite is the case. The laborious induction into the system of characters, seemingly so wasteful of time and energy, so inefficient as a means to mass literacy, is an integral part of the traditional system of socialisation. It inserts a dominant ideology, of both class and gender, into the very form of the language, which is then repeated endlessly in everything that is written or read.

Much more is at stake here than mere practical efficiency or inefficiency, though that too is an important issue. A defence of the writing system, even in its simplified forms, is essentially a defence of an ideological machine of massive efficacy. The operations of this machine have, however, remained covert, of necessity, to maintain their effectiveness. Most discussion around simplification and romanisation revolve around 'myths' such as universality and indispensability, myths which have been convincingly debunked by John DeFrancis (1984). But ideology is an important and often neglected issue. The ideological system is to be found in many other aspects of the language. It would by no means disappear if the traditional Chinese script were to be eliminated. Yet such a disruption of the function of the written language would still have major repercussions for the ideological complex, not least because any disruption would bring the ideological nature and content of the written characters out into the open for the first time. If this were done, then the claims for the neutral and unifying nature of the traditional script would not be so easy to sustain. A new and different kind of debate would open up, and new alignments might form to produce a very different language policy, a shift from the present policy of tacit endorsement of the *status quo*.

From this we can see the possibility of describing the nature and function of the system of radicals, the sheer number of which otherwise seems to defy any attempt to abstract a simple pattern. Even if we look only at the fifty most common radicals, rather than the full set of 200-odd, we still seem to have too many, a system that is too diverse. However, we will argue in what follows that underlying both the complete and reduced sets is a system of classification that has the same essential qualities as we have seen with the five agents and the *yin–yang* pair. The radicals are used in two broad senses, one material (the entity classified by the radical is made of or materially like the radical) and the other ideological (the entity concerned is constructed in terms of the meanings associated with the radical). This difference itself is often ambiguous, since the material reality is constructed in ideological terms itself through the overall scheme, so that the material fact may also carry ideological meanings. We see these ideological meanings as organised through homologically related taxonomic subsets, which give rise to massive redundancy, since the same ideological prime may underlie a large number of these subsets. Along with this redundancy goes systematic contradiction, since a substantial proportion of the content of the subsets will be devoted precisely to the task of opposing neat oppositions. As a result there will be what at first appear to be numerous exceptions, whose explanation will be found however to be derived from a simple and consistent set of functional principles.

To illustrate the process we will begin with the radicals that are associated with the five agents: water 水, fire 火, wood 木, metal 金 and earth 土. In the P-form, the most obvious examples are the characters formed by the binary pair: fire, the male element in the *yin–yang* transformer, and water, the female element. As well as being the female element, water is associated with qualities such as black, north and winter, while fire is associated with the more 'masculine' elements such as red, south and summer. In the characters formed by these radicals, the evaluative divisions are equally clear. In modern Chinese, there are some 450 characters formed by the radical 'water' and about 100 formed by 'fire'.

Most of the characters in both categories are materially constructed, for example 'river' 河 and 'sea' 海 for 'water' 氵, and 'lamp' 灯 and 'furnace' 炉 for 'fire' 火. However, for the 'water' radical, there are more than twenty characters which have clear ideological values. For the 'fire' radical, there are about a dozen. This is in keeping with our observation above that the feminine tends to be more developed in the quantity of terms to describe (or abuse) it.

Some characters formed by the 'water' radical such as 'dirty, corrupt' (污) and 'licentious, debauched' (淫) leave little to the imagination when the gender associations of water are considered. Others are less clear. Many that seem materially constructed such as the three characters for 'vast' (汪, 浩, 汰) all describe vastness in terms of water, but they also carry connotations of vastness to excess. There are some characters which seem to carry positive values. Examples are '*qing*' 清 and '*jie*' 洁. In both of these the second component is phonetic and does not affect the meaning, which in both cases is 'cleanliness and purity'. They are interesting S-form concepts because like the virgin–whore complex, these characters form the 'virgin' aspect of a predominantly negative trend. In fact, these characters are often used in the names of nunneries and temples.

By contrast, 'fire' radical characters carry predominantly positive values. For example, there are many terms which are materially engendered and they have meanings such as 'bright, luminous and brilliant' (for example 灿, 炳,

燎) and, like their English equivalents, carry positive connotations in the ideological realm. Those that are obviously negative, such as the characters for 'dust, disappointed' 灰 and 'disaster' 灾, have as their other component radicals meaning 'to grab with the hand (to contain)' or 'to cover'. Thus it is the masculine element, fire, which is restrained or contained when disaster and disappointment is implied.

While water and fire are two elements which are meant to represent the male–female poles of the *yin–yang* opposition and thus are most obvious in revealing the oppositions involved when they are used as radicals in the characters, two of the other elements in the *yin–yang* machine which are opposite each other – metal and wood – are situated in areas which are less unambiguously *yin* or *yang*. We may thus expect characters formed by these radicals to be of the S-form and to exhibit less 'antagonistic' contradictions even though they still show ideological dimensions, just as wood is situated in the same point as spring, and metal in autumn, and spring and autumn are not seen to be so diametrically opposed. This is in fact the case. Of the 200-odd characters formed by the metal radical and the 300-odd formed by the wood radical, only a dozen or two in each category carry clear ideological meanings which are not directly related to concepts having to do with metal or vegetation.

These two radicals generate almost equal proportions of characters having positive or negative connotations. There are more characters formed by the wood radical, not surprising given the fact that wood is the site of east and spring, thus giving rise to the idea of 'the origin or stem' 本. In keeping with its S-ideology connections, 'wood' 木 characters embrace concepts which are directly opposite in their implications. Thus while 柔 means 'soft', 权 means 'power'. However, in Daoist philosophy, as is well known, 'soft' does not imply 'weak', but quite the opposite. Thus, while it may seem superficially that power and softness are conflicting qualities, the seemingly contradictory implications of the 'wood' radical in fact only reinforce the Daoist and *yin yang* ideological message.

Characters formed by the 'metal' radical also carry both positive and negative meanings. For example, while 错 means 'wrong, disorderly', 锐 means 'sharp, clever'. On the whole, though, metal is seen to be stronger and, according to the *Book of Changes*, more masculine than wood, so that many of the characters have meanings such as 'to subdue' 镇, 'to lock, to confine' 锁 and so on. While 'wood characters' also contain categories like 'to regulate' 格, the tone implied by the word is not so forceful, showing that the action derived from the wood origin is not as hard as that of metal origin.

This has significance for the P-ideology. Just as words from the 'fire' radical can be contrasted with words from the 'water' radical to show the gender bias of these groupings, so it can be seen that 'metal' characters take on meanings such as 'sharp' 锋, 'brilliant' 锦, and 'to subdue' 镇 whereas many 'wood' characters have meanings such as 'to rot' 朽, 'to infect' 染, and ' mixed' 栽.

Just as many more words are formed by the 'water' radical than by the 'fire' radical, so too more words are derived from the 'wood' than from the 'metal' radical. This conforms with the general rule that the 'masculine' needs fewer adjectives to describe it than the 'feminine'.

Lastly, following our argument, the agent which lies in the centre of the *yin–yang* machine, earth 土, should as a radical be even more ambiguous in its transformations than 'metal' and 'wood'. Of the 100-odd characters formed from the 'earth' radical, those with negative meaning and positive meaning are about equal in number. Thus, the character 'bad' 坏 is formed from the earth radical. In its simplified form, the 'no' component to the right suggests that the language policy makers also viewed the earth element ambiguously – no earth is a bad thing. Other examples where earth appears to promote a negative ideological content are 'collapse' 塌 and 'sink' 堕. On the positive side, true to its mother-earth origins, characters such as 'to nourish' 培 and 'to sustain' 堪 form part of the repertoire generated by this radical.

No discussion of the radicals would be complete without mentioning characters formed by the 'woman' radical 女, a component which also illustrates vividly the points we have been arguing in this chapter. The most ancient Chinese dictionary, the *Shuowen jiezi* of the Han dynasty, listed only three characters under the 'male' 男 radical (Xu Shen: 698–9), namely 'male' 男, 'maternal uncle' 舅 and 'nephew' 甥. There were so few characters in the 'male' category that this classification was dropped from later dictionaries and the three characters were reclassified. By contrast, the *Shuowen jiezi* has 258 characters formed by the 'woman' radical 女. Modern dictionaries have rather fewer, about 180, but the contrast with the meagre 'male' category remains striking. Regarding characters formed by the 'woman' radical, we can make several interesting observations: in terms of the *yin–yang* dichotomy, we would expect the 'woman' radical, being *yin*, to resemble the 'water' radical in generally having negative connotations yet at the same time forming some characters which seem to suggest a positive value.

Many characters, of course, derive from the biological meaning of the 'woman' radical. Words such as 'mother' 妈, 'elder sister' 姐, and 'younger sister' 妹, for example, carry little ideological import separate from the social meaning of women. Apart from ones derived from nature, many characters with the 'woman' radical are clearly derived from the female gender and carry strong ideological messages. We will look at some very simple and common ones.

Certain characters formed from the 'woman' radical denote actions involving both sexes which are considered unsavoury and immoral, for example, 'slavery' 奴, 'prostitution' 娼, 'treachery' 奸 and 'adultery' 奸. Other characters formed by the 'woman' radical denote emotions seen as negative, for example, 'jealousy' 嫉 and 'avarice' 婪. This indicates that these emotions were thought of as particularly characteristic of women.

These blatantly negative concepts belong to the P-mode of the power–

solidarity split. Of the radicals which have to do with 'human' qualities – 'person' 人, 'self' 己, 'child' 子 etc. – none has as many emotionally and morally charged negative concepts as the radical for 'woman'. In *yin–yang* terms, this shows conclusively that despite the assertion that *yin* and *yang* are complementary concepts which integrate and influence each other and are themselves beyond human values, this is in the abstract only.

Naturally, proponents of *yin–yang* as neutral do not stop at the characters we have looked at. In fact, there are many characters formed by the woman radical which at first glance seem to suggest very good qualities. Some common examples are 'good' 好, 'peace' 安 and 'excellent' 妙. Closer inspection shows, however, that these characters contain two contradictory messages, and reveals the extent to which the female gender takes the role of the oppressed. 'Good', for example, seems a perfectly good character; but as well as the 'woman' radical, it also contains the 'son' 子 radical. It seems then, that the concept and what it represents is a good thing to have (for men). 'Peace' is again a composite character which seems to have been invented and used by men. The character has woman in it, but on top of the woman is the 'cover' or 'roof' radical. Thus, it implies that to achieve peace, one must keep the woman indoors or under cover. In the same way, 'excellent' 妙 has woman in its composition, but the other component is 'few' 少, so that the usually negative notion of woman here is reversed to form a positive concept.

It is also possible to explain characters such as 'good' and 'peace' by the S-form of the *yin–yang* machine: that even in the *yin* part, there need to be concepts which would make the *yin* seemingly favourable. In fact, in terms of S-ideology, there are many characters formed by the 'woman' radical which denote positive qualities, more, for example, than are formed by radicals such as 'fire' and 'jade'. Most of these characters have meanings such as 'charming' 娇 and 'beautiful' 妍. While such characteristics seem desirable, there is no doubt which gender they are attributed to and which gender and class they ultimately serve. Beauty not only is in the eyes of the beholder, but is used and abused by the beholder as well. An apt example is the character 'bewitching' 妖. The meanings attached to words formed from this character range from 'pretty and coquettish' 妖艳 to 'evil spirit' 妖魔.

Reforming the Chinese character

In the next two chapters, we will examine in more detail linguistic structures which go beyond simple characters and word. Here it is sufficient to acknowledge that the Chinese script, while difficult to master, carries with it the ideological underpinnings of traditional Chinese culture. The process of learning Chinese characters is in part a process of committing to memory cultural values – about power relationships, categorisations and social norms. Given the fact that political and social power and privilege rest on a knowledge of these characters, it is not surprising that those who have made the effort and succeeded in mastering the written language would be reluctant to support drastic reforms which would result in the simplification or abolition of these characters. As Wang Li, a prominent language expert in the Language Reform Committee, remarks, the greatest opposition for language reform 'comes primarily from intellectuals, especially from high-level intellectuals' (quoted in DeFrancis 1985: 63).

Most people would agree that simple things are easier to commit to memory than complicated things. Nevertheless, the belief that the traditional complicated forms of characters are superior to any simplified versions is so strong that experiments have been conducted again and again to show that simplified characters are easier to learn than complicated ones (see for example Dong Yuequan and Song Jun 1987: 13–17). However, there is a widespread contrary belief amongst linguists and psychologists that reducing the number of strokes may not make the learning of Chinese characters any easier. Even Western linguists writing books on comparing different writing systems, such as Geoffrey Sampson, argue that the language reform in China is 'misguided', and that if 'the visual distinctiveness of the elements' of a character are taken into consideration, then 'the reformed characters are inferior to their predecessors' (1985: 160). One of the most common reasons advanced by people such as Sampson who believe that the Chinese script may be easier to learn and to read than an alphabetic script is that each character is like a Gestalt, that is, the various parts of the characters form a total image which relates to what it signifies.

What we have shown above, however, is that when the Chinese or foreign student learns the Gestalt, it is one which uses the P and S ideologies for the benefit of groups of people from the upper classes and of masculine gender. Thus, when opponents to simplification say that the simplified characters are 'not beautiful', (Wang Tian 1988: 131) they are expressing an appreciation for a Gestalt which is culturally determined.

Another, and more important, version of this argument against simplification is that simplified characters would lose their original significance and thus become harder to learn. Such arguments only demonstrate that a particular notion of what is a universal and correct representation of the world has been accepted. In this way, as we have stressed before, compared to an alphabetic language, the script may not be efficient to learn initially, but it is an extremely potent cultural carrier which educationally is very efficient and powerful. This is in fact a point often made by those who are against romanisation, and largescale experiments have been done to attempt to show that Chinese children initially find it harder to learn to read than American children, but after the initial difficulties they cope better (Dong Yuequan and Song Jun 1987: 17).

The arguments for simplification and alphabetisation of Chinese characters have been debated most vociferously in this century. The establishment of the PRC brought in a government which was ostensibly more prepared to change for the sake of making the written language more accessible. Barely nine days after the new Republic was proclaimed, the Chinese Language Reform Association was formed. By 1955, the 'Draft of the Chinese Character Simplification Scheme' was announced. The Draft has three sections: a list of 798 characters where the number of strokes have been reduced; a list of 400 variant characters which are to be abolished; and a list of 251 radicals with two standardised versions of their handwritten forms. Over 200,000 people took part in discussing the Draft Outline, and 5167 submissions were received. In 1956, the 'Chinese Characters Simplification Scheme' was announced. This was the scheme which formed the basis of the 1964 'Comprehensive List of Simplified Characters' of 2238 entries which is still current today.

The creators of the new simplified forms tried where possible to retain the semantic component, thus leaving the ideological trace as well as creating characters which had a phonetic clue. The semantic component is crucial to their decision making on reforming the characters. For example, the character for 'brilliant, bright' 灿 with a fire radical and a phonetic mentioned above was simplified in 1955 by simply dropping the fire radical and keeping the phonetic part 粲 unchanged. However, it was obviously felt that this was not as good an abbreviation as keeping the fire radical and substituting the more complex phonetic 'can' (fresh, smiling) 粲 with 'shan' (mountain) 山.

This switch performs several functions. It reaffirms the connection between 'fire', the masculine element, with brilliance and shine. At the same time, although 'shan' (mountain) is not as good an approximation for phonetic reasons as 'can' (fresh) in the 1955 version, it does mean that 'mountain', again a masculine aspect in our *yin–yang* chart, is tagged on to the concept of brilliance. This character and its simplification show very clearly the demand for ideological encoding. It is a good example because the word 'can' (brilliant, bright) 灿 does have clear connotations. While most of the other characters do not carry such a convenient message, it is in fact possible to work through the list of differences and show that on the whole, the connotations inherent in the characters are not lost in the simplification. This shows the extent to which the committee members were making sure that in the simplification process, the traditional Gestalt was not lost.

In order to illustrate the strength of traditional ideology in the characters, it is illuminating to look at one example from the failed 'Draft of the Second Simplification Scheme' of 1977. Here we can demonstrate how, when the ideological content in the Chinese character shifts, the Gestalt as a whole no longer congeals. The character which illustrates our point is 'xian' (suspicion, resentment) . The original was made up of the semantic radical for woman (*nü*) 女 and the phonetic '*jian*' (also) 兼. The new scheme has changed this to the semantic radical 'heart' (*xin*) 心 and the more accurate phonetic '*xian*' (first) 先. The compilers have actually provided an explanatory note to this new character, saying that since it has a derogatory meaning, they have decided to change the woman radical to a heart radical. This is the only case in the Draft where a radical change (in both senses) has occurred and been made explicit. It is unlikely that the compilers were ignorant of the feelings already generated by the woman radical and how demands for change had been dismissed. This shift, in the section of characters which are not yet in common use and which needed to be tested, was indicative of some of the thinking of the Cultural Revolution period, when the traditional ideology surrounding women was being questioned on a mass scale.

There were many factors which worked against the Second Scheme. Apart from practical ones such as those made by linguists like C.C. Cheng which include the short amount of time allowed for general acceptance of the scheme and the obvious lack of support from above, it is clear by looking at the ideological implications of reforming the characters why support may have been so half-hearted. All the changes included in the First Scheme of 1956, which had been greeted with official fanfare and support, were ones incorporating shorthand versions of characters already in common use traditionally. These were not attempts to change the Gestalt, as it were. By contrast, the Second Scheme invented new characters which were more in keeping with the spirit of the Cultural Revolution. The result was still a Gestalt, but one with an image which changed traditional power relations.

In the political struggles of the Cultural Revolution, the leftists, who favoured simplification, lost miserably. Taking the Second Scheme of Simplified Characters as an example of the reasons for their failure, we can draw out several lessons. The most important is perhaps that voiced by those who criticise the general dictatorial style adopted by the 'Gang of Four'. It is ironic that for a leadership which constantly promoted the 'mass line', the line was in fact the creation of a small group of people – 'the vanguard' in Leninist terminology. Language is a living thing which cannot be forced on people. One reason the 1956 list of simplified characters was acceptable was precisely that they were already in general use anyway. By inventing some, no matter how few, new symbols and expecting the general public to use them, the compilers of the Second Scheme were begging for a rebuke. The scheme in fact died not long after without even a whimper.

Reading ideology in written texts

We have stressed the ideological content and significance of Chinese characters because usually this aspect is completely left out of descriptions of the language. However, we do not want to go to the other extreme, and imply that characters have an overriding role in carrying ideological content in Chinese. If that were so, then readers of Chinese texts who do not know Chinese would, for good or ill, be completely unaware of the ideological content of most texts, unable to be affected by it, and incapable of giving an ideological reading of any text. On the contrary, in our view language acts as a set of vectors which carry complex ideological forms, which are always massively and redundantly present in innumerable other sites and systems of meaning.

This position has immediate consequences for anyone who seeks to read Chinese texts more deeply. The redundancy between language and other systems is so massive and systemic that in many cases it is possible to use an ideological analysis of non-language codes as the basis for projecting what is happening in the system of writing, and even vice versa. Therefore someone who cannot read the characters as such can still get a pretty good sense of what is going on in a text by drawing on the *yin–yang* machine. In some ways their understanding could be better than that of someone who can decode the characters but is blind to the presence and complex work of ideology. Of course to be able to read both characters and ideology is even better: justification enough for the long and tedious task of learning all those characters.

We will illustrate the range of tactics of reading and interpretation and the issues that they raise by discussing a single story, 'Lilies' by Ru Zhijuan (1958, reprinted 1985: 7–18). Our aim is to show how the text works to construct its meanings by complex interactions between meanings carried at three levels: the narrative level (the world represented by the text), the symbolic level (objects, qualities, etc. given particular ideological values by the ideological machine) and the graphemic level (meanings encoded in characters, drawn from the same ideological machine and interacting closely with meanings from the symbolic level).

Ru Zhijuan has been an important writer since the 1950s. Her early work had many of the qualities of Socialist Realism typical of this period, portraying 'typical' people demonstrating exemplary virtues and reinforcing various current dogmas of the Chinese Communist Party. This particular story, first published in 1958, is only nine pages long, and deals with a minor incident in the struggle between the Communists and the Nationalists in 1946, three years before the Communists achieved their final victory.

The action is seen from the point of view of the narrator, a woman who is in the army as part of the support forces. It begins with her being escorted by a young soldier to a first-aid post just behind the front line, immediately prior to a Communist offensive. He intrigues her by his strength and sensitivity, but nothing of an explicitly sexual nature happens between them. The two approach people in the local village to try to obtain quilts and mattresses for the wounded (it is mid-autumn). The young man tries unsuccessfully to borrow a quilt from one young woman, so the narrator makes a second approach and asks the woman again. The woman this time agrees, and brings out a splendid quilt, red with white lilies embroidered on it. Clearly, she felt that handing this item over to a young soldier was a breach of sexual etiquette. It turns out that she is a bride of only three days, and this quilt is her wedding dowry. Yet she is willing to donate so precious an item to the Communist cause. The young man is so agitated that he tears his jacket. The bride offers to sew it up for him, but he declines. The young man is then fatally wounded in the offensive that night, sacrificing his life to save a whole squad. The bride is deeply affected by his heroic death. She frantically and futilely stitches up the tear in his shirt, and instead of reclaiming her quilt she drapes it on the dead body of the young man.

The moral of the story is clear even in this bare summary – a celebration of the heroic peasant-soldier and the selfless bride, each in their own gender-appropriate way sacrificing what is most precious to them to the Communist cause. This is closer to propaganda than ideology, which normally functions far more subtly. The story is dealing with two potent sets of opposition: between men and women, and between traditional values and the new values of modern socialist China. In the story itself these oppositions are constantly at play. The narrator explains in the first paragraph that she was held back from a dangerous posting by the commander of her regiment 'probably because I was a woman'. She does go to the front, as a modern woman, but cannot keep up with the young soldier because she has blisters. Once in the village itself she organises people, including the young peasant-soldier, but it is he who goes to the front itself, while she waits behind in the traditional role of tending the sick and suffering. Traditional gender roles are renegotiated under the pressure of wartime conditions but remain primary, in a typical oscillation between S-ideology and P-ideology forms.

At the outset, the narrator is contrasted with the bride, as modern professional woman to traditional wife; but the traditional woman makes a huge leap, from a traditional bride concerned only with her family to a woman who works with the narrator in the hospital and who sets the needs of the Communist cause over the family. But complementary to this movement is the ideological tug of the core ideology, with the terms of her climactic commitment to the state – the actions she performs, the meanings accreting to the quilt and its flowery symbols – coming from the rich resources of the ideological machine.

These elements weave throughout the story like a subtle commentary on the action, which we can track even through a translation. For instance, the first words of the story, seeming to set the scene in a minimally functional way, are 'Mid-autumn, 1946'. The year is the first word in the Chinese original, in Arabic numerals which lack any resonance from the ideological machine, locating the action in the well-known history of the war of liberation. Then follow the characters *zhongqiu* 中秋 meaning 'mid-autumn'. This has practical significance in the story, because autumn is a season cold enough to need quilts. The mid-autumn festival is a time when families unite as one, a point emphasised in the story when the narrator and the soldier discover they are from the same locality, thus establishing they are almost family. Autumn is also a season with symbolic significance in five-agents theory, a mediatory season opposed to spring. Ru Zhijuan elaborates and complicates this structure within its own terms. The weather is now fine, she writes, but it had just rained that morning, and 'the crops on either side sparkled fresh and green in the sunlight. There was a moist freshness in the air'.

The description sounds as close to spring as to autumn, with crops growing not leaves falling, a balance between hot and cold, fresh and moist, life and death. The landscape is understood in these traditional terms, as a generic landscape as much as the particular scene of a particular war. The narrator herself speculates along these lines (if not for the sound of gunfire 'you could have imagined you were on your way to a fair' [Ru: 7]). Later on, after the battle starts, a government official brings her a moon-cake. She remembers that it is the mid-autumn festival, and again her imagination invokes tradition, a shared tradition of food, songs and games that binds her and the peasant soldier just as strongly as their common service of Communism.

Signifiers of tradition are everywhere in the story, taken for granted as a common language for everyone, villagers and army alike. For instance, the bride's house has two large scrolls pasted up on the walls in bright red, presumably with an antithetical couplet on marital bliss. The quilt itself is red, the colour of masculine energy, with white lilies embroidered on it, which traditionally signify purity and death. All this is made explicit in the climax of the story: 'Her eyes were bright with unshed tears in the moonlight. I watched as they covered the face of that ordinary country lad, who had hauled bamboo, with this red quilt dotted with white lilies – flowers of true purity of heart and love' (Ru: 18).

In this last climactic passage, everything has meaning in terms of the ideological machine. The 'unshed tears' for instance are both psychologically realistic and also a complex play on moisture which is not moisture, the tears of a woman who is being supremely womanly in grieving for a man who is not her husband, while also transcending womanliness in her heroic act of sacrifice. The bamboo the man once hauled is an odd detail to mention at this point, which has the kind of double function that is typical of the discursive strategy of this story: signifying both his status as peasant, and the masculine object of his labours, contrasted to the lilies that the bride embroidered.

This reinforcement of traditional meanings by the same kind of meaning in the characters works in a complex way. It is not that the characters contribute any meaning that is not already signified in the words of the text and by the objects depicted. The effect is somewhat different: it is to stitch these meanings inextricably into the very means of thought and communication, into the written language that is the common medium of communication for all writers of Chinese, whatever their political or social position (though of course, the difficulty of the Chinese script means that not all Chinese speakers will be able to read and write the script). It produces the quintessential ideological effect, of making a specific set of meanings seem natural, inevitable, the only possible way of constructing the meaningful.

In the penultimate scene of the story, the complex and layered way in which this works is subtly illustrated. The bride performs two symbolic acts, sewing up the tear in the shirt, and covering the soldier with her quilt. At one level, the meaning of her sewing up the tear in the shirt comes from the gendered division of labour in terms of which this is woman's work, although done on this occasion for a man who is not a member of her household. The fact that she does it now frantically and pointlessly, since he is dead, demonstrates vividly how this ideology and the roles it assigns to women and men can make sense of the senseless. But the character for 'needle' 针 (*zhen*) contains the metal radical, which as we have seen is masculine. 'Needle' is again used when the doctor pronounces the soldier dead by saying 'there is no need to give him the needle'. The dead soldier's hands are said to be 'icy cold' 冰冷 (*bing leng*), both characters having the 'water' radical, which is the female form.

The final action, when the bride covers the soldier with the red quilt embroidered with white lilies, shows the same kind of process. Mostly the characters simply repeat and reinforce the meanings that we have explained as part of the associations of the words, but even this closure between script and object, signifier and signified, has a powerful meaning and effect. The reward for literacy – for Ru Zhijuan as for her readers – is to have this powerful machine working as beautifully in the 1950s or the 1990s as it ever did, offering seductive images for the harmonising of all oppositions, between men and women, Communism and Chineseness, tradition and modernity. The story itself demonstrates the effect, by drawing on all the seductive power of the ideological machine to underline its positive message about Communist heroism, its everyday tale about the activities of ordinary men and women in the real-life circumstances of recent history. Ru Zhijuan does not need to state that Communism is the heir of the Chinese tradition, or that the Chinese tradition is an indispensable resource in the Communist project of constructing Chinese socialism. Her skilful use of the resources of the tradition combines with the seemingly natural way the meanings are encoded in the script itself to make the statement overwhelming and redundant: ideology that is irresistible because it is invisible.

4 Grammar as ideology
Critical linguistics and the politics of syntax

In this chapter we will look at aspects of the complex relations between language and ideology in Chinese. Language forms in every language are finely adapted to the functions they typically serve, shaped by discursive constraints which themselves are minutely sensitive to effects of power and ideology. In these ways language appears as the highly flexible and ingenious servant of ideology. But language also plays an active role in ideological processes. In Chapter 3 we argued that the Chinese system of writing is ideologically saturated. In the present chapter we look at the other major specialised task involved in learning Chinese as with every other language: learning its grammar.

We should note at the outset that we take a different perspective to grammar from that which is normally found in the language textbooks for foreign students of Chinese, for example the DeFrancis series and the *Practical Chinese Reader* series. It also differs from approaches taken by some excellent studies which employ methods such as structuralism or functionalism (e.g. Chao Yuen Ren 1968; Li and Thompson 1981). Instead, we want to stress the explanatory value of always attending to the relationship between grammar and ideology. We will show that Chinese grammar, like the script itself, is highly ideological, and an understanding of the ideology dimension will enable the learning and teaching of it to become much more meaningful. As throughout this book, we hope that this chapter will be illuminating and relevant for readers with no grasp of Chinese and no current intention of learning it, as well as providing context, framework and motivation for those learning the language.

In contrast to the case with writing, the grammar of Chinese is often represented as not much of a problem for language learners (here understood primarily as students, native speakers or not, devoting most of their efforts to learning the written code). The difficulty of the language is seen to reside mainly in learning characters and associated vocabulary. The grammar is something that can be taken for granted while characters are being learned. In the official curricula for primary and secondary schools in China, for example, there is no work on grammar as such throughout the syllabuses. The emphasis is placed instead on the learning of characters (Zhonghua renmin gongheguo guojia jiaoyu weiyuanhui 1986). This is reflected in the language textbooks. In the twelve-volume primary textbooks, for example, the exercises are again mainly on learning the use of characters (Renmin jiaoyu chubanshe yuwen yishi 1984 and 1987). In textbooks issued for English speakers learning Chinese, particular 'sentence patterns' are fed in, but in no particular order and with little rationale or explanation. These patterns are presented as grids with specific slots that can be filled with appropriate categories of content (Liu Xun *et al.* 1981). The strategy is a structuralist one, and it has dominated Chinese teaching in the English-speaking world since the 1950s.

This strategy reinforces the high valuation of the written language as the 'real' language, and avoids having to understand the principles that make sense of specific constructions or kinds of usage in the spoken language. It presents a large number of individual structures as items to be learned through drill and repetition (see for example Li Dejin and Cheng Meizhen 1988). In this way a paradox arises: the grammar is treated as simple, yet its presentation is so fragmented that the learning of it can be surprisingly difficult. The learning of grammar is thus readily assimilated to a teaching strategy which operates primarily with the principle of the learning of characters; the main task becomes the accumulation of endless amounts of detail. This method is ideal as a means of habituating ideological forms so that they are learnt without question. It is however inefficient as a way of understanding and explaining the language and its different forms. Since learning is always more efficient if it proceeds with understanding, the method is highly inefficient in this respect. It induces a dependency of learner on teacher which is pedagogically unproductive while ideologically convenient.

For this reason we will look at the issue of grammar in Chinese from a perspective which emphasises grammar's social nature and functions and its role in making sense. We will base our analysis on the theoretical models deployed in *Language as Ideology* (Hodge and Kress 1993) and *Social Semiotics* (Hodge and Kress 1988). In these terms, Chinese grammar can be viewed as a set of rules, plus a specific set of extremely common items in the language whose function is primarily grammatical. The rules consist of a set of categories, classifications of parts of the language and parts of the world, and a set of rules of combination, i.e. what can, or must, or must not go with what. The items can be either lexical items (words or parts of words, e.g. *wo* as pronoun for 'I' or 'me', *men* as particle indicating plural) or structures considered as signs (e.g. word order as in *wo-men* meaning 'we' or 'us'). In most studies of grammar these rules and items are normally regarded as having either relatively weak meanings or none. We assume on the contrary that they will always carry important social meanings. The classification systems on which the rules are based always have a reference, even if it is sometimes oblique, to social or conceptual categories. The 'grammar items' are more difficult to connect to social and conceptual meanings, but in every case they constitute traces of processes of judgement which always have a cognitive basis, always deriving from some social context or purpose. Social meanings are continually enforced by rules, and every rule of the grammar is a social prescription, a form through which ideology is transmitted. So a reading of any text which attends to points of grammar is always at the same time an ideological reading.

A grammar in this sense is a set of regularities, recurring patterns and principles, whose origins and functions are always social. To learn these basic principles is to have a much more powerful and generative grasp of the language and of the culture itself. A grammar of this kind helps users of the language – speakers, readers, learners and commentators alike – to cope with the range of familiar forms, and with new forms as they emerge or are encountered. It locates basic social meanings carried by the language, and it makes the task of learning it much easier by making sense of what otherwise seems a morass of detail. In what follows we give an outline of key aspects of Chinese grammar and the 'sense' that they make, in terms of such a functional theory of language and society.

The grammar of culture

To many English speakers 'grammar' is so well-known and seemingly irrelevant a category that it has almost lost all meaning and value. 'Grammar' is what conservative teachers insist on in English classes, in contrast to feeling and content, and what conservatives writing to newspapers like *The Times* lament has been lost by modern youth: the trivial ability to scrupulously avoid split infinitives and to not use prepositions to end a sentence with. To deconstruct these sedimented attitudes to grammar we will begin by looking at approaches which take the category of grammar very seriously and in a broad sense.

The French structuralist Claude Lévi-Strauss (1963) argued strongly for powerful connections to be made between linguistics and anthropology, on the grounds that structures of language and society were produced by the same capacities of the human mind. From this point of view, the term 'grammar' as applied to culture and society acquires the precision of its use with language, and its use with language connects directly with the important and substantive issues of social and cultural meanings. Edmund Leach in this tradition wrote:

> I shall assume that *all* the various non-verbal dimensions of culture, such as styles in clothing, village lay-out, architecture, furniture, food, cooking, music, physical gestures, postural attitudes and so on are organised in patterned sets so as to incorporate information in a manner analogous to the sounds and words and sentence patterns of a natural language. I assume therefore it is just as meaningful to talk about the grammatical rules which govern the wearing of clothes as it is to talk about the grammatical rules which govern speech utterances.
>
> (1976: 10)

Lévi-Strauss and Leach did not want to say that for any given society there was only one grammar, one code, throughout the culture. On the contrary, they insisted on the analytic need to distinguish the different languages or codes that make up a given culture. The idea of a single unifying grammar across the whole culture and all its component languages is as ideologically constraining as the idea of a single unitary 'China', and that is not how we want to use it. Instead, in taking up this idea of a 'grammar' of Chinese culture we want to keep the notion loose and heterogeneous, as a way of seeing connections and differences across the network of codes and practices that make up the culture, enabling us to track the play of ideological forms and processes that crisscross every text.

To illustrate how the idea can be used in this open and exploratory way, we will look at a short visual and verbal text: the title of a story 'Drunk among flowers' 醉入花丛 (*Zui ru hua cong*), by the writer Li Jian whose work we will discuss in more detail in the next chapter, and the accompanying illustration. In this case, the words and image are very close. The picture in Figure 4.1 illustrates the title, and functions as a kind of translation from one code (verbal) into another (visual, artistic). This makes it especially useful for our purposes, to show the pattern of similarities and differences across the codes that make up the culture. We will start with what is common to the two. 'Among flowers' (*ru hua cong*) literally 'in-flower-s' (plural marker) is directly represented by the woman lying amongst many flowers, holding one in her hand. The relationship between the two codes seems so clear, and the meaning of each statement seems so transparent and simple that we might think that there is virtually no need for grammar here. Each code shows us reality directly, the same reality.

But there is one discrepancy, focused on the first word of the title. The woman is lying down, but she doesn't look particularly 'drunk'. This is partly a decision by the artist, who could have represented 'drunkenness' and in fact did so in another illustration to this story. But it also reflects a difference in the two codes. 'Drunk' here is primarily a judgement, not a picture. The word 'drunk' in English is close to 'drink', so that it reminds of the process by

Figure 4.1 Illustration showing woman Red Guard 'Drunk among Flowers'

which the person came that way, but a word like 'blotto' doesn't carry the same direct sense of the causal process. *Zui* in Chinese is more like 'blotto' than 'drunk'. It involves judgement or commentary, rather than representation. Verbal language, in Chinese as in English, can both comment and represent, but its greatest strength over visual languages is its greater facility to comment, to represent the complex actions of the mind directly. The grammar of verbal language, compared to the grammar of visual languages, is constructed very differently because of this.

There is another marked difference between the verbal and visual versions. The word 'drunk' is not marked for gender. In this respect Chinese is like English, and both are different from most European languages. This could be a man or a woman who is drunk. But the picture is clear on this point. This is a woman: more clearly a woman than a drunk. However, the way her gender is communicated is not as simple as it may look. Her face and hair encode her gender, as does her body, with its slim waist and full, feminine hips. These signs may seem to be simple representations of her – after all, she is a woman and can be expected to look like this. However this meaning is coded, not totally natural. It is an artistic code which in fact is not common in traditional Chinese art. Women in Chinese art are always easy to identify as women, but not because of their 'womanly' bodies, which are normally covered by many layers of clothing. It is the clothing that signifies gender, in traditional Chinese art as in social interaction, not body shape. The artistic tradition normally just takes over the language of clothes from social reality (organised, as Leach claims, by its own rich grammar that allows it to have many complex meanings, of age, gender and social status). This pattern is reversed by the artist in this case. The clothing is almost gender-neutral, reflecting the (almost) gender-neutral dress codes of the Cultural Revolution period in which the story is set. So the gendered body is made unnaturally visible, to communicate what the dress code refuses to do (though this is in practice a distinctly sexy version of the normal clothes of a Red Guard).

So in this single picture we have two codes at work, a clothing code and an artistic code. The clothing code in this case does not have gender markings (i.e. its 'grammar' does not have the category of gender strongly marked), but the code of representing bodies does (i.e. its 'grammar' does have gender). But in traditional art and social life, this pattern would be exactly reversed. What then do we say of the 'cultural grammar'? Does it encode gender or not, now or in the past? The situation seems hopelessly confused for any one period, and there is the same confusion across codes. The verbal code, as we have said, does not mark gender strongly, at least in its grammar. However, often though not always, the writing code does, through the system of radicals. In this case, the word for 'drunk' 醉 is made up of two characters 酉 and 卒. According to Guo Moruo's research into oracle bones, the former is the picture of a bottle (quoted in *Hanyu da zidian*: 1487), whose significance for drinking alcohol is obvious. The other character means a soldier, which has an implied masculine gender, since soldiers in China were almost always males until the Communist period. So the word 'drunken (woman)' has masculine gender, indicated through the characters but not through the grammar. Or, more precisely, like the woman narrator in 'Lilies' she is uneasily crossing gender lines which do not cease to exist just because they are being renegotiated.

In the light of this we can say that the 'grammar of culture' in Chinese does indeed have gender as a core category, but in code after code it equivocates with this category, providing ways of both insisting on it and seeming to deny it, or combining signifiers of gender and signifiers of neutrality in complex packages which are normally contradictory yet still legible. It is therefore especially dangerous to generalise from any one code to reconstruct a single consistent grammar that will give 'Chinese culture', or the 'Chinese mind'. In a famous phrase Wittgenstein wrote: 'the limits of my language mean the limits of my world' (1971: 5–6). Perhaps. But we need to ask: which language? The greatest value of the notion of 'grammar' that we are using here is that it allows us to see the unlimited variety of actual texts and ideological forms and meanings in different sites, on different occasions, for different purposes, by different users, including people as confused as Li Jian and his artist.

Linguistic ideology in action

In its October 1988 issue the *Chung Wah News*, the Perth Chinese community newsletter, published an article criticising the use of simplified and homo-phonic characters, complaining that they allowed a potentially dangerous level of ambiguity (see Figure 4.2). In this chapter, we are not concerned with simplification and romanisation, and will use this article as a source for a discussion of the ideological make-up of Chinese grammar.

To illustrate the dangers of simplification, the *Chung Wah News* article gave two instances where simplification would lead to semantic chaos. One was hypothetical: according to the author, if the simplified form of 'after', 后, is used in the expression *Qian long hou*, then we have no way of knowing whether we mean 'after the Emperor Qian Long' or 'the Empress Qianlong' as they are both written as 乾隆后 in simplified characters. The other anecdote was offered as a real possibility. An anonymous 'educated youth', who was sent to the countryside, in a letter to his parents wrote '*youxie tongxue shangdiao le, wo ye xiang shangdiao*'. In this letter, the educated youth had wrongly written the character for the phoneme *diao* (he wrote 吊, to hang, instead of 调, to transfer). Thus, instead of saying 'some fellow students have been transferred back to the cities, I want to get a transfer also', the sentence reads 'some fellow students have hanged themselves, I want to hang myself too'. The distressed parents feared the worst, and in the story 'nearly lost their lives' with needless worry.

The author of this article claimed that the article was excerpted from one published in a Taiwanese newspaper by the prominent Taiwanese linguist Wang Xuewen. Given the reference to 'educated youth' it probably had an

中國文字，不宜簡化，因爲中國字的構造乃基於形與聲。形體改變的字會使詞彙的意義更爲複雜，如乾隆後改成乾隆后就可能鬧出笑話來。其次更不可以用同音別字代替正規的字詞，以求簡化。例如，一位下鄉知識青年給家中寫信說：「有些同學上吊了，我也想上吊」。父母接信後，急得要死。後來才知道他是想上調，調回城市的意思。一字之訛幾乎送掉父母的老命。

漢字的好處是先難後易。學會兩三千個常用字，就可以無往不利，因爲漢語詞彙是常用單字組成的，如太空人、太空衣等。現在電腦在使用文字方面，發覺漢字的結構優于印歐語文的結構。漢字將成爲繼英文之後的人類第二大電腦語言。因此，對於漢字，我們不應廢棄它或打亂它，應當好好的愛護它、發揚它。

Figure 4.2 Full text of *Chung Wah News* article in original Chinese

immediate mainland source. That is, the same ideology of language has been able to migrate from the 'centre' (anti-Cultural Revolution propagandists from the mainland) via off-shore China to a marginalised part of diasporic China. The most important assumption is that there is only one form of the Chinese language, with different methods of encoding it, one of which (complex characters) is superior to the rest (with simplified characters assumed to be superior to romanised script, and spoken forms even less adequate).

In practice, the 'Qianlong' error would not normally arise in modern Chinese in either its spoken or written form. The single morpheme '*hou*', the source of the problem, would not be used in isolation without context and, as a word, it would either be written as the compound 皇后 (queen) or 以后 (after), thus removing the ambiguity. The spoken form of the language has developed its own grammar and conventions which are distinct from those of classical Chinese. Ironically, it is the classical form which suffers most from endemic ambiguity, so it is traditional Chinese and its script and not reformed characters which should be the target of criticism by these conservative critics.

Underlying these widespread views we can lay out a simple scheme which classifies various forms of language. This scheme is not normally seen as part of the 'grammar' of Chinese, but it is undoubtedly part of its 'grammar' in the broader sense. In each of these 'languages' which are part of 'Chinese', the encoding system and the form of the language, including its grammar, form a functional unity. In place of the idea that there is a single Chinese language with different means of encoding, we need to recognise an ordered set (see Figure 4.3).

This schema is not a value-free classification. On the contrary the map is laden with ideological values, as with all classification schemes in the 'grammar'. The 'rules' that complete the 'grammar' prescribe either who can use one or other of these 'languages' in what contexts, or what social judgements will be made on them. The educated youth who made the 'error' not only caused his parents needless worry, but failed to use the most prestigious code properly.

In this schema there are two organising tendencies. The meaning and social value of the initial opposition is replicated throughout the rest of the table, so that the opposition between written and spoken forms, or between *putonghua* and other dialects, including colloquial forms of the Beijing dialect, have the same social meaning as the opposition between classical and modern. Thus when the written form is linked with the operations of technology and power, there will be a paradoxical tendency to claim that the most prestigious and complicated form of the written code must be a superior instrument. Totally unsubstantiated claims are made, in the *Chung Wah News* article and elsewhere, that Chinese characters are highly compatible with computers, second only to English, and a close second at that.

There is a second tendency running counter to this. As the table moves to the right and downwards it moves closer to the present and to vernacular forms of the spoken language, in the direction that the language itself is

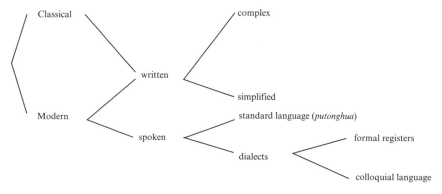

Figure 4.3 Schema of classifications of Chinese language

irresistibly heading, in spite of recent official attempts to reverse the process. The 'language' is a mass language, spoken in some form by China's one billion people and by many other overseas Chinese, so we can be sure that it will take and has already taken many different forms, following the lines of cleavage represented in the table, which will extend further downwards and to the right as the development of different dialects continues. But opposed to this understanding there is another ideological scheme, another part of the 'cultural grammar', which is superimposed on this model and completely contradicts it. This 'grammar' is a device for supposing that the majority of these forms do not really exist, or if they do they are not really 'part of the language'. They are just regrettable lapses from the perfection of the one true language in its pure state.

What we have here, as we had in the case of gender, is not one single consistent scheme that applies to all instances, but two or more contradictory schemes that are applied inconsistently at the service of particular positions. The set of grammars within the 'grammar of the culture' are organised like the ideological complex, around specific motivated sets of contradiction. We need to bear this in mind when we seek to understand debates on the topic of language. As one instance, we will look briefly at a recent article in the *Sydney Morning Hearald*. Headed 'Language loopholes bring a buzz to Beijing', it claims:

> China's street-smart masses are subverting the language, much to the dismay of the country's communist rulers.
>
> China's cultural commissars might be heartened by a new video on sale in Beijing: *Comrade Father*. It must be the first time since China stopped making 'tractor films' trumpeting socialist triumphs that anyone has tried to market a film with 'comrade' in the title.
>
> But the movie gives the Communist Party little to cheer about. In the underground argot of contemporary China, a comrade – 'tongzhi' – is a homosexual. *Comrade Father* is the Chinese title of *Priest*, a British film depicting the moral dilemma of a gay Catholic priest . . .
>
> The *People's Daily* fumes: 'The current linguistic chaos has two relatively prominent manifestations. One is the infiltration of Hong Kong dialect and the other is that vulgar and unbearable slang has moved from the corridors into the inner chambers.'
>
> (3 June 1993)

This report is partly structured by the Western myth of a popular rebellion against China's 'cultural commissars', the image of a joyless, rigid leadership who are out of touch and have lost control. We need to be careful in judging this kind of claim. This complaint might just repeat an old lament, as familiar in China as it is in conservative newspapers in Britain, about threats to the purity of 'Shakespeare's English'. But we can use the 'cultural grammar' to understand these anxieties about purity at a deeper level, and know where to look in order to evaluate them. Where the *Chung Wah* article identified the threat in the writing system, this article is concerned with an event closer to the core, a breakdown of boundaries between the standard language and other 'dialects', specifically Cantonese, the 'dialect' or language of Hong Kong and much of Southern China. In terms of the basic scheme, these fears are not wrong. While governments were resisting changes to the characters, written Chinese has changed dramatically over the century, incorporating far more from the spoken language than a few slang words from Hong Kong. The written language today is massively different from the language of the nineteenth century, far more so than is the case with English. By the standards of these things, there has already been a revolution in the Chinese language, affecting such structural qualities as the relations between the spoken and written languages, between the standard language and the other languages of China, and between different levels of class, status and region. Well might the *People's Daily* fume, but it fumes too late.

Sentence patterns and the ideological base

The rest of this chapter discusses details of the grammar of Chinese in a fairly technical way. We move between visual and verbal codes, bringing out basic principles common to both kinds of code as they function in a broader 'cultural grammar', concerned with the ideological contexts of making sense across the culture. The general points we make can be followed in English examples; the important thing is to get an impressionistic sense of how grammar works to encode ideology in Chinese, because that is how the system works: by the unnoticed accumulation of a series of repeated impressions, in which grammatical forms contribute to an inflection, an orientation through which the 'content' is continually filtered.

Every language is built around a small number of basic syntagmatic forms, which underlie the countless individual clauses or sentences that make up the language in use. These basic patterns are so common and so essential to specific acts of communication that they are normally taken for granted by all users, and treated as though they themselves were devoid of meaning. We argue the contrary. These models are chosen, they do not simply happen, and choice is always significant. It signifies a particular orientation, to the world and the discursive situation. It is ideological.

Clause types in all natural languages can be divided into two fundamental categories which correspond to the two basic functions of language, the mimetic (to represent the world) and the semiosic (to engage in social acts of making meaning). 'Semiosis' will be an unfamiliar term for many of our readers, but it is crucial for understanding the social functions of language, since the structures and meanings of semiosis are disregarded in traditional linguistic descriptions. It is these, however, which carry social meanings most powerfully and directly. (For a fuller discussion of these terms see Hodge and Kress 1988).

Actional models tend towards the mimetic function of language. They represent the world of events and their material basis. The picture of the young woman lying amongst flowers, and the corresponding phrase, are actionals. *Relational models* represent the set of semiosic acts that underpin discourse (e.g. perception, classification, judgement, thought, communication), the judgements that she is drunk, irresponsible, etc. The choice of a model is always significant, for a kind of discourse as for a particular clause or sentence. Actionals signify a commitment to representing the world-as-it-is, as an objective external reality. It is the language of no-nonsense common sense, with the relations it constructs between speakers and hearers anchored by a common reality. Relationals on the contrary foreground the work of the semiosic agents as primary. So the preponderance of relationals in any text, genre or language signifies the primacy of intellectuals, as the producers of knowledge, over the material world that the knowledge is ostensibly about.

It can be useful to count clause types, so long as we recognise that what we are reading is an ideological colouring, not some kind of truth about the nature of the topic. We can even do this with English translations. The broad tendency will be sufficiently common, and this is what matters. In the *Chung Wah* text there are thirty-six clauses, approximately twenty-two actionals and fourteen relationals. This count gives a misleading impression of the basic orientation of this article, primarily concerned with language and classification, not with events in the real world, but this impression is precisely what it seeks to give, since it wants to imply that its position on the language question is vindicated by what happens in the real world.

We will begin by looking at actional clauses, the basic way of representing action in every code. The first distinction we make comes from verbal language: between *transactive models* (where an action is understood as involving an agent who is responsible for it, and an object of the action) and *non-transactive models* (where the action is understood by reference to one main participant, who may be either the agent or the object of the action). These clause types are discussed more fully in *Language as Ideology* (Hodge and Kress 1993). Here we will bring out a few basic points about these two models as they apply in Chinese.

The picture of the young man defying army tanks in Tiananmen Square was, from the point of view of the West, an ideological triumph in the transactive mode (see Figure 4.4). It was published on the front cover of *Time*. As a transactive model, it is explicit about who is doing what to whom: in this case, the army acting against the people and this one man defying the army. Transactives represent causality in a sharp form and typically serve a P-ideology function, which on this occasion was suitable for the purposes of the Western media, representing a foreign government whose actions they deplored. Non-transactives more often serve an S-ideology function, working on behalf of a ruling group to blur the direction of action and the site of responsibility. The non-transactive model is conveniently more vague about responsibility, who has done what to whom. In the picture of Mao that

Figure 4.4 Young man defying the tanks on Tiananmen Square

presided over Tiananmen Square he is not shown doing anything to anyone, nor is he the object of the actions of anyone else (see Figure 4.5). That is typical of non-transactives. Thus Mao can be both leader of the nation, an active agent, and also the object of its reverence all in the one picture, seamlessly stitched together by this ideological form. He could have been depicted leading an army or defeating some enemy in one transactive picture, and being cheered by a huge crowd in another, and there are many examples in existence of both these transactive models. But the recurring staple model for Mao, as for his successors, is non-transactive, giving a vaguely inclusive and uncontentious image of benign rule.

These two models occur frequently in verbal texts; for example, in the clause discussed in the *Chung Wah News* article: *wo ye xiang shangdiao* ('I too want to hang myself'/ 'I too want to be transferred'). The two structures that make up this 'mistake', in their full form (the form in which they make complete sense) are:

1   *wo ye xiang (x) diao (wo) hui cheng li* [I also want (x) to transfer (me) back to the city].
2   *wo ye xiang (wo) shangdiao zisha* [I also want to hang (myself) and kill myself].

In this form, the two sentences have a different syntactic structure, as well as different meanings of *shangdiao*. Both are transactives, but in sentence 1 'I' is the object of the action, with an unknown x the real agent, who has the real

Figure 4.5 Portrait of Mao presiding over Tiananmen Square

power. In sentence 2 the agent and the object are the same, the self in a reflexive verb, so that the self has sole power as both agent and victim.

In practice language is more complicated. In this example, the form we have written it in is transactive, but the form in which it actually appears is a particular Chinese form for achieving a non-transactive effect. Chinese does this by using a construction organised as topic + comment (event). '*Wo shangdiao*' is a good instance of this, in both senses of *shangdiao*. In both, 'wo' is marked as the significant participant, irrespective of whether he or she is agent (the one doing the hanging) or object (the one who is transferred). English allows both transactive and non-transactive models with 'transfer': 'I want to transfer (non-transactive)/to be transferred (transactive, passive)'. The two meanings seem identical, but ideologically they are different. In the first instance the speaker retains the illusion that he is in control of his fate, while in the second he acknowledges who has the real power. In Chinese as in English, the main ideological function of the non-transactive is to mask power and responsibility.

There are many words coded as non-transactive in both English and Chinese. This coding is never neutral, never just a consequence of how reality or language is. Because the choice of model is of such crucial ideological importance, it becomes a dimension of the meaning of many important Chinese words or phrases. For instance, the Chinese phrase *wei renmin fuwu* 为人民服务 (literally, for-people-serve) would be translated as the English transactive 'to serve the people'. The English form encodes the position of agency and control of those who 'serve', so that the transactive model encodes a P-ideology while the meaning of the words indicates an S-ideology. The Chinese phrase, however, is non-transactive, whose ideological effect is to add the implication that the people are the dominant element and in some obscure way perhaps the real agents. The Chinese use of the different model is an important part of its ideological intent, though Chinese people were not necessarily taken in by it.

The functions of transformations

Transformations are a basic feature of every code, in Chinese as in English. The basic idea of 'transformation' is simple: anything that causes a structural change. No one can describe or learn or use any language across the normal range of its functions without a good grasp of the main transformational tactics and forms. However, language textbooks normally describe transformations in language indirectly and piecemeal, divorced from issues of ideology or practice, as a set of items to be learned rather than a set of principles which can be interpreted in various and sometimes devious ways. Also, transformations in language are treated as completely distinct from transformations in all other codes, which further cuts language learners off from the possibility of understanding the complexities of the transformational process itself.

To make some general points about transformations we will limit ourselves to two important types in visual and verbal language: the *passive transformation*, and *nominalisation*. These act on the basic actional forms, whose function is mimetic, to represent the world of actions. Thus we call them *mimetic transformations*. The passive transformation applies to transactives. It represents a transactive process primarily through the object of the action, who is foregrounded. Even the action itself, and many crucial details about it, are put in the background, left vague or even unknowable.

As an example of the passive transformation in the visual code, take the photograph of victims of Tiananmen Square (see Figure 4.6). This particular image was widely circulated at the time. It featured on the cover of *Time* and played an important role in ideological constructions of Tiananmen Square. This image foregrounds the object of the action, the victim in the foreground. The action itself is off-stage, represented only through its effects, the blood and the body. The soldiers who did it are also deleted. This deletion process, in verbal as in visual language, can have two apparently opposite effects. Sometimes, as in this case, the fact that the soldiers are not represented makes them and their actions unspeakable. The more intensely the feelings of the victims are represented, the more vaguely monstrous the main actors are made to seem.

This is a common ideological device at many levels. For instance, in the *Chung Wah News* article, the sufferings of educated youth occupy the foreground so exclusively that this kind of text cannot explore the more complex causal processes at issue. At other times, the elements that are

Figure 4.6 Foregrounding a victim of the Tiananmen Massacre

deleted are inconvenient, not mentioned so that no one will think about them. For instance, images of great public works are a kind of visual passive, since they represent the objects built but not the processes and agents, the workers who built them.

The passive transformation in the verbal code operates in rather different ways in Chinese as compared to English. The passive in English allows the agent of the action to be displaced or deleted. This is a fundamental ideological function. But Chinese has many ways of doing this, and does not need a passive form as such. The topicalisation transformation that we have already looked at can effectively delete the agent. We have called this a non-transactive form, but it could equally well be called a covert passive (e.g. *wo de tongxue shangdiao le* [my classmate has been transferred]).

There is one form in Chinese which looks like the English passive, but on closer examination it can be seen to have a rather different ideological function and place in the grammar. *Bei* 被 in modern Chinese is used in the same way as the English 'by', and looks like a marker of the passive in the same way as in English. However, paradoxically it has come to have almost the opposite function to the English passive. The primary function of the English form is to delete the agent (in over 70 per cent of cases, 'by' does not appear). But *bei* draws attention to the agent. It is normally used in sentences where the affected participant has been foregrounded by position, as in: *Yige xiaohai bei qiche zhuangdaole* 一个小孩被汽车撞倒了 (literally, a-child-by-car-was-knocked-over).

Since the position of first in the sentence signifies importance, this establishes that the victim is more important than the agent. With *Wo bei laoshi pipingle* 我被老师批评了 ('I was criticised by the teacher'), where the reader has a choice of siding either with the teacher or the person criticised, the *bei* form establishes the interests of the 'I' as primary, so that either the teacher (in spite of the honorific term *laoshi*) or the action is implicitly labelled as unjust. This form has a subtle ideological effect, and an interesting linguistic history. Traditionally, the *bei* form in Chinese almost always marked an event as having negative undertones. In modern Chinese it can now be used positively, a phenomenon which may have arisen initially because it was so often used to translate the English 'by'. Its expanded usage is also part of a general tendency in the spoken form to mark transformations more overtly than classical Chinese did, reinforcing the tendency we have already noted for mystification to become more curtailed in modern Chinese.

The next class of transformations we will look at is called 'nominalisation' in grammars. This transformation takes a process involving actions and verbs, and turns it into a noun, a thing. In this form it loses many of its features as an action or process, and instead is fitted into a relational model where it becomes subordinated to processes of classification and judgement. Verbal languages are more prone to nominalisation transformations than visual languages. Most of the important abstract words in Chinese as in English are nominalisations, for instance 'revolution' 革命 (literally, transform-life).

Chinese, like English, recognises a fundamental difference between things and processes, underlying a distinction between nouns and verbs as parts of speech. However, where most English words are marked in some way as noun or verb, this happens less often in Chinese. This means that movement from noun to verb is less obvious. However, the process still occurs and follows similar procedures to English. For instance, take a phrase from the *Chung Wah* text we have already looked at: *Zhongguo wenzi, buyi jianhua* (literally, Chinese-writing-not-suitable-simplification).

Jian, which means 'simple', is at the base of this transformational series. It is an adjective with an understood object, 'characters', which is deleted but easily recoverable. The addition of *hua* is similar in effect to '-ise' in English, turning it into a process: 'simplify'. This process can be presumed to have agents, but they are not specified. Finally it follows *buyi*, 'not suitable', classifying *Zhongguo wenzi*. *Jianhua* then performs the role of defining what is unsuitable. In English, this would be translated by a nominalisation ('for simplification') or by an infinitive ('to be simplified'). Thus '*hua*' performs the dual functions of the English '-ise' and '-isation'. In Chinese it isn't necessary to call this a nominalisation, because it does not need to be marked as a noun to perform all the functions served by nouns and by the process of nominalisation. But the three stages that would underlie this as a nominalisation in English are all present in the Chinese, and are part of its interpretation.

Wenzi illustrates another dimension of transformation. This word could be translated into English by either the nominalisation 'writing' or the noun 'characters'. *Wenzi* however is a noun, not a nominalisation, thus giving rise to a different ideological effect. It refers to the product of a process (Chinese people know that characters are produced by specific agents) but all markers of this process are deleted from the word, no longer part of its interpretation, unlike *jianhua*. The suppression of process in this case is achieved not by a visible and recoverable transformation (nominalisation) but by a prior act of choice that is now encoded in the lexicon itself. We need to realise that the basic ideological effect can be achieved, in both Chinese and English, by either of the two basic methods, transformation or choice, and that these methods can be arranged along a continuum in terms of how overt the shift is, and therefore how reversible.

In understanding the resources of the Chinese language we need to recognise the major ideological functions that it serves, and also the variety of subtly different ways it can carry out these functions, as well as the different contexts of use of the variants: who uses them and why. But this ever-extending inquiry into different particular forms is best carried out in the context of an ideologically informed functional framework. Otherwise the set of differences will seem like an unordered accumulation of separate items, rather than what it is: a dynamic and open-ended but basically coherent and comprehensible system.

The grammar of judgements

The other basic clause type, the relational, is mainly used to represent semi-osic acts: classification, judgement, etc. Verbal codes are much richer in this model than visual codes. In English, there is a single main form for the relational: X is (a) Y. Grammars of Chinese make a distinction between two forms of relational: the descriptive and the determinative. We take two examples from the *Chung Wah* article:

1   *Zhongguo wenzi, buyi jianhua* (descriptive)
    (Chinese writing is not suitable for simplification)
2   *Hanzi de haochu shi xian nan hou yi* (determinative)
    (The good point of Chinese characters is that first they are difficult, then easy)

The formal difference between the two in Chinese is the presence of *shi* 是 to mark the determinative. This difference is lost in most English translations, which use 'is' for both forms. The crucial difference is that the determinative makes it overt that an act of judgement is taking place. In descriptive clauses the statement, as in sentence 1, is offered as description rather than assertion. This subtle difference has a powerful ideological effect: to make the statement seem more obvious, less contentious.

To show the power of relationals we can look at a translation of sentence 1 into an actional model: 'Chinese writing should not be simplified.' The mimetic meaning of the two versions is more or less the same. The use of the relational, however, has significant effects. It shifts attention from the action ('simplifying' language) to the use of this process as a criterion in an act of judgement. There is no attempt to dispute the reality of the action. On the contrary it is taken for granted. The tactical value of the move is to shift the focus from the processes involved on to the self-evident rightness of the judgement 'is not suitable'.

These tendencies of the relational model work even more effectively at the level of the phrase. The basic principle is that the more that acts of judgement are embedded in other acts of judgement the more self-evident they seem, less in need of justification. For instance, *Hanzi de haochu* 汉字的好处 (Chinese-characters'-good-point) links the two elements (Chinese characters – good point) through *de*, before making its claims as to what the good point is. So although *shi* warns us that what follows is a judgement that may be open to dispute, the real judgement has already been made and is now a taken-for-granted part of the meaning: that Chinese characters have a good point.

The *de*-form functions very like the apostrophe-s possessive form in English, and is usually appropriately translated by this or by 'of'. But as in English, this form often does not mean an act of possession. In both cases a relationship of classification is treated as though it were like a relationship of possession. So 'good point', a judgement on Chinese characters, is treated as though it was a possession of Chinese, 'enriching' it, whereas it is strictly only a personal judgement about the language.

Built into the *de*-form is an ideological potential which is added unobtrusively to every particular act of judgement, contributing to features of the use of *de* which are otherwise inexplicable. In sentence 2 for instance *de* has negative connotations compared to sentence 1:

1   *wo shi laoshi* 我是老师 (I am a teacher).
2   *wo shi jiao shu de* 我是教书的 (I am a teacher/one whose function is to teach books).

The positive value of sentence 1 is partly due to the connotations of *laoshi* (teacher), but the *de* form in sentence 2 further devalues the position of the teacher, or indicates a low self-esteem in the person making this statement. This is because *de* establishes the subject ('I') as like the possession of the position, and therefore by analogy inferior to it. The negative connotations are relative not absolute, but whatever the evaluation of the item before *de*, what follows it must be inferior in status. This is why *de* has no negative connotations in the phrase *Hanzi de haochu*. What happens here is that *haochu* retains its high positive value, and thus lifts *Hanzi* even higher (*Hanzi* is even more than its good points).

The *de*-construction differs from the two relational clause types by foregrounding the act of judgement less, just as the descriptive clause foregrounds it less than the determinative. There is a continuum here. At the other end is the most covert and therefore ideologically unassailable form: the union of two or more elements bound so tightly that they are treated as a unity, a single word. Some instances in this text are *Zhongguo* ('central country' i.e. China), *Hanzi* (Chinese writing) and *fumu* 父母 ('father-mother' i.e. parents).

In all these instances, the link between the two elements is so close as to seem unbreakable, part of the language itself and no longer open to individual dispute. Yet each of these encodes a judgement that is problematic and disputable, in the present as in the past. To call China the 'central country' is to see the world organised around China. It is conveniently vague about where the circumference is that pivots around this centre – whether for instance it includes Taiwan, or Singapore, or even Chinatown in Perth. *Hanzi* combines *Han* (Chinese) and *zi* (characters) with its own ideological effect, as we can see if we compare this to the equivalent form *Zhongguo wenzi*. *Han* refers to the majority Han ethnic group within China, so it is less comprehensive than *Zhongguo*. More importantly, it does not do the same ideological work as *Zhongguo*. *Han* expresses a P-ideology, *Zhongguo* an S-ideology. In this case *Han* is linked intrinsically with *zi* to form a single concept, which is not exactly equivalent to 'Chinese characters'. *Zhongguo wenzi* links *wenzi* closely to *Zhongguo*, but not *as* closely, so that the join still shows, and we can recognise the possibility that there could be another form of writing (e.g.

phonetic script) that could also be classified as Chinese. This possibility is ruled out by *Hanzi*, where Chineseness and characters form an indivisible unity – precisely the point that the writer wishes to make.

The final example, *fumu*, is slightly different. This compound is formed out of the two elements *fu* and *mu*, which can also occur separately and retain their distinct meanings of father and mother. Their combination in a fixed form carries an ideological meaning about that relationship. In this meaning, the order is a crucial dimension. *Mufu* would theoretically be possible, but is unspeakable. Many Chinese speakers would say that it is incomprehensible, since *fumu* functions as a single word. This is probably overstating the situation, or rather, it is a claim about what is acceptable masquerading as a claim about comprehensibility. Certainly *mufu* is 'un-Chinese', so powerful is the prohibition against it. What it encodes through the word order is the primacy of the male in the family. Other familial words with the same fixed male–female order abound, for example, *fuqi* (husband and wife), *zinü* (sons and daughters), *dimei* (younger brothers and sisters). Seemingly an opposite meaning is encoded in the word order of 'ladies and gentlemen' in English. The difference between the two languages might tempt one to the judgement that word order is not important, or that English society is not a sexist, male-dominated one. Both judgements would be mistaken. Both Chinese and English societies are sexist and build a similar set of values into the language. The difference is that at this point, English encodes an S-ideology and Chinese encodes a P-ideology. But in the *yin–yang* pair, as we have seen, Chinese foregrounds the S-ideology.

In Chinese as in English, wherever word order is either fixed or significant (so that a different word order would produce a different meaning or effect) we can be sure that the word order is itself a signifier, and carries meaning. So all rules that concern word order should be explained in terms of the meanings of the order and the functions served by those meanings. An important meaning of the order of words in a complex phrase, in Chinese as in English, is the order of the acts of judgement it encodes, an order which recreates or signifies a social meaning over and above the sum of the individual parts. This meaning comes in two distinct forms, formal and symptomatic. For instance, in English we can say: 'English definitely relies on word order, absolutely for sure'. English speakers would recognise that this person is making a statement about word order, then reinforcing it three times over. Formally that makes it a very emphatic sentence. But symptomatically we also recognise that the person has felt the need to add 'definitely', then 'absolutely' and 'for sure' in that order. Paradoxically, this repeated emphasis signals anxiety, a sense of opposition that has to be crushed by all this repetition.

Much the same happens in Chinese, as we can see in this sentence from the *Chung Wah News* article: *Hanyu cihui shi kao changyong danzi zucheng de* (Chinese words rely on often-used single characters for their formation). A problem in interpreting this text focuses on the use of the '*shi . . . de*' 是 . . . 的 construction. The sentence makes good sense without either *shi* or *zucheng de* at the end. In this form it would have been a simple 'narrative' sentence. *Shi* converts it to a determinative, making it more emphatic. We can reconstruct the order of the acts of judgement, in this case first a simple descriptive, describing Chinese, then the addition of a modality emphasising the act of judgement.

Zucheng de is the last word in the sentence, and also the last act of judgement. We can tell this because *zucheng de* cannot be construed in relation to *kao*, and must be interpreted as governed by (and following) the *shi*-stage in the production of the sentence. Formally speaking, *zucheng de* implies a deleted element which can be supplied from the previous text: *hanyu cihui* 'the formation of (Chinese vocabulary)'. It functions to rephrase and re-evaluate what has been said previously, another indication that it follows later than the previous stage. The effect is that it comes across as an afterthought, which adds nothing to the original form and therefore detracts from its certainty.

This of course is a symptomatic judgement. The writer presumably didn't want to give this impression. However it remains a social meaning of this text even if not consciously intended, because it is formed by regular processes which carry social meanings. A similar thing is happening here to when anxious speakers display nervousness in spite of themselves, letting slip a word or phrase that reveals more than they intend, using signals which convey a meaning which everyone, themselves included, reads in the same way. For example, the statement '*wo shi zuotian lai de*' (I came yesterday), seems to emphasise 'yesterday' more strongly than the simple alternative '*wo zuotian lai*', but in practice raises more doubts. The words are not incorrect, but the traces of social processes that underlie the word order are still precisely revealing. Such aspects of language provide fruitful material for symptomatic readings.

So far, most of the points that we have looked at have reasonably close similarities between English and Chinese. There is, however, one kind of classification within the noun phrase which English almost requires but in Chinese is optional. That concerns number, whether nouns are singular or plural (marked also in the verb, which agrees with its subject), and determiners ('the' etc.). For English speakers learning Chinese this may seem simply a difficulty that Chinese spares them, of no further significance. However, the difference is more significant than this suggests. It is only invisible to English speakers because they do not consciously recognise what singular and plural mean in their own language.

The system of number in English is part of the system of determiners which classify the status of the main entities in an utterance. This system is concerned with the scope and certainty of the claim made by an utterance. It is not just a judgement about how many things are being talked about: it concerns ideological issues of definiteness, certainty and unity. It isn't the case, as we might think, that English speakers always use the plural when more than one thing is involved. *Wenzi*, for instance, could equally be translated by 'writing' or 'characters'. The singular not only emphasises the unity of the object, it constructs it. With the singular, a whole series of judgements become easier and more plausible than would be the case with the plural form: for example 'Chinese writing is ancient' (not 'characters are ancient' because not all of them are equally old).

The different Chinese conventions concerning determiners and number allow an ideological operation of great power: automatic generalisation from individual instances. The difference between individual and general is a fundamental one in Chinese thought as in English. However, this aspect of Chinese has the effect of naturalising a particular form of argument, the form used in the *Chung Wah* article like many others. The example from the article draws on one anecdote, concerning one couple, the parents (*fumu*), but these are also stereotypical individuals, a replicated mass. The effect is to make an argument based on a single case seem a compelling proof.

In practice, Chinese does use plurals, drawing on a range of ways of signifying the underlying concept of plurality. As in English, plurality affects how certain or definite a statement is. In Li Jian's title, the plural added to flowers is more significant precisely because it is optional. The fact that there are 'many flowers' (as in Mao's 'one hundred flowers', see p. 107) implies the ideologically dangerous possibilities of multiplicity, uncontrolled plurality of meanings.

The *Chung Wah* text has other instances which nicely illustrate the ideological effect of the choice of singular and plural. Near its climax come these words: '*women bu ying feiqi ta*' ('we should not abandon it', i.e. Chinese characters). Here we have the plural form of 'we', but a singular form for *Hanzi*, 'Chinese characters'. The writer could have used a singular form for *women* (e.g. *Zhongguoren*, Chinese people), and a plural or non-specific form to refer to *Hanzi*. The effect of what was in fact used is to give less unity and definiteness to those who should respect the language, a vaguely inclusive 'we', while emphasising the unchanging unity and abstract truth of '*Hanzi*', a unity which spans history and all other differences. Unity is a highly desirable ideological prime, in Chinese as well as English. Chinese makes it easier to achieve.

Modality and the reality factor

The reality factor is crucial to every semiotic effect, everything done through language. We term this function in its broadest sense the system of *modality*. In linguistics, 'modality' is normally concerned with modal particles, like 'may' and 'can' in English, or *hui* ('will') or *yao* ('must') in Chinese, which are attached to verbs to indicate the degree of probability or authority of the action concerned. We use it in an extended sense, to refer to all aspects of text or discourse which serve this function, including all signifiers of power or respect, and all states of possibility, including negation. (See Hodge and Kress 1993 for a fuller discussion.) Language only affects behaviour insofar as it influences belief, and belief rests on judgements about the credibility of speakers and messages, the fit between message and reality: that is, on modality. So all aspects of language which are concerned with this function are of the first importance – an importance they are not normally given in most textbooks in current use, in China or elsewhere. But because it is so crucial an aspect of any use of language, the forms it takes become complex and devious. Where language functions in a condition of struggle, it is important to be able to create belief in spite of facts to the contrary, and conversely to be able to see past the efforts of others to deceive or mislead. To fulfil the first function there is need for a set of elements and strategies to construct belief; for the second, there is the corresponding need to dismantle the structures and claims of others. These purposes are of course contradictory, yet it is a single language which is required to hold them both. We do not expect, then, to find a simple, clear and consistent system in any language or community. Rather, we expect the opposite: truth and mystification so inextricably intertwined that finally only continual alertness can distinguish between them.

We need to be very careful in coming to terms with so complex an aspect of language. Written Chinese has many fewer markers of modality than English. In response to this fact Alfred Bloom (1981), an American linguist, took as his starting point the Whorfian proposition that language determines thought and on this basis tested whether Chinese people have a 'less firm grasp of reality'. Using written texts he got some positive results. However, all that he in fact established was that the written code does suppress a range of markers of modality, and this has effects on the typical response to such use of language. But all readers of Chinese are also speakers of forms of Chinese, and it is these spoken forms which complement the written form with a richer set of modality markers. Speech flows around the mystified modalities of the written code, constantly mediating its messages and supplementing its claims.

Issues of modality apply to every code. In the case of visual conventions, modality systems are less clearly codified, but they are still important, with a multiplicity of different systems in common use. For instance, the following picture shows the God of Longevity riding a deer, holding a peach blossom in one hand and a staff in the other, with a fir tree and clouds close by (see Figure 4.7). In one sense, this image has a single meaning and a single modality, since all these are iconographic signs of the single meaning of longevity. But there are subtle differences in the degree of realism, and hence the modality. The deer is the most realistic, the symbols the man is carrying the least. His clothes are more realistic than his face, and the fir tree and the clouds somewhere in between. This pattern represents the overlaying of two principles of modality, which are the reverse of each other. The more realistic an image, the more believable it is as a thing, but the less full it is of potent, authoritative meanings. Conversely, the symbols of longevity, barely able to be decoded as real objects, and the unrealistically deformed head of the man, carry the highest modality meaning, since they refer more closely to a world of metaphysical truths than to material reality.

Figure 4.7 The God of Longevity depicted on a mug

In English, the clause type with the highest modality is the 'simple present' declarative sentence, for instance 'Chinese is easy'. In spite of its seeming simplicity, this form is reinforced by a number of modality factors. Paradoxically, one is the absence of markers of truth. This sentence form is the simplest way an English speaker can link the two concepts. In Chinese this corresponds to the difference between the 'descriptive' form (*Zhongwen hen rongyi*, Chinese very easy) and the 'determinative' form (*Zhongwen shi rongyi*, Chinese is easy). As we saw above, although '*shi*' is normally translated as 'is', it is more emphatic, more marked. And precisely because it makes stronger claims it is more contentious, signalling opposition at the very moment it is trying to stamp it out. The emphatic 'is' in English has the same effect: 'Chinese *is* easy' indicates the strong insistence of the speaker, but also the opposition of some listener who needs persuading. The *shi*-form is thus not very frequently used.

The most explicit way in English of indicating varieties of modality is through modal auxiliaries, words such as 'can', 'may', 'might' and 'should'. These terms fall into two functional categories: S-ideology forms and P-ideology forms. The S-ideology forms are systematically ambiguous. For instance, 'can' means either ability to (a fact about the state of the world) or permission to (an expression of power relations). The P-ideology forms are unambiguous, for example 'are able to' or 'are allowed to'.

Modern Chinese particles fall into the same broad categories, for the same ideological reasons. For example, like the English 'can', the S-form '*keyi*' 可以 means either 'ability to' or 'permission to', whereas the P-form '*yingdang*' 应当 is unambiguously 'should'. Because the S-forms are systematically ambiguous and misleading, it is those that need to be deconstructed for language learners, so they will recognise that problems and complexities of use come not from their own limited intelligence, but from the varieties of use.

In the text we have been considering, the phrase *bu keyi yong* 不可以用 (can't use) illustrates some other aspects of the operation of such terms in Chinese. *Keyi* means either 'can' or 'may', with the same ambiguity between ability and permission as the English 'can'. But here it is used with the negative *bu* before it. The effect of this is to narrow the scope of the word and emphasise the social meaning (prohibition) rather than the referential meaning (whether people are in fact able to do the action in question, which in this case they unfortunately can). The interaction of the explicit negative, which expresses the force of the P-model, helps to disambiguate the meanings of the particle. This is the normal effect of *bu* on these ambiguous S-forms.

Other particles exist which do not have any ambiguity in the first place. At the climax of this article comes this clause: *Yingdang haohao de aihu ta* (literally, must-well-love-it, i.e. we must love the language). *Yingdang* is a modal particle which expresses exclusively a moral imperative, not a state of probability. This is a P-form, because at this point in the article the writer has no wish to mask the fact that he is exhorting and commanding the reader.

To illustrate further the use of modal auxiliaries, we should consider one of the most common modal particles in Chinese, *yao* 要. The root meaning of *yao* is 'to want', and it is sometimes used in that non-modal sense (as is 'need' in English). But as a modal particle it has what seem to be a bewildering set of possible meanings. For example, *wo yao shangdiao* can mean:

1 I want to be transferred (desire).
2 I will be transferred (future).
3 I *will* be transferred (modal imperative).
4 If I were transferred (hypothetical).

But it is not correct to say that the word *yao* has four (or more) different meanings, as illustrated by these sentences. The truth is that *yao* has an ambiguous meaning potential, and in particular contexts some of these potential meanings are treated as more relevant. For instance, in some contexts sentence 1 could express simply a wish to be transferred. At the same time it also necessarily has the sense of a future action. But this same sentence, said in a context where the reason for transferring is clearly another person's wishes, would carry an implication like the English 'must'. Sentence 3 shows the same double meaning. Said in a context where the speaker, A, is more powerful than the hearer, B, and B is able to carry out that task, then *yao* is treated as a modal imperative: 'should'. But where the sentence is said by B as she picks up the laundry basket, *yao* would be interpreted as 'will'. Because the agent is deleted and because the empty meaning is filled by the surrounding social context, organised by relations of power and solidarity, the nature of the power concerned is mystified even more than it would be in English.

In English, every verbal auxiliary carries a modal function. This explains the otherwise puzzling uses of what is called the system of tense and aspect in English. The 'simple present', for instance, is not so simple and normally refers to past and future as well as or more than the present. Chinese, especially in its classical form, has very few markers of time, and none are obligatory as in English. This does not mean that the traditional Chinese, who were obsessed with tradition and history, had no sense of time and no interest in it. On the contrary, precisely because it was so crucial a frame for reality it was removed from the surface of the written code, for the same reason as markers of modality were.

In modern Chinese, the *le-* 了 form illustrates the same mingling of time and truth-value as in the English system. The particle *le* is often called a marker of tense indicating the past, but it also has a modality function. In '*Youxie tongxue shangdiao le*' (some students have transferred), it performs both functions. Here, it has a lower claim to truth than the unmodified simple present. It indicates the relative and partial truth of a specific event (about which someone might lie) rather than a general truth.

Other aspects of the language carry a modal function. In Chinese as in English, the question form indicates uncertainty, even though the speaker may in fact know the answer to the question. In both languages, intonation patterns provide a further message system to regulate modality. Chinese indicate the modality of question by a raised pitch more or less throughout the clause or, more commonly, by the addition of the modal marker '*ma*' 吗. English speakers raise their voice mainly at the end. But in both codes it is possible to send a counter-signal through intonation patterns or modal markers. In English, a question form with a downwards intonation pattern is interpreted as a command, just as a statement with a rising intonation pattern is interpreted as a question or a request. In Chinese, substituting the particle '*ma*' 吗 with '*ba*' 吧 would transform a question into a request.

The effect of all these markers of modality is to carry a complex form of negation. The English 'may', the Chinese '*yao*', etc. all carry an implication that the world is not entirely as described in the message itself. Negation also expresses in a particularly direct form the fact of conflict: either denying a truth or claim, or forbidding an action. For this reason full negation signifies the presence of conflict, while partial negations, as carried by the rest of the modality system, mask or modify it in some respect. Precisely for this reason, all modalised forms imply that someone somewhere thinks the opposite, whose opinions in some way have to be countered or acknowledged, if only by suppression. That is, all negatives necessarily invoke their opposite, reconstructing a dialectic process in which the opposite has a necessary place.

In the clause *women bu ying feiqi ta* ('we should not abandon it' i.e. Chinese characters) we can see the process at work. *Bu* is an emphatic negative, seeming absolutely definite in its stance. *Ying* (should) seems equally emphatic. But together they imply that there are some people who are doing precisely that, 'abandoning' Chinese characters. 'Abandon', *feiqi*, is formed out of not one but two characters, each by itself meaning 'abandon'. Again this ought to reinforce the meaning. On the one hand it does emphasise where the speaker stands, but on the other it paradoxically lends this strength to the opposition, because it is they who are abandoning these characters. 'Abandon' itself contains a negative meaning, incorporated into what is apparently a positive form. Again the negative implies a previous positive form, in this case the bond that must exist before something is 'abandoned'.

Here, as with other processes such as transformation, classification and the different forms of modality, the final effect of the utterance is given by a reconstructed history of its production, a history which encodes the oppositions and conflicts that lie behind its generation. In this instance, the sequence is: strong bond (to characters) → breaking of the bond (abandonment) → negation of abandonment (*bu*) → negation of fact/affirmation of value (*ying*). Strategically, then, this utterance recognises the opposition to its position, and incorporates that opposition into its reconstructed history. But that history has as its base line a state in which everyone, whether for or against characters now, was once united in an attachment to them. This complex history is one way of establishing the 'real' affiliation of all Chinese speakers on the side of the traditional script. The passage then concludes with a positive form: *yingdang haohao de aihu ta* (literally, should-well-love-it). But here the positive forms act as a reminder of the continuing opposition. *Yingdang* (should) instructs these intractable people, implying that they need it, and the reinforcing *haohao*, seemingly totally positive, serves to carry the negative meaning as well.

This instance shows what is an important general truth about modality and forms of negation in Chinese. These markers are never absolute; they always work dialectically. This dialectic is inscribed into their very form, and even if it is not, it is inferred or reconstructed by all users. The dialectic so reconstructed is not 'the truth' but just a best guess or a coded message. It is a reminder of what should never be forgotten about Chinese, as about every other living language: speech arises out of social interaction and social struggle, and everywhere it bears the marks of its social origins, meanings and functions.

5   Living with double-think
Ambiguity in discourse and grammar

In China today, change is clearly visible in almost all aspects of life, but some things continue with apparent imperviousness to change. The Communists dismantled much of what they saw as the apparatus of imperial China, but they continued to govern a highly unified nation with an iron hand. In the post-Cultural Revolution era Tiananmen Square was a brutal reminder that a free-market economy was not the same as a free society. Tang Xiaobing noted in 1993 of the then leadership: 'Any innovative thinking and unorthodox, not even necessarily revolutionary, language poses a fundamental threat to a regime that secures its absolute hegemony through relentless ideological homogenisation, rigid social stratification, and political terrorisation' (1993: 281).

The Chinese language has been the medium in which power in China at every level has been exercised, negotiated and resisted for millennia. These political functions have shaped it to its core, leaving no part of the language unaffected. Grammatical and linguistic forms are part of a functional complex that rests on a set of discursive rules so intricately interrelated that the grammatical forms could not function without the discursive rules, or vice versa. It is this formidable discursive achievement that is bequeathed to each successive regime, however different its policies and aims. This complex is not unchanging but acts as a massive inertial force on the ways in which change can be managed and understood.

In this chapter we want to examine one important aspect of this discursive complex: its systemic combination of two qualities which initially sound like contradictions. On the one hand, the Chinese language, especially in its written forms, is so radically and endemically ambiguous that it might seem that the Chinese have always lived in a post-structuralist heaven in which every meaning is polysemic and indeterminate. On the other hand, Chinese discourse, especially political discourse, has been tightly controlled and governed by 'ideological homogenisation' as well as by 'political terrorisation', to use Tang's description, across different periods and under different regimes. This is far more the case than in any current Western democracy.

The discursive rules we are talking about here are akin to what Foucault has called discursive regimes, by which he meant systems governing what can be said or meant about what topic with what authority by which speakers. In Foucault's view discursive regimes operate across whole fields of discourse, not only in cases of clear censorship in political discourse. We extend the idea of discursive regimes in the concept of semiosic regimes (see Hodge and Kress 1988), a set of regimes in a variety of semiotic forms, including linguistic and many other codes, governing action and meaning across a range of situations. Such discursive regularities can be broader and more long-lasting than a particular political group. In the case of China, successive dynasties drew on a substantially common discursive resource. There was a major transition between imperial China and Communist China, separated by the turbulence of the war with the Nationalists and the Japanese. And there have been other moments of rupture in the operations of this discursive machine over shorter time scales. At such times, the system reveals its nature far more starkly than during periods of 'business as usual', where these underlying features operate more smoothly and effectively for being taken for granted.

There are three boundary moments in Chinese discourse and semiosis over the second half of the twentieth century that are of special interest from this point of view, throwing the nexus between ideological function and linguistic and semiotic form into sharp relief. First is the period immediately after the Communist accession to power, when the party deliberately and consciously attempted to define the new conditions of language and discourse for China under socialism. This debate took place in what may seem a dry and academic terrain, the so-called 'abstract inheritance' debate within philosophy. But this particular debate dealt with central ideological issues for the new regime, whether or how the terms and concepts of traditional philosophy could be incorporated into a Marxist framework (see Louie 1986 for a fuller discussion of this whole debate). A second major rupture occurred between 1976 and 1980, when China negotiated a route back out of the discursive regimes now associated with the Cultural Revolution. The 1990s have witnessed another period of discursive and semiosic instability and change, as Deng and his successors have tried to balance the contradictions between central controls and a measure of freedom.

Discourse at the limits: the unfortunate case of Li Jian

To make this kind of point with the necessary precision and contextualisation we will draw mainly on a small set of texts written in 1979 by a writer, Li Jian, who is not in himself either well known or important. What gives these texts such value for our purposes is that the debate to which they contributed took place at one of these crucial times of rapid change in the evolution of Chinese discursive politics. Li Jian provides an illuminating instance of language and ideology not because he was successful or influential but because in some respects he was catastrophically and symptomatically *un*successful as an ideologue. In 1979 he wrote a fiercely debated article which seemed to support the cultural policies of the 'Gang of Four', arguing that writers should 'praise virtue' and celebrate the achievements of the masses. By 1980 he had totally changed his position, writing a number of stories which seemed to attack the ideas of the 'Gang of Four' more savagely than anyone else. His views were castigated on both occasions by both reformists and conservatives (see Louie 1983 for a fuller discussion). There was nothing particularly out of date with Li Jian's views, he was simply 'caught out' by the rapid ideological shifts in the aftermath of the Cultural Revolution, when political rhetoric had to be handled with extreme care.

The discursive regimes of modern China are distinct and complex, but we don't want to suggest that there is something incomprehensibly different in the way they work, in the ways linguistic forms and political and discursive systems mesh together in a single functional whole. English speakers reading our analyses will recognise generic similarities, with shifts in political rhetoric, in their own countries. For instance, in Australia in 1996 a fierce debate began after a speech given by the new Prime Minister, John Howard, over the issue of 'free speech', which Howard opposed to what he called 'political correctness'. His words as reported were: 'One of the great changes that has come over Australia in the last six months is that people do feel able to speak a little more freely and a little more openly about what they feel . . . I welcome the fact that people can now talk about certain things without living in fear of being branded as a bigot or as a racist'.

These words skilfully use the capacity of English to be vague. 'Freedom' and 'feelings' are generally regarded as good things, and 'certain things' is not specific about what these 'things' might be. But his words caused a furore because they coincided with a speech by an Independent MP, Pauline Hanson, which was strongly racist against Aborigines and 'Asians'. Howard's words were scanned for their 'real' meaning as intently as if he was an enigmatic representative of the Chinese government in the glory days of Sinology and Australia was made up of a nation of China-watchers. As one commentator said: 'In politics timing is everything – and these comments were sufficiently vague to be interpreted in some quarters as an endorsement of the call by outspoken Independent MP Pauline Hanson for a review of immigration policy and the abolition of multiculturalism' (Short 1996: 2).

What Short and others were doing here was assuming a secret intention behind Howard's words (or claiming to assume – Short's careful 'interpreted in some quarters' may be professionally cautious, since most readers and commentators were fairly sure on this occasion what the 'real Howard' thought, a position close to Hanson's). They then interpreted this according to what they understood of his 'real' motives and meanings, in terms of generic rules of Australian political discourse. But this was a relatively new government, whose attitudes to multiculturalism were shrouded in ambiguities, hence the 'real' meaning could not easily be taken for granted. Howard was criticised as failing in terms of what was presumed to be his intention: not to say what he personally 'really' thought or felt, but to give a definitive ruling on what his government decreed it was correct to think and speak, to deliver the kind of meaning that could then act to interpret the statements of himself and his government. His vagueness was meant to be safe and at the same time create discursive stability. Instead it destabilised discourse and provoked a debate which flourished excessively vigorously and out of his control.

In Li Jian's case the error of judgement arose because the particular debates he initiated occurred at a period of crisis in Chinese discursive forms, when the transition from the Cultural Revolution period had to be negotiated in such a way that the social and political fabric remained intact. This crisis brought out in an acute form a phenomenon that is endemic in Chinese political life: a systemic form of double-think held in place by unstated and unstable systems of discursive control, the whole constituting an ideological formation which is still inseparable from the specific forms of the language itself.

The debate surrounding Li Jian is especially suitable for our analysis of the Chinese language and its ideological functions because it produced a windfall in ambiguities in language use and awareness of systems of control which are normally taken for granted and therefore not mentioned explicitly. We will pick out from the debate examples of language use which we feel illustrate most clearly our argument that the ambiguities of the Chinese language, commonly constructed by juxtaposing contradictory terms, are a necessary part of the ideological formation of the Chinese consciousness. In the process we will show that the contradictions and ambiguities in the written language have been used by the elite ruling group as a means to social control.

Staking the terrain

We will begin by looking at the title of Li Jian's first article, the one that aroused such heat, because it functions in many ways that are typical in its use of the forms of Chinese written language. We are concerned here mainly with the official written language. Spoken Chinese, like other spoken languages, is typically less ambiguous than written because the context is normally clearer. Spoken Chinese also employs many more modal particles to clarify situations. The title, ' "Praising virtue" and "lacking virtue" ' ('*Ge de*' *yu* '*que de*') 歌德与缺德 (Li Jian 1979: 5–6), is typical in both its ambiguity of reference and its unambiguous stance, and in both ways it is typical of Chinese language in use. We do not know who is praising virtue, or what people and actions are to be regarded as virtuous or lacking in virtue. But we are in no doubt that the first are to be regarded as good, and the second not.

The first effect is achieved by mimetic transformations, which we discussed in Chapter 4. These transformations act on the structures of representations, changing the 'content' or its orientation. We interpret '*ge de*' ('praise – virtue') by assuming it comes transformationally from a prior form which has an agent, since '*ge*' here is a verb, and someone must be doing the praising. This agent has been transformationally deleted, and has to be guessed at to make sense of the phrase. But the form of the text does not indicate who this is, whether it is one person or many, or whether it includes the author. Similarly we know nothing about those who 'lack virtue' beyond the fact that they must exist for us to make sense of the phrase. English has many transformations of this kind, and they serve the same broad kind of ideological function. We may not know who John Howard's 'people' are who 'feel able to speak a little more freely', but we know we're meant to think they're good.

The most straightforward translation of the phrase '*ge de*' into English has similar enough linguistic and ideological qualities to the Chinese, even though formally they are such different languages. The problem with translation is not so much the inherent and incommunicable difference between English and Chinese, but the scope that translation gives for ideological work by the translator. As illustration of this point, in an illuminating article Perry Link translated '"*ge de*" *yu* "*que de*"' as 'praise and shame' (1987). In this English version the agents are deleted even more than in the Chinese and in the case of 'shame' all traces of an action by those who 'lack virtue' are also deleted. It seems that the same vague agent does the praising and the feeling of shame. This very different version not only illustrates the well-known difficulties of translation, it also shows how the indeterminacies of the Chinese text leave the way open for the insertion of the perspective taken by the translator. Link in his article discusses cultural change in the context of social transformations involving many people and political forces. This change was not necessarily caused directly by individual agents. The ambiguity of the language – the Chinese language, not just Li Jian's particular use of it – allows a translation which makes Link's claim about post-Mao Chinese society plausible or even inevitable.

The mimetic transformations are complemented by another set which operates in a parallel fashion on the conditions of semiosis itself (i.e. the social processes of producing meaning, involving speakers/writers and hearers/readers and the relations between them which make communication possible). These we call *semiosic transformations*, since they act on semiosic structures and meanings. One instance here is the use of quotation marks around the two phrases. Such use of quotation marks is a post-classical feature of the Chinese written code, part of the language that it adopted and adapted from the West because it served Chinese ideological purposes equally well. It is analogous to the use of so-called 'scare-quotes' in English, where the tactic is used extensively in newspapers. It is used even more extensively and differently in contemporary Chinese. The quotation marks serve to indicate that someone has said the phrase concerned, but that the actual speaker has been deleted. So again, the reader does not know exactly who this person is, whether it is one person or many, reliable or unreliable, living or dead. Howard's speech included another variant of this tactic, when he talked of people 'living in fear of being branded racists and bigots'. In this case he is referring to people who have never been in any danger of Ku Klux Klan-style violence, but still claim they 'live in fear'. But this claim is put as a fact, not a claim. It is the 'enemy', those who 'brand' them as 'racists and bigots', whose words are drawn attention to, and this move is enough to discredit the enemy's assertions.

In both English and Chinese, the incorporation of markers indicating a specific speaker has an effect on the authority and reliability that is assigned to an utterance. This is what is known as the *modality* of the utterance. Modality in Chinese as in English works in very complex ways. As seems obvious, the utterances of authoritative speakers, or ones 'like us', are normally assigned a high truth value; and the opposite is the case with utterances of low status or hostile speakers. What is less obvious is that where quotation marks are used, drawing attention to the fact that this phrase has a specific source, they reduce the modality status of the phrase. Even though a presumed source can itself be of high or low status, and this judgement is incorporated into the overall modality value of the utterance, the mere mention of a source detracts from the modality of an utterance in both English and Chinese. In the instance we have mentioned, there are two phrases, each with quotation marks indicating that they are the view of a particular group, and therefore to be viewed with some scepticism.

However, in this article Li Jian is not neutral in regard to these two groups. He goes on to argue that it is right to 'praise virtue', and that those who oppose this tendency 'lack virtue'. This very different valuation enunciated by Li Jian is constructed by a parallel semiosic transformation which is very common in Chinese. This pivots around the term 'virtue' (*de*). This term not only has a mimetic meaning, it also has a semiosic value. It constructs not only a kind of object in the world (virtue) but also a kind of speaker and context. It is associated with traditional moral discourse, going back to the classics of Confucianism and Daoism. As with the quotation marks, it therefore recalls a semiosic context which has been deleted. But unlike the quotation-mark strategy it does not draw attention to the fact of transformation or its dependence on a particular source, so that it does not problematise the modality of the phrase to the same degree.

Li Jian's linguistic move here mirrors the strategies of the 'abstract inheritance' theorists of two decades earlier. During this debate the Chinese intellectual elite, now servants of a socialist state not an imperial regime, tried to construct a reworked version of the classic tradition, but in an 'abstract' form. That is, they wanted to select from the tradition and transform it to obscure its roots in the social forms of imperial China. These traditional concepts and values with their quotation marks removed could then be reinserted into a Communist republic as legitimate, valued forms of thought. But the strategy of 'abstract inheritance' grew out of a struggle in which the label of 'traditional' lost its previous automatically positive value for some 'radical' groups. The struggle left a potential instability in the new system of semiosic values, since the traditional virtues were no longer taken-for-granted positives, certainly not in a marked, 'non-abstract' form. In fact, the ideologues of the Cultural Revolution aimed to attack and root out from the past non-revolutionary ideas such as 'virtue'.

So Li Jian's title in some respects is a typical and legible example of the language in use; but it employs these normal forms with a complexity that becomes, under pressure, a source of instability. As the article unfolds it seems to become clear that the 'praise virtue' faction is good and the 'lack virtue' faction isn't, but this interpretation is anchored by a conventional ideological value given to '*de*' 德. '*De*' has a strongly positive value in traditional thought, which the 'Gang of Four' and the Li Jian of this article were supposed to reject. If the traditional system of values is accepted, then the deleted agent who 'lacks' virtue ought to have a negative value. Following this line, it is hypothetically possible that this speaker may be giving a negative value to traditional thought, and therefore *praising* the person who 'lacks' virtue. In the 'abstract inheritance' debate, for example, radicals like Guan Feng, though in the minority, were adamant in criticising all the basic 'virtues' of traditional thought. Conversely, the taken-for-granted positive value of 'praising virtue' assumes someone who accepts traditional values without question. This may all sound confusing, and it is; but this is precisely the confusion that Li Jian was unable to manage in this debate.

We have discussed this title at such length because it illustrates so many crucial aspects of Chinese. One is the ambiguity of reference, the mimetic ambiguities that conceal precisely who or what is being talked about until further information or prior knowledge comes into play. The second is an ambiguity of ideological value, so that different readers can assign different allegiances and therefore overall meaning into the text, depending on what their own allegiances are and how they judge the author. Li Jian drew on traditional values to support a group whose primary commitment was to challenge those values. The result was a potential contradiction which is stable when a whole group is committed to that contradiction, but is destabilised when the political forces that hold that contradiction in place are weakened.

In the normal course of events, readers of any persuasion would tolerate, indeed participate, in such ambiguities and contradictions in the language. But 1979 was not a 'normal' time. Although the Cultural Revolution was clearly over, ways of apportioning blame or praise on those for or against its policies were certainly not clear. Political allegiances were still volatile, with groups forming and re-forming in rapid succession. With the ideological framework shaken, the Chinese language was also being destabilised, and disoriented writers and readers alike scrambled for any familiar signs and markers which would return them to a sense of security and 'normality'. In fact, 'scar literature' – literature produced in the first few years after the Cultural Revolution about people's unhappy experiences of the event itself – was basically a search for a new but familiar system of signs. This literature was clichéd even when it was new; and this was the precise reason it was so popular. Clichés, however, do not necessarily disambiguate, nor do they free language of contradictions, as Li Jian was to find to his cost.

Clichés pointing everywhere and nowhere

In English the term 'cliché' is used negatively, as a mark of bad writing. But in spite of this official disapproval clichés are widespread, especially in politics and advertising, because in practice they are highly functional (Hodge 1986). Clichés, in English as well as Chinese, have two major effects. Semiosically they construct solidarity, uniting a community by their recognition of the familiar, and as a result they come to acquire a kind of truth-effect for the community which is united by its recognition of their predictability.

In Chinese, most idioms and set phrases (*chengyu*) are four-character expressions. Thousands of four-character expressions from traditional discourse such as 'adding legs when drawing a snake' (*hua she tian zu* 画蛇添足), meaning a superfluous act, survive in modern Chinese, and are actively reinforced through language textbooks and other media. Thus, even during the Cultural Revolution, nearly all political slogans were framed in the *chengyu* form. For example, the virtue of 'self-reliance' was *zili gengsheng* 自力更生 (literally, self-strength change-live), and a slogan targeting Confucius was *pi Lin, pi Kong* 批林批孔 ('criticise Lin Biao and Confucius'). In many respects this form is the linchpin of the dominant discursive strategy. A precise knowledge of their social meanings is essential for anyone who wants to understand the underlying dynamics of specific exchanges, since this knowledge is part of a semiosic survival kit for all participants. English speakers are liable to feel superior over the Chinese use of slogans, as though clichés are inherently simple and they themselves do not use them. The opposite is true: English political life is full of clichés (like 'freedom of speech') and these forms can be highly complex and ambiguous in use.

Li Jian's 1979 article was a tissue of 'clichés', potent four-character expressions, and in this respect was typical of its genre. The problem for Li Jian was that his article was written at a time of profound shifts in the complex alignment of the various strata of slogans. Chinese speakers recognise the conventionality of all four-character expressions. But they also understand them as typical of different kinds of period, group and values. As an instance of how these forms function in an unstable semiosic situation we will take a single passage of his text, the last sentence in the first paragraph:

> But to eulogise the Chinese people's great leader Chairman Mao and his glorious thought, to establish legends and erect monuments to the proletariat and the labouring masses, and to loudly rally for the four modernisations – what is wrong with that? 但是, 歌颂中国人民的伟大领袖毛主席和 他的光辉思想, 为无产阶级和劳动群众树碑立传为四个现代化事业大声激呼, 这又有何不好? (*Danshi, gesong Zhongguo*

renmin de [weida lingxiu] Mao Zhuxi he tade guanghui sixiang, wei [wuchan jieji] he [laodong qunzhong] [shubei lizhuan]), wei sige xiandaihua shiye dasheng jihu, zhe you youhe buhao?

There are three distinct strata of four-character expressions here, each oriented to a different social grouping, each therefore with a different semiosic effect. First is 'great leader' *weida lingxiu* (literally, great-big-lead-sleeve). This expression was a conventional epithet for Mao. As such, it is locked into a syntagmatic bond with Mao himself, so strong that at certain periods it could be understood to mean Mao, even if he was not mentioned. But the more strongly these items are chained together as almost a cliché themselves (*weida lingxiu* + *chairman Mao*) the weaker the links between each item and the reality it refers to.

This principle applies to the components of these expressions, too. *Ling* for instance has a range of meanings, including 'neck', 'collar' and 'lead'. *Xiu* literally means 'sleeve', but that meaning is inappropriate to the point of incomprehensibility in this context. It recalls a symbolic feature of dress in imperial times, but was not applicable to Mao's style of dress or the signs of power in the People's Republic. Syntagmatic bonds (its place in the four-character expression) exert a force that overrides the link between this character and its concrete meaning, but this is only a different balance of the same forces acting on the other units. Each character is doubly determined by a vector of forces: by the chain binding the component elements of the expression and by the bond between the character and its referent.

The syntagmatic bond also draws strength from the semiosic context, from the need for political solidarity that it expresses. Its 'truth' is its signal of political allegiance, not its correspondence to how-things-are. But this expression was unstable because of its close connection to Mao himself. This epithet is not a conventional term for Mao's successors. This is because with the change in Mao's position in the construction of the Chinese political community, its 'truth' inevitably changed. This change was well under way as Li Jian was writing. So a term that would have given status and authority to his text three years previously, mobilising a large community around its 'truth', was already approaching obsolescence, leaving Li Jian isolated on the shrinking other side of the fissure that was opening up beneath the formerly safe term.

Three years previously, there would not have seemed to be much difference between this epithet for Mao and the equally orthodox pair of four-character expressions *wuchan jieji / laodong qunzhong*. The first of these (literally, no-produce-rank-step) is the orthodox way of referring to the Marxist category 'the proletariat'. But, unlike the term 'great leader', this predated Mao's rule, so that the community that it organised was larger, more diffuse, and therefore better able to survive political changes.

The four characters are strongly bonded to each other, to form what is normally understood as a single concept, but its component items still have semantic force. *Jieji* can stand alone, as the word for the Marxist term 'class'. It is a paratactic compound, with both terms having a meaning of 'step' or 'rank'. That is, both terms imply a social order organised hierarchically. They incorporate elitist values into the core vocabulary of Chinese Marxism. In this respect they are no different from the term 'class' (German *Klasse*) which incorporates elitist values which are seemingly neutralised in the syntagmatic unit 'working class'. *Wu chan* is even more paradoxical. *Chan* can mean 'giving birth', 'produce' or 'property', while *wu* is a negation. Together the negation plus this set of meanings of *chan* gives an ambiguous specification of what defines this crucial class for Marxist thought. If it means 'property-less' it is still unclear exactly what constitutes 'property', whether for instance it could include the class of intellectuals and bureaucrats who did not own property in the same way as the landlord class. In the post-Mao years, it is precisely this ambiguity which has enabled the party political machine to redefine intellectuals into the proletariat class (see Wu Naitao 1987: 21–2).

So this key term, *wuchan jieji*, yokes together vagueness, contradiction and elitism. It ought to be unacceptable as a primary positive term in Marxist discourse, its life even shorter than *weida lingxiu*. In practice it has lasted, precisely because of these apparent defects, since its weakened links with its mimetic meanings allow it to incorporate different forms of Marxism and even non-Marxist ideologies. Again, the parallels between this and the 'abstract inheritance' method are striking. Feng Youlan, the Peking University philosopher who devised this method, was in fact verbalising what was already in place on a linguistic level. But its meaning is not entirely open. The weakness of its links to referents is held in place by the strength of its syntagmatic links within the sentence, and by its semiosic links to a particular group. It is unusable by Taiwanese, except as a form of quotation, since its meaning incorporates those who can use it, not simply what it mimetically refers to, in the material world. It is interesting to note that in recent years, *wuchan jieji* as a term is going out of use in China as well. It is being taken over by *gongren jieji* 工人阶级 (working class, literally, work-people-rank-step), which is in many ways even more ambiguous, for 'work' can be and has been defined in a great number of ways.

The third kind of four-character expression we will look at, however, is most definitely used in Taiwan. *Shubei lizhuan* ('establish legends and erect monuments') is a classic four-character expression, which originated in the pre-revolutionary period but is still entirely acceptable in current usage. The mimetic content of this phrase is frankly traditionalist. *Bei* refers to imperial monuments that commemorated heroic achievements on behalf of the imperial state, and *zhuan* refers to Confucian classics or celebratory biographies. Its form is also a significant feature which carries important ideological meanings. The overriding quality is its symmetry and balance. Syntactically it is verb-noun-verb-noun, with the two pairs expressing a complementary meaning. *Shu* and *li* can both be translated as 'erect, establish', but *shu* implies movement upwards, while *li* refers to the stability of what is set up, its firm anchoring on the ground. *Bei* refers to material records of military achievement, whereas *zhuan* refers to written records of intellectual/'moral' excellence. The phrase thus carefully balances opposites in a harmonious structure that reconciles them. This is not the case with either of the other two phrases we have looked at, which do not pivot around their midpoint. *Weida lingxiu* is adjective-adjective-noun-noun, and the repeated meaning ('big-big') is confined to the first half. Nor does the paratactic form itself have the delicate internal contrast that gives it a further aesthetic dimension.

The same is true of *wuchan jieji* (proletariat).The phrase itself acquires political complexity by being applied to the 'proletariat', and it is in fact the combination of the double four-character expressions *wuchan jieji* and *shubei lizhuan* that is the operative cliché that survives in post-revolutionary discourse, not the phrase on its own. Its overall semiosic meaning (i.e. the community that it integrates) is one that affirms the coexistence of traditional culture and values with a Marxist society. In this form it guarantees a kind of 'truth' that transcends past and present in a new universality. As such it has a high modality in post-Cultural Revolutionary China.

In the one sentence, Li Jian has yoked together four-character expressions from three different strata. These organise the 'truth' of three different communities, three different stages of Chinese society which are still part of their semiosic meaning in contemporary use. If they stayed yoked together, this diversity would have been a strength, since what is acceptable to otherwise distinct and antagonistic communities must have a high level of acceptability indeed. But in the unstable situation in which Li Jian was writing, the text came apart at the seams, splitting along these lines of cleavage, alienating all groups instead of bringing them together.

In order to understand this set of meanings and effects we need to assume that readers and writers share a simple classificatory system of kinds of four-character expressions, attaching a semiosic meaning to each of them which recognises their source and allegiance, and assigns them a political meaning as a result. The system partly works with formal markers. Here the symmetrical form of the traditional phrase plays an important role. Partly it relies on the component meanings which single out and assign specific social values to marker aspects of reality. But partly it is the link between kind of text and kind of writer that is established by many repeated instances. This last link is difficult to recognise from particular examples of text, but it is as readily accessible to members of the community as the other kinds of marker.

Drunk among slogans

Li Jian's original article attracted such hostile criticism that he not only retracted his argument, as many Chinese ideologues have done in similar circumstances, he also engaged in a radical rethinking of Chinese language and Chinese ideological processes. This change of mind did not take the normal form of another article acknowledging the errors of the past and enunciating the new 'correct' position. Li Jian changed the form of his writing activity as well as his political stance, writing a series of ten short stories in a brief period of time. The stories adopted a common strategy. They attacked the discursive strategies of the Cultural Revolution by showing characters who 'misread' common slogans, taking them too literally and too idiosyncratically. These 'misreadings' were set in a context of a material world which did not conform to the meanings of the slogans and which took savage revenge on the idealist protagonist. The gap between the 'truth' of the slogans and the nature of material reality was traumatic for this protagonist, producing a pathological scepticism that was close to madness. So obsessively do the stories probe a specific pathology of Cultural Revolution discourse, we can guess they also correspond to Li Jian's own painful personal experience.

In the defence that he wrote in response to attacks on these stories, Li Jian described the basic strands of his strategy (Li Jian 1981a: 54). In it he foregrounded a method of 'stream of consciousness', an attempt to represent in an uncensored form the actual thought processes of his characters. Since inevitably this 'thought' was expressed in language and concerned with meanings derived from actual texts, his stories are at the same time an attempt to articulate the basic processes of the construction and interpretation of meaning in language. These 'stream of consciousness' elements were then set against what he called 'realism', which represented his attempt to demonstrate the erroneousness of these forms of language and thought.

We will take his story, 'Drunk among Flowers', to illustrate the theory of language and linguistic processes that is common to them all (Li Jian 1981b: 29–37). The title itself refers to the central character, a young female Red Guard who at the start of the story is slightly drunk and lost in a poor rural area. She shelters with a poor peasant who complains that he needs a woman. Influenced by a phrase from Mao, the young women sees it as her duty to sleep with him and become his wife. However, the decision proves unwise in a number of ways, and by the end of the story she is very unhappy and mentally deranged. The 'flowers' of the title could refer to the flowers in the grass on which she collapses, but they could also refer to the thoughts of Mao, which intoxicate her and lead her to behave in an irrational way which she lives to regret. (In 1956, Mao Zedong initiated the 'hundred flowers' movement in which Chinese intellectuals were encouraged openly to express their concerns about national policies. Tens of thousands thought that genuine free expression was possible and criticised the Communist Party. Within months, the anti-Rightist campaign was launched and the critics suppressed. Notwithstanding the ruthlessness of this campaign, later generations seemed to continue to believe Mao's pronouncements.)

Mao's 'hundred flowers' seems to have intoxicated Western readers as well, as evidenced by the number of books on contemporary literature with titles like *Stubborn Weeds* (Perry 1983), *Roses and Thorns* (Perry 1984), *Fragrant*

Weeds (Jenner 1983), and *Blooming and Contending* (Duke 1985). At the key point in the story, after the peasant has made his request, Li Jian writes as follows (1981b: 30):

> In her mind appeared a supreme directive: 'Without poor peasants there is no revolution. Denying them is denying the revolution. To attack them is to attack the revolution.'

This is a well-known quotation from Mao himself, of the kind that was studiously memorised by Red Guards. As Li Jian's critics were later to insist, the words were not normally understood to mean that good female Marxists should agree to the sexual advances of every frustrated peasant (Li Jikai 1981: 52). The young woman's reading is aberrant, but the linguistic process she employs is not. In the opening, the quotation is described as 'appearing' (*chu xian*) 出现, an intransitive verb which obscures the agency of the process itself, making the words appear with a magical authority. But they come with the kind of semiosic labelling that we have referred to in the previous section. 'A directive of the highest order' (*zuigao zhishi* 最高指示) recalls, as part of its meaning, not only its source (Mao) but also its status as a marker of orthodoxy. This status we suggested can carry a stronger force than the particular meaning. It can mask contradictions and inconsistencies and even common sense. So although this particular foolish misreading would normally have been policed out of existence, the overall response to the phrase has a kind of parodic truth. In practice the Cultural Revolution abounded in such 'misreadings', with tragic consequences.

The misreading exploits certain general qualities of Chinese that give rise to systematic ambiguities. Another phrase in the story, *Meiyou pinnong* 没有贫农 (literally, no-have-poor-peasant), which we have translated 'Without poor peasants' is in fact built around an agentless verb, *you,* whose understood agent could be singular or plural, whose tense and modality are not specified, as is normal in Chinese. Similarly, *pinnong* could be one or many peasants. At issue is the crucial difference between a general or abstract statement that applies to all peasants and all revolutionaries, as in the normal reading of the text, and a specific reference to an actual peasant, the one in front of the girl, an actual Red Guard. The difference between individual and collective is a very important one for social and political thought. We can see here the consequences of a linguistic system which systematically obscures the difference, if there are no overriding systems that then control the ambiguity.

The person doing this misreading is not Li Jian himself. He is careful to specify the conditions of the misreading. The story opens with a quotation, the words of a song: 'Beautiful wine and coffee' (*Meijiu he kafei* 美酒和咖啡). As with the four-character expressions and the words of Mao, these words are readily identified and assigned a specific social value. Both sentiment and form are pre-revolutionary and 'decadent'. To find that the singer is a Red

Guard is already a shock, a contradiction which then affects the reading of her misreading. By the laws of modality a double negative approximates a positive, so the misreading by a non-Red Guard ought to leave the correct reading intact, and Li Jian ought to be safe from the accusation that he was attacking 'real' Red Guards. But a double negative does not have the same effect as a simple positive, and Li Jian's device leaves open the possibility that he thought that many actual Red Guards were not 'real' Red Guards, i.e. were not as they were meant to be.

Li Jian's technique has made the evaluation of the Red Guard's interpretation ambiguous. The same is true of his treatment of the narrator of the story. The morning after the Red Guard has slept with the peasant, for instance, the scene is described as follows (1981b: 30–31):

> The sun rose in the east as she welcomed the first bright and beautiful morning in Baligou.
> She leant against the door frame and faced east. The golden quilt of the sun covered the blushing face of the young woman who faced the dawn.
> She cried.

Sun, east and dawn have positive meanings in Chinese as in many other languages. This description therefore implies that she has done the right thing in sleeping with the peasant. But the description also has a political meaning, since the positive meanings of these terms were taken over in political discourse, exploiting a pun on Mao's own name, *Dong* 东 'east'. In his earlier article, Li Jian gives a typical polemical use of this set of connections (1979: 5):

> The flowers and plants that face the sun and open up their beautiful faces to the golden sun. But those animals that are good at living in damp, filthy places can only curse the red sun. Those who can't 'sing virtue' 'lack virtue'.

Facing the sun here has a double meaning, in which both terms reinforce its positive value: orientation to the sun as a 'natural' response to beautiful things, and orientation to Mao as equally 'natural'. As an ideological ploy it may seem obvious and crude, but in the article it has the merit of allowing readers to know where Li Jian stands, and therefore how they should orientate themselves to his text. The story uses this ploy in an even more obvious way, repeating the words 'sun' and 'east' to emphasise their importance, in a phrase that is like a parody of 'The East is Red', the most well-known hymn to Mao. But the effect of this is to seem to incorporate a political judgement of approval into the narrator's text, as though he is asking the reader to accept that the young woman's interpretation of the original Mao quotation was politically correct. So as readers we do not know whether to take this narrator as deliberately false, who simply repeats the mistakes of the young woman and is an extension of her consciousness; or whether he/she is closer to Li Jian, endorsing as author this judgement at this point in the text. This doubt only doubles the earlier doubt about how this text is to be read, and what its allegiances are. This is then further complicated by what was understood to be Li Jian's own position, as a defender of Cultural Revolution thinking of the kind displayed in his well-known article of only a year before. The accumulated effect of these doubts was to make Li Jian's second kind of intervention as unpopular as his first. His critique of the dominant modality strategies was so radical that his own meaning and position were unable to be understood. In the same way, Prime Minister Howard could not easily praise multiculturalism and be believed.

Policing the discourse: ambiguity found and lost

A further value of Li Jian's work for our purposes is that it provoked critiques that brought out the normal bases of judgement of the dominant strategies of reading. Li Jian's stories represented a threat to the systems that controlled the proliferating ambiguities of the language, so in response to them, his critics described the relevant rules that set limits in practice. Hua Ming, for instance, criticised 'Drunk among Flowers' in the following terms:

> In *Drunk among Flowers* he puts together the wild enthusiasms of the modern religion [Mao-worship] and the sacrifice of the 'virtue' of a woman Red Guard. By mixing together 'the liberation of all mankind' with satisfying the carnal desires of a poor peasant he has created a filthy and wicked (*wuhui, xie'e*) 'romance'. And how can he expect people to believe a story which is against the common logic of everyday life and which does not correspond with normal human feelings?
>
> (1981: 4)

Hua Ming is not a well-known critic, but he was writing in *China Youth*, a journal through which the Party set standards for China's younger citizens. His tone is thus conservative and didactic. He objects to the mixture of categories from different genres (political discourse and romance), but he also has a double objection to the resulting text: it is immoral ('filthy and wicked', terms that recur in the outraged response to Li Jian's stories) and it is unbelievable. There is both overlap and contradiction between these two criticisms, since if it is so unbelievable, it should not have such a damaging effect, and its 'immorality' ought to be a reason why it should not be believed.

The measuring stick that is used to judge the credibility of the text is a form of 'common sense', a concept which has been influentially theorised by Gramsci as applied to Western political discourse (1971). The nature of this common sense is described by Hua Ming as *shenghuo changli* 生活常理 (common logic of everyday life) and *ren zhi changqing* 人之常情 (normal human feelings). Important to the operation of these phrases is the term *chang*. It basically means 'common, everyday', but it is also an important term in Confucian-Daoist thought, referring to a constancy which is almost a universal principle. *Li* means reason or principle in everyday speech but in neo-Confucian discourse has the meaning of a universal principle. *Qing* also plays a key role in the construction of this 'common sense'. On its own it can refer to passion or feeling, even the kind of erotic feeling that Li Jian was too fond of exploring, in Hua's view, but in the context of this syntagm it is controlled, closer to 'reason' than 'feeling'. The ideological effect of this is intriguingly similar to the English 'sense', which outside the phrase 'common sense' refers to physical senses, but in that context refers to a socially constructed perception which is opposed to sensuality (see Williams 1986).

As a final component of this measuring stick that is used to beat Li Jian, we will note the ambiguous role of *ren* 人. This word is normally translated 'man', as though it were neutral, but this neutrality was brought into question in the debates about 'abstract inheritance' in the pre-Cultural Revolution period. Since these debates were also about the contemporary uses of the vocabulary of the classic texts, they are relevant to our present concern. Guan Feng and Zhao Jibin argued with convincing evidence that in Confucian texts, *ren* was always distinguished from *min* 民 on grounds of class and status (see the discussion in Louie 1986). The same distinction has survived into modern usage, where *min* has a different range of contexts. Again we can see an analogous phenomenon with the English word 'man', whose gender content has been attacked by feminists, but which also carries covert class values, in this case lower class. So for instance it is possible to say 'Very Important Person' but not 'Very Important Man'. Users of English show their recognition of the covert class and gender meanings that are erratically part of the word by patterns of use, not by making this meaning explicit; but this covert status only makes the ideological function more effective. The same is true of *ren* in Chinese, where the need to cancel out its class meaning is shown in the combination *renmin* to describe the 'people', still divided on class lines but with the boundary of that division now masked and rendered unproblematic. So the 'common sense' that Hua Ming invokes as a measuring stick of truth is ideological, not a simple appeal to experience. It is firmly anchored by traditional values and traditional morality, including the elitism that was a dominant feature of the old tradition.

In his earlier article, however, Li Jian was not challenging the systems of control of ambiguity, he was exploiting the manipulative uses of ambiguity that are equally endemic to political discourse in Chinese (as in other languages). So the critiques of the article show a different aspect of Chinese reading strategies: how they cope with ambiguity and mystification in others, and remain in control of those who attempt to manipulate language.

Another critic, Wang Ruowang, gave an influential and authoritative critique of the article, quoting extensively and giving a detailed discussion.

Wang was a highly placed critic whose literary activities led to his expulsion from the Communist Party in 1987. He was imprisoned after he supported the marchers for democracy in Shanghai in 1989, and released a year later. He is so highly regarded as a liberal in the Chinese context that even in the West he is described as 'Keeper of the Flame' and 'Moral Critic of the State' (Rubin 1987: 233–50). After quoting the passage that we have discussed earlier, he comments:

> This is to say, the most important criterion for judging whether a literary creation adheres to the 'four basic principles' is to see whether the writer in his writings has established legends and erected monuments for the worker-peasant-soldier heroes. If he has, then this is a 'concrete manifestation (*juti biaoxian*) 具体表现 of the principle of adhering to the Party nature in literature and arts'. Otherwise, I am sorry, but 'What's the use of these people?' To the author, adhering to the 'four basic principles' is not the general demand (*zongde yaoqiu*) 总的要求 placed on the content of a piece of writing, it is merely a concrete demand on the choice of topic and characterisation.
>
> (Wang Ruowang 1979)

Wang Ruowang employs a form of common sense on this text, but it is a very different kind from Hua Ming's, because of his different ideological stance and purpose. What he does is first to translate the vague content of the passage into a specific narrow mimetic content, what Li Jian is 'really saying'. Then he draws attention to the broader semiosic context that allows him to be so sure what Li Jian 'really' means, connecting Li Jian precisely to the dominant group in the Cultural Revolution. In the same way, Short knew what Howard 'really' meant about multiculturalism.

It is no accident that Wang uses the same framework that was invoked in the 'abstract inheritance' debate. The key terms are the distinction between 'general' (a level of meanings which is indeterminate) and 'concrete' (specific meanings that operate in a specific context). The leading ideologue in that debate, Feng Youlan, used the same term for 'concrete', *juti*, as Wang Ruowang, but employed two different terms for the problematic other pole. His first formulation was *chouxiang* 抽象 (abstract), which through *chou* carries the sense of selecting out, extracting an essence and leaving the dross – the dross of the contexts and values of traditional Confucian society. Thus the term contained an elitist conviction that the imperfections of the former elite can be safely removed by the new elite. Under pressure Feng shifted his ground, and referred to the consensus core as *pubian* 普遍 (general). This term swung to the other extreme, since *pubian* means general, with connotations of being common. This contradicted the elitism that was at the centre of Feng's position, but he was under considerable pressure at the time, and the strategy of incorporating oppositional meanings into key terms was endemic, as we have argued.

Wang does not use either of these more technical terms. *Zong* is a single character expression that refers to a kind of meaning that either comprehends others in a new synthesis, or asserts a new consensus. It ambiguously asserts the possibility of ambiguity as freedom (opposed to the strict Party line that Li Jian had argued) while reasserting the existence of norms that will continue to control and limit this freedom. This is the kind of position that Feng Youlan would have wanted to argue in the 1950s and 1960s but couldn't, since he could not claim that the situation was governed by a single set of understood norms. Wang Ruowang is able to do so in the new climate of 1979, even so early in the thaw. This is the triumph not of a particular position but of the old conditions of discourse, and its triumph was so speedy because it had never really been destroyed.

So we see that Li Jian's two moves, seemingly at opposite poles of the political spectrum, in practice were simply different kinds of offence against the normative modes of discourse. Similarly, Wang Ruowang and Hua Ming represented different political interests, but they both support the discursive regime that enabled them to operate as members of an intellectual class. The interest of this class is to sustain the semiotic system that was inherited from pre-revolutionary China, one that allowed similar levels of ambiguity to coexist with the same mechanisms of control.

If the levels of ambiguity are too excessive, of course, they would disable the communication process altogether. This would be the case if it were not for the systems of control exercised by semiosic rules governing discourse. But the need for control systems makes submission to these systems the prerequisite for effective communication. This submission involves long training in acquiring knowledge of the characters and also the less obvious training in recognising what meanings and authorities count. Yet new times and conditions generate new meanings for new groups, which exert their own pressures on language and discourse at every level. Both change and stasis turn out to be complex and ambiguous phenomena. Sometimes change seems dramatic and irreversible, but at another level mechanisms continue that keep the system in a more or less steady state. At other times, change goes deep to the core of the system itself. In the case of China it is important to be able to see how familiar patterns of language, power and discourse are able to reassert themselves almost intact in spite of seemingly catastrophic changes. It is equally important to recognise that some changes are powerful, systemic and irreversible. China in the twenty-first century will be a fundamentally different form of society and culture compared to China under the Qing dynasty, though it will still be China.

Mapping discursive change in contemporary China

In this chapter and the previous one we have been arguing that the Chinese language has the features that it has because of the functions that it serves. We have emphasised the capacity for ambiguity of the language, especially in the written form as used in public discourse. In our account, this tendency towards ambiguity in the language is normally constrained and controlled by discursive rules, to give a set of interpretations that mesh with 'common sense'. To simplify, the language allows the vagueness and inclusiveness of S-ideological forms, while discursive rules are based on the stricter P-ideological forms: who is a recognised, authoritative speaker and who is not, what is an acceptable statement and what is not. The result is typically a kind of double-think in which two kinds of meaning coexist, with discursive rules the over-riding principle of interpretation, always decisive in the final instance.

The case of Li Jian is therefore interesting because it shows the vulnerability of this system at times of ideological or political change. Li Jian was a particularly unfortunate case but he is by no means a complete aberration. The impression of monolithic certainty of beliefs and truths in Chinese politics is an illusion created and sustained only with effort by the ruling group at any time. The Li Jian phenomenon was an accident always waiting to happen. Languages in general tend to change slowly, glacially, but they do change. Similarly, discursive rules have a longer life than a single political regime, but they too change over time. It is important to be able to discriminate between superficial changes and those that go deeper, signifying and contributing to deeper processes of change. Foucault (1981) described the project of history as identifying continuities and discontinuities at different levels, so that history is made up of discontinuous series overlaid on series of series marked by slow change, and massive continuities. Maps of these series-of-series, macro-patterns over a long period of time, are liable to seem simplistic and contentious, but that is how they can best fulfil their role: not to be banal and comprehensive, but to make largescale change visible and speakable.

With discourse, there is a myth currently popular in the West which pivots around the symbol of Tiananmen Square as representing the 'old' discursive regimes maintained by relics from the Communist era. From being the execution grounds in imperial times to a gathering place for freedom fighters in modern China, Tiananmen (Gate of Heavenly Peace) has been a symbol of the great changes sweeping through China this century (Spence 1981). Since 1989, China has been seen as opposed to the new discursive freedoms that are seen as the inevitable products of free-market capitalism (Lee 1996: 242). This is a narrative of economic motives versus human rights, the old (Communism, repression) and the new (Capitalism, freedom) combined in a package whose imminent use-by date is part of the myth.

For instance, a recent article in the Australian press was headed: 'Spice sells as media frees up'. It claimed:

> The lure of profits and circulation is stimulating some adventurous journalism in China as signs emerge that the media is inching free of Beijing's rigid shackles for the first time since the Tiananmen Square massacre.

Small unofficial newspapers, the so-called 'xiao bao', carrying punchy or sometimes scandalous stories, clutter the newstands, where they compete with the giant and incredibly tedious party organs such as the *People's Daily* and the *Guangming Daily*.

(Lague 1997: 12)

This story is organised by the new Western myth of Tiananmen Square as symbol of Communist rigidity and repression, opposed by the profit motive and the pleasure principle irresistibly combined. There is an important half-truth here: things now are certainly different. In Beijing today there are many signifiers of discursive change. The official party organ, *Red Flag*, is no longer the centrepiece in a monolithic party machine, and in fact is no longer published. But against this, even in the period when the press was most tightly controlled by the Party, significant positions and policy changes were often tested first in minor publications or provincial papers.

This was the case with Li Jian, whose first article was published in 1979, thus giving it the dangerous status of being both sanctioned and not sanctioned, leaving Li Jian open to being supported or repudiated. The Cultural Revolution itself started by a discursive back door. Mao and his allies, excluded from the Beijing press by his powerful enemies in the Party, launched the Cultural Revolution with a series of articles in a Shanghai paper, followed up in Beijing itself with a famous Wall Poster. The success of that poster showed how views from below could be expressed with powerful effect, if supported by powerful players within the core of the Party. The new situation is not an absolute break with discursive regimes of the past. There were controlled sites for plurality of meanings then, and there is still tight control now. The proliferation of papers, the multiplicity of discourse, does not represent a new freedom that has thrown off the 'rigid shackles' of a repressive regime. Foucault has argued in a different context against the 'repressive hypothesis', the myth that an earlier period (for instance, the 'Victorian era', the Communist regime) was repressive and was followed by freedom to speak truth. In practice, more discourse does not necessarily mean more 'truth'. A new organisation of media in China is emerging which undoubtedly produces more discourse; but it by no means guarantees full revelations of a formerly unspeakable 'truth'. For Chinese citizens now as for the China watcher, 'truth' is more directly available but more dispersed, sometimes harder to get at because you need to read so much more, to sort out the different versions to see what you can trust. Yet there is a difference, and it matters.

On the other hand Tiananmen Square, since 1989 an unambiguous symbol in the West for an older, ruthlessly repressive politics, is in fact positioned in complex ways against changing discursive rules. In some ways it was as much a mistake by the authorities as Li Jian's intervention, and for similar reasons: a failure to understand that the ambiguities in the meanings they were trying to construct would not be controlled by the discursive rules that they relied on. Tiananmen Square was a show of force displayed for domestic consumption, picked up and elaborated by Western media to become a highly complex signifier, symbol not only of the operations of traditional Chinese discursive systems but also of new forces and forms of communication.

The demonstrations in Tiananmen Square in 1989 were broadcast worldwide from the beginning, giving them a scope that was outside the control of the traditional system. Amongst the images beamed out to a non-Chinese world, unmediated by intervening Sinologists or government-controlled media, was one particularly potent image: a plaster replica of the Statue of Liberty being crushed by advancing tanks. Paradoxically, this powerful image was co-constructed by the demonstrators and the government alike. The demonstrators provided the statue, unimpressive in itself, while the government provided the tanks that turned it, with all its foreign tackiness, into the symbol that it became. The statue in itself was ambiguous – Western in origins, Chinese in its present use – but ambiguity, as we have said, is no problem for Chinese discursive systems. Tanks are similarly ambiguous, no more Chinese than the Statue of Liberty, and yet very Chinese if used under the control of the legitimate Chinese government. But these ambiguities could not be controlled outside China, and therefore could not be controlled inside. Tiananmen Square as a carefully constructed symbol for the repression of discourse continues to provoke more discourse than it discourages.

We need to step back from these local controversies and claims to get a broader picture of discursive rules and discursive changes. From this point of view, we believe, there has indeed been a series of major discursive shifts over a century or so, a systemic shift which is massive and consistent across many codes, not just in verbal language in its standard and written forms. Contemporary discursive regimes may still be less 'open' than is claimed, but there is a consistent movement in this direction. We can contrast the present government with the socialist discursive regime that held sway for four decades, and both with an imperial discursive regime that maintained common forms across many centuries and different dynasties.

Non-verbal codes are useful to present the contrast between these three discursive regimes. As signifiers of the new discursive regime we will take the phenomenon of department stores that now are so striking a feature of the streetscapes of Beijing. These look so like their equivalents in Taiwan, which in turn look so similar to the Western archetypes of Paris or New York, that it is easy to see them merely as yet another uninteresting instance of the Westernisation of China. But they function in ways that are different from their Western counterparts, and mark a sharp break with earlier Chinese forms.

Beijing department stores indulge in conspicuous displays of luxury and wealth. They are part of a regime of spectacle. China in the past has had regimes of spectacle, but they were organised differently. In the imperial regime, the Emperor and his court displayed their immense wealth mainly behind closed doors. Peasants were excluded by great gates enclosing wealth they could only imagine, protecting a life they had no experience of and could not understand. Similarly, nobles behind their gates hardly knew what the life of a peasant entailed. Within households there were similar boundaries between the lives of men and women. The discursive system was organised by large, overt barriers, impermeable boundaries.

In Maoist China, barriers continued to exist, but they were constructed primarily by rules and regulations governing access, policed by officials whose primary function was to act as gate-keepers. This discursive and political system very successfully blocked movement, controlled knowledge, and mystified power and privilege. In the new post-Mao discursive system, the wealth and privilege that go with political power have not disappeared, but they are now overt. Politicians are expected to be corrupt, and the pursuit of wealth, which has always been part of Chinese political and economic life, is accepted as part of the scheme of things. Deng's dynasty, for instance, has secured its place even after his death. It's official: there are wealthy Chinese people, on the mainland and overseas, and it's OK for them to spend large amounts of money buying commodities that most people could never dream of affording.

A crucial difference can be seen in the behaviour of Chinese people today in relation to these palaces of luxury. Where the peasants in imperial China were excluded from the Forbidden Palace by high walls and armed guards, and ordinary people were excluded from various places in Communist China (such as 'Friendship Stores' designated for foreigners) by red tape and innumerable officials, those who do not now enter the new palatial department stores exclude themselves. No one officiously turns people away at the door; but in practice, almost everyone in these stores has the air of wealth that signals they are the right people to be there. In simplistic terms, we can say that walls in the imperial regime were made of solid materials. In the Maoist period of Communist control they were made of rules and regulations, administered by officials. Now the rules and barriers have been internalised by enough of the populace for the system to be sustained more economically by a new form of discursivity: the discourse of the 'free market', the 'market economy', the 'profit motive', which directs people to go without constraint to where they want to go, i.e. to where they know that the commodities that they can afford are sold.

This is not freedom but a new discursive system, with different effects. It is found in the dispersal of forms of information, in the multiplicity of media springing up. It is found in the greater tolerance of different forms of speech, of different dialects even within China. The China that it constructs or allows to exist is more dispersed, less controlled from the centre. This postmodern China does not consist of an essential China, located on the mainland or carefully preserved on Taiwan, surrounded by various debased or contaminated forms of Chineseness. In terms of this emerging discursive system, there is no definitive Chinese 'inside' that excludes or is contaminated by influences from an alien 'outside'.

This new discursive form is not yet dominant in mainland China. It coexists with the old discursive system, with an outcome that is not stable or predictable. What we have tried to do in this chapter is to give a framework within which this ongoing dialectic can be tracked and analysed. From this point of view, the unhappy Li Jian demonstrated an important truth too large and complex for him to manage. His first fatal intervention relied on the complexities of the old discursive system, supported by the coherent and cohesive central government that was indispensable to its mode of operations. His second intervention opted for the complex indeterminacies of the new modes of discourse, avant-garde and postmodern; but where the first intervention was behind the times, the second was equally dangerously ahead of them. Both positions were equally uncomfortable. But if it is part of the role of a writer and artist to reflect truly the shifting moods and currents of his time Li Jian was a great success, as a beautifully comprehensive illustration of the major patterns and tendencies in Chinese discourse.

6   The cult of the hero

Masculinity and popular culture

In earlier chapters of the book we have dealt with various forms of ideology and politics in Chinese culture. We have seen that every cultural artefact, whether it be language, literature or philosophy, is heavily politicised by gender. We have hitherto examined this more extensively as regards the position of women. In this chapter we want to turn our attention to issues of sexuality and the construction of masculinity. In the process, we want to extend the scope of our analysis to take in some of the forms of popular culture that are so important in forming and mediating attitudes to gender and sexuality. These ideological themes run throughout the culture, from high culture to everyday practices, and we need to track them across the full range to understand the variety of their transformations and the complexity of their effects. As focus for the discussion we will examine the meaning of the term *yingxiong* (hero) and its manifestations in a classic novel the *Romance of the Three Kingdoms* (Luo Guanzhong 1988) as well as various forms of popular culture such as icons in temples and comics.

For a number of years most approaches to gender in Chinese Studies have used the insights of contemporary feminist theory (see for example Gilmartin *et al.* 1994) to look at the position of women and the discourses that have constructed them (Edwards 1994). This has been important work. But ideologies of gender consist of a complex of definitions of forms of masculinity and femininity and different genders and sexualities, including heterosexual and homosexual forms, and it is in that kind of theoretical context that specific ideologies need to be situated. Chinese masculinities have only just emerged as an important component of gender studies, with a concentration on literary studies (Louie 1991, 1992), and much of that is in the investigation of homosexuality (Hinsch 1990).

To pursue this theme we will mainly draw on a study of the multiple forms of one particular god, Guan Yu, carried in different kinds of text in different sites at different times associated with different values and practices. In all his manifestations, Guan Yu is associated with versions of masculinity, and through this figure we can see how masculinity and its refractions have complex linkages with other important ideological themes such as nation and identity. In the process we will deploy a wider range of methods of analysis than we have so far, since Guan Yu figures in so many different kinds of text requiring different kinds of analysis, from an ethnography of cultural sites and practices surrounding Guan Yu as 'god' to semiotic and literary analyses of Guan Yu as hero in popular comics and in literary classics.

'In China Confucius is worshipped as the greatest man of scholarly learning, and Guan Yu as the greatest man of military prowess' writes Zhu Zhengming (1996: 2) in a recent book devoted to the cult of Guan Yu. The importance of Confucius is well recognised in the West, but Guan Yu is much less well known outside China. Confucius' influence is pervasive in Chinese thought and social life. The Cultural Revolution that tore China apart between 1966 and 1976 was in many ways a concerted assault on the hold of the Confucian tradition on Chinese minds, and the speed with which traditional ideas returned to China after the collapse of the Cultural Revolution shows clearly the tenacity and strength of Confucianism, and its powers for adaptation and legitimation in the core of 'Chinese socialism' (Louie 1980).

Guan Yu's image is everywhere inside China as in the various diasporic communities, easily recognised by his trademark red face and fierce expression, but his significance is much harder to see and describe. In his day, Guan Yu (AD 160–221) was only one of many military leaders at the end of the long and prosperous Han dynasty, the 'Three Kingdoms' period, from which China plunged into five hundred years of civil unrest and warlordism. He was probably illiterate and not obviously religious, and he made no attempt to save 'China' or serve any emperor against any foreign enemy. Yet over the next 1600 years his status rose and rose. He was praised by successive emperors from different dynasties, sanctified by different religious leaders, and celebrated in numerous works, in both high culture and popular culture. It is difficult to find any close parallel to him in the West. He is perhaps a combination of St George and St Peter, Robin Hood, El Cid and Ned Kelly, John Wayne and Arnold Schwarzenegger, but the analogies are far from exact, and the combination is unique.

The figure of Guan Yu provides a useful way to problematise both Western and Chinese stereotypes of sexuality. Orientalism, as Said (1978) has argued, has typically tended to feminise orientals. In some respects Chinese men, at least in China, seem to confirm something like this stereotype. On the streets of Beijing or Hong Kong, as well as in the media, they do not seem to fit the 'macho' stereotype that has been diagnosed as still dominant in Western discourses of masculinity (Connell 1995). And recently some contemporary male Chinese writers have come up with a damning judgement on Chinese men by applying these standards, concluding that they are feminised or neutered (Sun Longji: 206).

There are certainly differences between contemporary China and the West, but equally, within both 'east' and 'west', there are differences across different classes in different regions at different times. In fact China does have its own macho tradition, the *yingxiong* or *haohan* tradition. The *haohan* has his origins among the lower classes and criminals, exemplified by the bandits of *Water Margin* (Shi Nai'an and Luo Guanzhong 1980). He is rough, tough and has no ambitions to succeed within the established social order (see discussion of *haohan* in Jenner 1992: 203–6). Recent 'Chinese westerns' in both fiction (Zhu Hong 1991) and film (see for example Zhang Yimou, *Red Sorghum* 1988) feature such *haohan* characters who take on rude, brutal, decisive and invincible macho roles. The role of this stereotype in Chinese constructions of masculinity does not exactly match its occidental counterparts.

In part, this is due to the related Chinese masculine ideal of the *yingxiong*, and for this the exemplary model is Guan Yu. In this chapter we will examine Chinese masculinity by focusing on this model. The sheer range of Guan Yu's manifestations presents a methodological challenge. Our 'reading' of Guan Yu takes us into an ethnography and psychoanalysis of popular culture and a semiotics of mass culture forms, as well as into the domains of philology, philosophy and literary studies that are at the core of the Sinological tradition. These are not alternative or complementary approaches to a common topic, but part of an ideological struggle in the politics of culture, in which constructions of masculinity and definitions of the nation are what is primarily at stake.

Wen–wu and Chinese masculinity

In trying to understand discourses of masculinity in Chinese it seems obvious to start from the terms that Chinese would typically use: in this case two powerful and pervasive pairs of terms, *yin* and *yang* to describe primary oppositions between men and women, and *wen* and *wu*, to describe two fundamental categories of masculinity. We have already discussed the *yin–yang* pair in Chapter 3, and this is one Chinese philosophical term which is used in the West. We will now look more closely at another binary concept *wen–wu* 文武, which can be roughly translated as 'mental–physical' or 'literary skills–martial skills' (see Louie and Edwards 1994). In Confucianism *wen* virtues, skill in literature, culture and the arts, are represented as superior to the military *wu* virtues, though both are important and should be combined in a full education. The two sets of virtue play a crucial role in the Confucian project for the training of the self, the production of suitable agents for the state. Since a career in public life was confined to men for most of China's history these terms acquired a masculine gender, so that they operate in effect as an ideology of masculinity which is more influential because it is not identified as such.

It is important, however, to recognise a severe problem associated with a concentration on the meanings of words in isolation. Gods also are 'goods to think with', nodal points in a complex discourse on gender which overlaps with but also destabilises verbal discourses focused around the meaning of terms. So Confucius and Guan Yu are exemplars of *wen* and *wu* qualities respectively, but they are also complex and contested signs, in which Confucianism is the dominant ideology and Guan Yu the site of a recurring set of subversive meanings that are always being appropriated, worked over and used, but continue to escape and circulate with their own recalcitrant force.

These terms have played a key role in organising discourses on gender in Chinese for over a thousand years, embedded in so many cultural forms that they are ubiquitous and inescapable. Consequently they are a key to ideological readings, a pre-existing meaning that can be relied on to come up again and again as a preferred, 'culturally appropriate' meaning. But that is also a problem if it encourages a reading process in which the primacy of this ideology is guaranteed in advance, since it elides the ideological process by taking it for granted as always already complete, beyond dispute or contestation.

Here is where a precise knowledge of the Chinese language is indispensable yet also part of the problem. *Wen–wu* belongs to a set of terms in Chinese that have become ideologically saturated, subject to endless commentaries that attempt to fix the correct complex and unobvious meaning which at the same time constructs the ideal Chinese subject: the 'real' Chinese whose reality is demonstrated by the effortless correctness of their understanding of Chinese. The ideological strategy of lexical commentary is more elaborate and central in Chinese discursive practices than it is in English. The commentary on *wen* and *wu* has continued in an unbroken tradition since Confucius in the sixth century BC.

The commentary on the English word 'man' has equivalent functions, though a different content and a much shorter and more intermittent history. These commentaries can be mobilised by the merest reference to 'real men' in everyday speech, or even by secondary signifiers, stereotypes like hairy chests, certain clothing codes, speech styles, etc. But in the English-speaking world the feminist assault on this as a taken-for-granted meaning of 'man' has been so successful that it has lost any 'naturalness' it might once have had. 'Real men' bleat that they are now a threatened species, huddling together in male-bonding groups or being self-consciously 'blokey' (see discussion in Morton 1997), but the marginality and absurdity of these practices contradicts the arrogance that is intrinsic to definitions of masculinity. There is a danger, however, in taking this discursive triumph at its face value, as though at one time the practices and values inscribed in the notion of 'man' more or less corresponded to the values and actions of the majority of men, so that its overthrow, so surprisingly swift and easy, is not only the signal of a new gender order, it is the actuality.

Ideology is never as simple as this. As we have said, ideology operates minimally as a complex of contradictions, and no one element functions or has meaning independently of the complex. In the English case, the majority of men have never been 'real men' even during periods when gender relationships were organised most strongly to favour the interests of males. The

'Marlboro man' today sells cigarettes to men who don't ride horses, and he inhabits a landscape without women to dominate or relate to. If English speakers were trying to describe discourses of gender to someone from a Chinese background it would be tempting but misleading simply to expound these stereotypes naively, as though they were a reliable and sufficient guide to the ideological complex, or even to the material and ideological processes in which gender identities are formed and reformed, promoted and contested in various spheres of social life.

In the same way, we have seen in previous chapters that some writers have typically been dangerously half right in their account of 'the Chinese mind'. They have emphasised the specificity of Chinese language, which is essential, but in the process they transmit a conservative ideology in a purer and more coherent form than it is ever lived in practice. They see and describe this unitary ideology so well that they see nothing else, and they present it as though to doubt or dissent from this version is definitionally un-Chinese. This dominant ideology is indeed important and powerful and widespread, but it is not beyond debate or dispute. On the contrary, it is only comprehensible in the context of ongoing tensions, struggles and differences.

For the official 'doctrine' of *wen* and *wu* we must go to Confucius and his commentators. But even within this tradition we find S-forms and P-forms of ideology. The S-form emphasised the principles of harmony and balance between these two principles, these two forms of musculine ability which the 'ideal man' must possess in order to achieve successful self-management and good government on the personal and national scale. This ideal, however, is in practice more often found in the Kingly Ruler than in his loyal servants. So the Emperor was typically constructed as the possessor of this rare balance, promoted as a goal for all yet meant actually to be possessed by only a few. This exclusiveness, the co-existing P-ideology within the ideological complex, was recognised and institutionalised from early times. Sima Qian describes the custom in the Han dynasty of having the *wen* officials lined up on the east side of the imperial court, on the Emperor's left-hand side, with the *wu* officials to his right, on the west. He sat above and between them. This custom survived into the twentieth century, and it has traces in many other iconographic images and practices as we shall see.

Within the *wen–wu* complex, the two forms were both equally valued and in harmonious interdependence, as in the S-form of the *yin–yang* duality, and also asymmetrical, with a P-form that underwrote uneven distributions of power: 'The virtues of *wen* are superior, the greatness of *wu* is lower, and this has always and will always be the case' (Huang Kuangzhong 1980: 389). This has not always been the case politically. What has always been the case is that Confucian scholars have been in control of the historical record and the values it is seen to demonstrate. The underlying elitism of this group can be illustrated by the Song dynasty dictum: 'A good piece of metal does not become nails and a good man does not become a soldier' (*hao tie bu da ding, hao han bu dang bing*).

The S-form of this ideology was inclusive, an ideal that was ostensibly available to everyone in society, its exclusions (of almost all women and almost all foreigners) and its discriminations (primarily along class lines) not foregrounded. In this form it functioned as a universal prescription for the basis of successful rule, whether over nation, family or self. This form functioned hegemonically, incorporating ordinary men into an ideology which legitimated their power as men within the sphere of the family in the same terms as it justified the greater power of the rulers in the political sphere. As also happens in European ideologies, discourses of patriarchy were mobilised as part of an overarching ideology in support of the power of the state.

The *wen–wu* complex was designed to both legitimate and control men's powers and desires. The element of control operated differently in the two terms. The discipline built into acquisition of *wen* qualities was so extensive that it did not need special emphasis in the ideological scheme. To become a good scholar required arduous training over many years, with few sensuous satisfactions on the way. The ideology of *wu* not only emphasised the different skills to be acquired by training and discipline of the body, it included an insistent puritanical asceticism. In this ideology the *wu* hero shows his masculinity by rejecting the allure of women. One of the most well-known incidents in the life of Guan Yu as *wu* exemplar is the occasion when he is set up by his antagonist Cao Cao to 'look after' the wives of his 'sworn brother', Liu Bei, in a single room. Instead of exercising his masculine rights as Cao Cao hoped or expected, Guan Yu ostentatiously spends the night outside the women's room reading from the Confucian classics, thus proving his loyalty to Liu Bei and the self-control that goes with being a good Confucian *wu*.

In contrast to Guan Yu's abstinence, classical literature is full of instances of scholars as successful lovers. Passing the imperial examinations was normally the best of aphrodisiacs, and the 'talented scholar' got the girl in imperial China. His sexuality was unrepressed and in no need of repression, though of course he was not outside the obligations of the Confucian ethic. Sexuality was feared and repressed in the *wu* figure, but promoted and provoked in the *wen*. So *wen* was constructed as more of an S-form, including sexuality as well as learning, whereas *wu* was represented more in P-forms, in which *wen* discipline controlled and repressed active male sexuality. This gave rise to a recurring stereotype of Chinese male sexuality that confirms the Orientalist notion of Chinese men as not fully masculine in the supposedly 'Western way'. Van Gulik sees this image as especially the product of the Ming and Qing dynasties. In his account, in the Manchu occupation the 'Qing barbarians' monopolised martial arts, and the Chinese literati tended to avoid them. In this context there emerged an image of 'the ideal lover' as 'a delicate, hyper-sensitive youngster with pale face and narrow shoulders, passing the greater part of his time dreaming among his books and flowers, and who falls ill at the slightest disappointment' (Van Gulik 1974: 296).

This image, in practice, is not so unfamiliar to the European tradition.

This is the Keatsian lover, a pale, swooning but desirable male: James Dean competing more than well with John Wayne. The image undoubtedly had great currency in China, as for instance in the depiction of the archetypal 'delicate, hyper-sensitive youngster with pale face and narrow shoulders' Jia Baoyu, the hero in *Dream of the Red Chamber* (Cao Xueqin 1973), one of the classics of Qing literature. In neither case should the image be taken as the reality, or even as an uncomplicated instruction to men on how to be male. Both images were part of a set of discourses of masculinity that underpinned the patriarchal order of society of their respective times, in which families and society at large were not typically run by pale and youthful aesthetes but by mature men whose power in their own sphere was not to be questioned.

The role of the intellectual class was problematised by ideologists of Communist China, especially during the period of the Cultural Revolution, when there was a determined effort to tackle the elitism and sexism of the Confucian tradition. As an example of this work, take the poster in Figure 6.1. Its caption reads 'Good at both *wen* and *wu*', thus directly invoking the classical doctrine in order to challenge it. It reproduces the traditional iconography in having *wu* to the left of the picture, *wen* to the right, with the two figures in front both women. The *wu* line includes peasants as well as soldiers, the standard Communist transformation of the meaning of *wu*, while the *wen* line includes factory workers, and no specialist intellectuals. Behind them soldiers stand reading wall posters, demonstrating their classic combination of *wen* and *wu*.

This kind of self-conscious and direct attack on the classic tradition would no longer be found: it is marked as 'Cultural Revolution', dangerously out of date in the new China of the 1990s. Its attack on the old values is obsolete not because Chinese society has now achieved gender equality, but the opposite: a radical gender project is no longer on the agenda. But in spite of the deliberate inversions, the poster still shows how powerful is the hold of this tradition on ideological processes in contemporary China. It is an S-ideology form, creating the image of a harmonious society in which everyone is happy, in which the old exclusions – of women and peasants and workers – no longer apply. But the group still forms two lines, as in the emperor's court. The woman who is the new bearer of *wen* is one step in front of the woman with the gun, who is sturdier, less elegantly dressed. The *wu* qualities are still given a lower value, however subtly, even in this image whose point is the old traditional one, the harmonious balance of opposites in the creation of a very Chinese utopia.

Guan Yu and images of nation

Ideologies of gender play an important role in the construction of images of nation in which popular energies can be recruited and invested. Confucian ethics are presented as definitionally 'Chinese', and the figure of Guan Yu has been involved in different personal and public practices of inventing China.

Figure 6.1 Cultural Revolution poster with traditional *wen–wu* symbolism

To illustrate something of the process we will take a recent book entitled *Legends about Guan Yu of China*, written by Zhu Zhengming and published by China Today Press (1996). This glossy and well-produced book has a text in English and Chinese, but is directed more to Chinese speakers than to

English. The China Today Press has this kind of outreach function. This book is aimed at Chinese of the diaspora. The shrines of Guan Yu pictured in the book are located in Taiwan, Hong Kong, Tibet, Sydney and New York as well as in mainland China. The book is designed to construct an image of China which goes beyond the borders of the People's Republic. Guan Yu is presented as the ideal figure to carry out this task.

The Preface, entitled 'The spirit of Guan Yu unites the Chinese nation', explains how he does it:

> [Guan Yu's] influence on the morality and practices of the Chinese people has been far-reaching. The Chinese, including those living over-seas, especially in Southeast Asia, pay great respect to Guan Yu. In recent years, many from Hong Kong and Taiwan have visited the mainland in order to pay homage to Guan Yu. Some of them prostrate themselves in front of Guan Yu's image weeping with emotion.
>
> The brilliant culture of 5000 years of Chinese history is a cohesive force of the Chinese people. The worshipping of Guan Yu inside China and in Chinese communities in other countries is a display of the love of this great culture. This picture album is published to promote this culture so that the Chinese can be more united in their effort to build a stronger China.

The intent of this passage is clear. There is a deliberate slippage between the idea of China as a nation state and the more abstract idea of 'Chinese culture' as a way of uniting 'the Chinese people', wherever they may live, inspired by the second idea to build a stronger version of the first. The flow of money and expertise from diaspora communities into the mainland has indeed been an important force in the Chinese economic 'miracle', but polit-ical union is a divisive topic as it applies to Hong Kong and Taiwan and Tibet. This softer, vaguer and more seductive construction of 'China' has its uses, and Guan Yu is being used as a device to achieve this task. In practice Guan Yu has been used in this role many times before. In spite of his adoption by many emperors, historically he was never a warrior on behalf of China nor a loyal servant of any emperor. The pattern was on the contrary that emperors whose claims to Chineseness were doubtful in some way, such as the Manchu emperors of the Qing dynasty, appropriated Guan Yu's recalcitrantly native popular definition of what it was to be Chinese, which seemed to survive all these successive appropriations.

Zhu's book includes some examples of dedications to Guan Yu in fine calligraphy, some by emperors, which typically emphasise his conventional Confucian virtues and often mention his status as a Chinese hero. For instance, there is a picture of an inscription attributed to the Qing emperor Tong Zhi (1862–75), which is translated as 'Fame is known far and wide in China' (Zhu Zhengming 1996: 34) where the word for 'China' is *huaxia* 华夏, which is a term encompassing 'China' in all its historical and geographical manifestations. In the same way, there is another inscription reproduced which comes from Guanling Temple in Taiwan which is translated as 'Military saint of the world' (Zhu Zhengming 1996: 35). 'The world' here translates two characters, 天 and 下, which mean literally 'under heaven'. In earlier times these referred to China as being effectively 'the world', the known or civilised world, the secular realm. In the postmodern diasporic age its vagueness is still functional, allowing a convenient blurring of the differences between the whole of the globe and the Chinese communities scattered throughout it, integrated by their common worship of Guan Yu, the 'military saint'.

Guan Yu mediates other oppositions, as the book makes clear. This figure from early Chinese history, whose traditionality is not in doubt, is also worshipped as a god of wealth. The book observes: 'Today China is developing a market economy. Many people have become rich and many are trying to be rich. Guan Yu, God of Wealth, is once again worshipped in the central halls of common houses, department stores, hotels and public bars' (Zhu Zhengming 1996: 11). The move towards a market economy, with its risk of exposure to contamination from Western capitalism, is a highly contentious one which has raised debate over the 'Chineseness' of this move. Guan Yu is a useful god to legitimise this development, as a traditional god who has been important for many overseas Chinese who have lived and sometimes thrived in capitalist societies. The book does not mention the fact that Guan Yu has also been taken up as patron god by the Triads. This makes slightly better sense in relation to the historical Guan Yu, a kind of bandit with a fierce code of honour in lawless times but not notably successful in accumulating capital. But the historical Guan Yu has never been an impediment to his protean roles as a popular god.

Guan Yu along with other icons and practices of traditional China has provided a focus for a sense of ethnic identity for overseas Chinese for many years. Guan Yu features prominently in joss-houses built by Chinese sojourners across the USA, Australia and Southeast Asia. For instance, he is one of the gods with a shrine in the Chinese Temple in Brisbane. A leaflet given out to tourists gives something of the temple's history as seen by its present custodians:

> Little evidence remains of the involvement in the development and adaptation to the social and economic life in the Pioneering Days of the Brisbane settlement by the Chinese community of that period, the only remaining indication of their presence here over 100 years ago is The Temple that was built in 1885 by the members of five clans from Guangzhou (Canton) the most southern province of China who had settled as immigrants in Brisbane at that time.
>
>   The Chinese have a great regard to their place of origin and the traditional customs of their Home Culture . . . and in keeping with this traditional culture the Chinese of that time in Brisbane built the temple to

unite their people with a common place of worship and to feel the security of home ties whilst living in a new country.

This account minimises the racist discrimination that the early Chinese community would have suffered in Brisbane in the 1880s, as in the rest of Australia and throughout the Western world. They were deprived of basic civil rights and excluded from many areas of employment; 'adaptation' is a euphemism for stoic endurance of nearly intolerable conditions of life. As this document explains, the temple was neglected and fell into disrepair between 1945 and 1965, and was restored by a new wave of immigrants, with ethnic Chinese Vietnamese now constituting almost half the users of the temple according to the pamphlet: 'Before they were aware of the Temple location, they felt bewildered and found it hard to settle, now that they have found a Traditional Culture and Religious Characteristic Tie to the Home Land they left in a world of change, and a place of peace where they now often meet friends and relatives they have not seen for years, their new life is a joy to them.'

This micro-history of one diasporic community is now part of the meaning of the temple, framing and contextualising the unifying message of the 'Home Culture'. The gleaming gold and fresh silk of the restored temple signifies a self-confidence in the new home, as well as a link with the old 'Home Land', which in the case of the ethnic Chinese of Vietnam is not China. The temple's role in the past was as a lone place of relative security in a hostile dominant society. Now it takes its place alongside other public signifiers of Chinese identity, pre-eminently the celebration of the Chinese New Year, in which the traditional dragon of China takes over the streets to the aggressive sound of fireworks, but also in each city's local 'China Town', where small statues or paintings of traditional gods like Guan Yu mark and defend the boundaries of shops as they do the doors and entrances of private homes. Even among many 'enlightened' modern Chinese, these effigies are believed to provide a magical protection, a protection which was needed many times more strongly in the past against a racism which still infects the Brisbane air.

The Brisbane temple is not dedicated to Guan Yu, but it has a shrine to him, in an annexe to the left. The statue is large, typically aggressive, with his traditional 'dragon sword' and a dragon on his tunic. As a signifier of China Guan Yu presents as arrogant, militant, macho, unapologetic, unassimilated, reminding the isolated and oppressed members of the Chinese community more of the political and economic power of China than its rich intellectual and artistic culture. But to balance this statement of a masculine Chinese identity, on the right of the temple is a shrine to the Goddess of Mercy Guan Yin. As the most popular female deity in China, Guan Yin is mostly worshipped by women; and she is in a sense the female counterpart of Guan Yu, representing the complementary virtues of the feminine in traditional culture, nurture and mercy. It is the two principles together, not Guan Yu on his own, that constructs an image of China and a sacred space in which a Chinese identity can be sustained in a foreign land, in the many different and changing conditions of the diaspora. Nonetheless, it is Guan Yu not Guan Yin who is used to signify China itself, in a temple which served the overwhelmingly male early Chinese settlers in Australia.

Guan Yu and the cultural unconscious

The Guan Yu who appears in so many different kinds of text clearly does not have a single stable or consistent meaning. In his case the Guan of history and the Guan of patriotic and moralistic discourses are almost entirely distinct, and they are as distinct again from a third Guan, the object of popular veneration, immersed in common structures of feelings and desires. It is the third Guan who is the key to his ideological effectiveness in the present as in the past, yet these meanings are hard to find in public texts. They can be usefully located in what we call a 'cultural unconscious', meanings that are not 'unconscious' in the Freudian sense, not formally 'repressed', since they do emerge in some kinds of discourse, but they are consistently marginalised or ignored in dominant discourses. But however elusive they may be, however vulnerable to specific over-interpretations derived from hermeneutic methods that are excessively powerful, these meanings are too important to be left in an analytic 'too-hard' basket. In this section we will try to show how a combination of ethnographic and semiotic approaches can produce a form of psychoanalysis of culture which is not unverifiable, not inaccessibly interior and asocial, or formed according to specifically Western assumptions and categories as has been criticised in the Freudian tradition.

The historical Guan began to acquire the attributes that were to make him a god at some time between his death in AD 221 and the first stage in his deification in 592 when, according to legends, a Buddhist priest dreamt he saw Guan Yu, who asked to become a Buddhist. Popular stories accreted around him, independent of the historical record and the dominant religious traditions of the courts, Confucian, Daoist and Buddhist. These stories and beliefs were part of a strong current of beliefs in Chinese life, existing alongside the mainstream religions, mostly despised by the Confucian literati as superstitions, and excluded from their account of the culture except in the forms in which they managed to appropriate it. In the case of Guan Yu, the Confucians made huge efforts to incorporate him and the energies he represented into the Confucian moral tradition. The classic novel on Guan Yu's life, *Romance of the Three Kingdoms*, was reputedly written by Luo Guanzhong, a Confucian scholar of the Ming period, stitching together the historical Guan with the folk tradition within a Confucian framework, to construct a popular Confucian saint.

But the folk tradition, preserved through the oral culture, was never fully silenced or incorporated, and it has continued its subterranean existence into the present day, in the form of 'superstitions' and 'folk observances' as well as in popular literature. Its location in lower-class culture meant that it typically had an oppositional character. This can be seen when it emerged into the clear light of the dominant literary culture, most notably in the work of the famous Qing dynasty poet, Yuan Mei, who entitled his collection of stories of ghosts and the supernatural *Censored by Confucius* (*Zi Bu Yu*) (Louie and Edwards 1996). It refers to a phrase from the Confucian *Analects*: '*Zi bu yu guai, li, luan, shen*', 'The topics the Master did not speak of were prodigies, force, disorder and gods' (Confucius 1979: 88).

Yuan published his book in 1788, within two decades of the fairy stories of the Brothers Grimm in Germany. These served the same function in Europe of bringing a rich tradition of folk tales to the attention of a previously indifferent dominant literary culture. Yuan's collection has a wider scope than the Grimms'. Writing in the stifling Confucian orthodoxy of the Qing court, he dealt, in his stories, with a range of social practices that were 'not talked of' (or 'censored') in the prudish and moralistic Confucian tradition, such as homosexuality, transvestism, corruption and hypocrisy. The 'ghost stories' themselves often act out fears or desires that were normally not satisfied – such as exposure of the corruption and perverse sexuality of magistrates and officials, or dramatic returns of the repressed in the form of unacted desires or excessive punishments. In the case of European fairy stories, psychoanalytic readings such as those of Bettelheim (1976) bring out the unconscious meaning behind the recurring themes of incest, cannibalism, decapitation, etc., but in Yuan Mei's stories these meanings often lie closer to the surface.

We need to be careful in proposing a simple division between conscious and unconscious meanings in either case, and Foucault's warnings (1979) against a simple acceptance of a 'repressive hypothesis' apply to Chinese discursive regimes as well. So it is in the first place a discursive fact that talk about 'wonders, feats of strength, disorders of nature and spirits' – the kinds of stories that attached themselves to figures such as Guan Yu in popular traditions – was mostly excluded from official written discourse. It was devalued in the dominant culture but continued a vigorous life in spoken discourse at all levels of society. Thus these meanings and beliefs were not so much unconscious as unofficial and illicit, speakable (in some contexts) but not easily writable, implied but not clearly stated, and not supposed to be read or understood in the written record. Sinology, born in nineteenth-century Europe at the height of a Victorian discursive regime, took over the Confucian role of censor and sanitiser of the Chinese Mind, policing the clean readings of a clean set of texts. Given this, we need to develop a suspicious hermeneutics as applied to the official versions of Chinese culture, one which will often have many strategies in common with psychoanalytic forms of criticism in the West.

One set of meanings of Guan Yu is fixed in his iconography as it appears in temple after temple (see for example Wang Shucun 1996), drawn more from some lost popular religious tradition than from history, and now glossed by folk stories that explain his attributes. He is quintessentially and exagger-atedly masculine: nine feet tall with a two-feet-long beard, which he is normally represented holding more or less sensuously as he sits, legs wide apart, on his throne. He is identified by a large, distinctive sword, which either he or his companion holds erect to his right. There is normally a dragon on the blade of the sword, which is often named the 'green dragon sword', and displayed also on his jacket, on his breast and over his groin. His expression is fierce, and his face is bright red.

The phallic meaning of the sword does not need much help from Freud to recognise, and in any case it is underlined by the meaning of the dragon, which has frequent associations with the male organ (see Chou 1973). The dragon, according to the legendary Cao Cao, another character in the 'Three Kingdoms' saga, represents the true nature of the *yingxiong*, the hero, who like a dragon is able to be at ease in the universe, and to shrink and extend at will. But as we have seen the dragon is also used as the symbol of the Emperor and, by association, of China itself. 'The Dragon' is China as a masculine destructive force, not as the feminine earth or nurturing mother.

The sexuality represented by Guan Yu is aggressive, uncontained within any domestic or familial context. One folk story, dramatised in a Yuan play, describes how Guan Yu dealt with a beautiful woman, Diao Chan, who is presented to him as the spoils of war. Guan Yu cuts off her head with his Green Dragon sword, so that he will not be tempted. But from another point of view the abuse and hatred of women is seen in this story as the subtext of his masculine virtue, necessary to overcome his presumed natural male desire.

His red face, the colour of the masculine *yang* essence in five elements theory, is explained in one legend where Guan Yu saves a woman from rape by killing her assailant with his sword. Guan Yu then washes his face to disguise himself, using sacred water provided by the Heavenly Queen Mother. The process of washing in this sacred water gives Guan Yu's face its perman-ent red colour for which he has become famous. The story is hard to interpret as an explanation of how a face became red. But it seems to explain his quintessential masculinity in his repudiation of violent male sexuality (the rapist's, his own masculine potential), affirmed by a female god and by means of water, the feminine element in five elements theory. Far from removing or moderating his masculinity the act of cleansing increases and fixes it. As with the killing of Diao Chan, the logic of the story expresses a form of extreme sexual puritanism that literally marks the 'real man', the *yingxiong* hero, masking a subconscious hatred and desire for women and sexuality.

All of this sounds like the description of a psychopath of masculinity, a critique of the psychopathology of the classic male hero with similarities to an occidental tradition that may go as far back as Homer and Virgil, and forward to Clint Eastwood's film *The Unforgiven*. The connections via Freud with a three-thousand-year-old European tradition may seem danger-ously anachronistic enough, but in this case it seems worse because we are talking about a god who is venerated by many Chinese people. Guan Yu is conventionally represented as a complementary god to Confucius, and his meanings have been strongly controlled by the Confucian literary and religious tradition. The construction of Guan Yu as a god drew on careful work by Confucian and other religious traditions.

Two aspects of the iconography of Guan Yu carry this kind of meaning. One is the slogans usually written close to the images. At Guanling for instance, there is a stone tablet in the hall headed 'The teachings of Master Guan' (Zhu Zhengming 1996: 37). It describes 'Four Goods': 'Read good books; speak good speech; do good deeds; be a good man'. These somewhat unspecific pieces of wisdom are conventionally Confucian in spirit, with no obvious connection with the historical or mythological Guan Yu. This kind of association of Guan Yu with generic virtues, putting Confucian platitudes in his mouth, is common in temples which contain his statue.

His shrines typically have him as one of a group of three men, with him in the middle, sometimes holding a book in his right hand. His lieutenant Zhou Cang stands to his right (but on our left as we look at the group) often holding his sword, and his adopted son Guan Ping to his left, usually holding a large seal of office. The lieutenant often has a black face and a bushy beard, and is relatively short and muscular, while the adopted son has a white face and is taller. This triadic structure is typical in the design of Chinese shrines. The central figure normally represents the most important figure, who unites the qualities of the two on either side, mediating or incorporating and transcending the qualities of the others. The figure on the left of the group (from the point of view of the worshipper) is usually less valued than the figure on the right. In this case it is the lieutenant who represents the militaristic virtues and masculine attributes associated with Guan Yu in legend. There is thus a double displacement of the core meanings of Guan Yu: his masculine attributes are carried by his lieutenant, and his heir is an intellectual.

Underlying this scheme is the *wen–wu* dichotomy of forms of masculinity. The figure of Guan Yu is recoded by these means to signify not the *wu* virtues of which he was the primary exemplar, but the Confucian ideal of the integration of *wen* and *wu*, cultural and military expertise. But this recoding is only ever partial. He still sits glowering at the centre, legs spread wide, body fleshy and vigorous, face red and scowling, sword close by, clearly a military man not a scholar, not even a thinking person's military man.

From cult to comics: forms of circulation in popular culture

The relation between high culture, popular culture and mass culture is organised differently in China compared to typical patterns in European countries. One important difference is the extent to which a common stock of traditional themes, characters and narratives circulates across all forms and genres. In English-speaking cultures, some classic authors recur in popular forms – pre-eminently Shakespeare, but also writers and works like Jane Austen, *Dracula, Frankenstein,* Arthur Conan Doyle and the Arthurian cycle. But the scale of the presence of Guan Yu in so many forms goes well beyond any comparable example in contemporary English-speaking culture. He is the central character in major classic novels and in Yuan plays, in Beijing Opera and in various texts (statues, pictures, objects, festival performances) circulating around his cult form. In contemporary media there have been a number of television programmes dramatising the stories of Guan Yu. And there is a series of comic book versions of his story that have a huge circulation.

In this different discursive system, popular forms like comics operate with complex forms of intertextuality. Exactly how these intertextual linkages are activated in a variety of specific reading strategies for different categories of reader – older and younger, inside and outside China – is still a matter of conjecture. In all cities and towns in China, it is still common to see children and adults alike reading comics outside the local 'comic rentals'. The comic featuring Guan Yu which we will examine, 'White Horse Slopes' (Number 13 in the *Sanguo yanyi* series), was originally published by Shanghai People's Fine Arts Publishers. The series has gone through a large number of editions with print runs of a million copies by many other publishing houses. These small, convenient texts can be read anywhere – in trains or waiting rooms as well as in the privacy of homes, and the readership covers all ages. Given the way that these texts are shared, the total number of readers is likely to be hundreds of millions.

In many ways this series is a highly masculine genre. Its readers are predominantly male. Form and content are organised in many respects by the *wen–wu* ideology. Almost all characters are male. The main characters fall into three main categories: *wu* characters, like Guan Yu, *wen* characters, mainly advisers, and leaders who combine *wen* and *wu*, including Cao Cao, prime minister to the Emperor, the Emperor himself, and Liu Bei, 'sworn brother' to Guan Yu but, as his elder brother, of higher status. The locations of the action also fall into *wen–wu* categories. Although this is ostensibly an action comic, almost half the frames show events in the Emperor's court, usually a set piece debate: *wen* action. About a third are *wu* scenes, set outdoors, usually a battle with Guan Yu performing heroic feats. The remainder are set outside the court, sometimes in a forecourt, sometimes in the countryside, but depicting *wen* action, some kind of discussion or informal debate.

Figure 6.2, the opening frame in 'White Horse Slopes', shows many of the typical features of the *wen* mode. It is a static, posed picture, framed by a curtain to the left. The drawing style follows the conventions of European Renaissance art, Western but not contemporary in style, while the scene is reminiscent of a stage performance in a Beijing opera. Cao Cao occupies the central position, seated and receiving advice from Cheng Yu, one of his advisers. This is a *wen* scene, in which Cao Cao the ruler listens to the advice of Cheng Yu and weighs it up. The textual elements of visual (the picture)

（1）汉献帝建安五年（公元二〇〇年）正月，董承谋杀曹操的事被人告发。曹操杀了董承、王子服等人后，打算进一步除掉马腾和刘备。程昱认为：马腾屯军西凉，未可轻取。刘备分兵驻守徐州、下邳、小沛，也不能轻敌。

Figure 6.2 Illustration from 'White Horse Slopes', showing Cao Cao with his advisers

（76）胡班悄悄地来到厅前，望见烛光下面，有一个将军正在看书，生得相貌堂堂，威风凛凛。胡班见了，不由得失声赞叹。

Figure 6.3 Guan Yu, the God of War, reading the Confucian classic *Spring and Autumn Annals*

and verbal (caption plus balloon) repeat the *wen–wu* opposition, with the picture satisfying the simpler *wen* demands on cultural training. The speech in this balloon is longer than usual : this is the opening scene in the comic. On this occasion the caption does not contain any speech, but it often does. There is a systematic difference between the contents of the caption, including any speeches. Speech in a balloon is often simpler and more direct, and usually advances the action, whereas speech in captions gives background understanding, part of the *wen* orientation of the captions generally.

Because the text is structured so consistently in *wen–wu* terms, it signals three possible reading positions that engage with this ideology. One, which appears as the dominant or preferred reading position, would integrate *wen* and *wu*, interest in both the verbal and the visual text, argument and action, historical and cultural background and plot and character. Such a reading would be an edifying performance, a repetition in a popular form of the dominant practices of self-formation. But the series of captions make up a self-contained narrative, mainly a potted summary of the famous classic novel, complete with improving moralisations, which could be read as such, with the pictures serving only as illustration for what would then be a simplified *wen* text. But it is also possible to read the text primarily as a *wu* narrative, carried mainly by the artwork, dwelling more on the action narrative frames than on the clearly signalled debate frames, with the speech in the balloons helping with the understanding of the meaning of the pictures. In this reading the captions would be secondary to the pictures, read only in enough depth to make sense of the pictures. And since these comics are read privately for pleasure there is no one to carry out an examination to test whether the comic has been read dutifully, as part of a process of self-formation carried out in the reader's own time, or whether it has provided only the illusion of docility, instant and unearned *wen* status and indulgence of *wu* fantasies of heroic action.

These comics are not all ideologically of a piece. Sometimes they offer exemplary images of the *wen–wu* ideology in so overt a form that it is difficult to read them in any other way. In Figure 6.3, for instance, Guan Yu the *wu* hero is shown reading the *Spring and Autumn Annals*, a classic Confucian text. The junior officer who observes him says, in the balloon: 'He's absolutely incredible!' This incident is a well-known and often cited one about Guan Yu, its importance coming from its construction of Guan as fully *wen–wu*. In the novel and other sources it plays no particular role in the plot, and he does not come up with any insights worth recording: for him to read this text is (ideological) work enough. (For the illiterate historical Guan to have read at all would have been a miracle, but that's another issue.)

The ideological effect of this image comes from its strong intertextual links. The incident it records comes from the classic text supported by innumerable commentaries. The pose itself is reminiscent of the image of Guan Yu in temples, where he is often shown with a book in his right hand replacing the *wu* sword, sitting with his legs wide apart, as though poised for vigorous action not contemplation, stroking his famous beard/phallus with his other hand. Yet the image troubles as well as confirms the temple iconography. The drawing style and narrative of the comic suggests a level of energy that is not fully constrained by any disciplining of the body or the demands of the *wen* act of reading.

Guan Yu's posture here and throughout the comic is an important signifier of his *wu* meaning. In the comic, all main (i.e. high status) characters stand with their legs apart, but *wu* characters are marked by having their legs wider apart than *wen* characters. This is in marked contrast with the crouched stance and shuffling walk which is the common signifier of the docile, well-educated Chinese body. If legs held close together signify protection and confinement of the genitals, then legs wide apart signify the opposite: a careless, aggressive and exposed sexuality. The hero in Westerns, the John Wayne figure, similarly walks with legs wide apart, in a swagger that signifies hyper-masculinity, though in Westerns as in Guan Yu comics, the macho hero always gets his man, but often doesn't get a woman.

This ideological content of the comics – the image of aggressive masculinity and active sexuality which is still visible underneath layers of Confucian *wen*-dominated orthodoxy, inscribed in particular stances of bodies – has intertextual linkages which have their own important effects. People who spend a lot of time in Asia can often make rapid and usually accurate judgements on which 'China' a Chinese man comes from by looking at how he stands and walks. The advertisement in the *Far Eastern Review* for Hongkong Bank which we discussed in Chapter 2 draws on this coding system. The two men in the image sit with legs astride in the Guan Yu pose, leaning forward aggressively, the one on the right thrusting his chopsticks/sword at the other. The caption anchors a meaning of a reconciliation of tradition and innovation: 'Everything has changed. Except the relationship, and the barbecued duck.' The relationships and styles have changed dramatically: these men are in some ways 'not really Chinese' in terms of traditional markers of Chineseness. But the combination of *wu* aggression and *wen* business suits is comprehensible in traditional terms, and the echo of Guan Yu's stance legitimates this as a thoroughly Chinese option. No wonder Guan Yu has been nominated also as the God of Wealth, especially popular amongst overseas Chinese like the men in this picture. He can fulfil this function better because of the images that circulate in the comics, connecting with and supplementing the meanings of his icons in temples.

Deconstructing the classics

In recent literary criticism the project labelled 'deconstruction' (see for example Norris 1982) devoted a major part of its energies to attacking the notion of a 'literary canon' as a core premise in the discursive regimes involved in the processes by which literary meaning is constituted and authorised. The 'canon' was a closed set of texts which were infinitely and inexhaustibly interpretable, in a process which nonetheless operated to transmit the core values of the culture to new generations. In this section we will suggest that something like a 'deconstruction' project could play a useful role in the study of Chinese culture too. Traditional Chinese culture was built around a relatively small number of classic texts, which were subjected to two main processes. A network of allusions established a strongly bonded field of intertextuality for the community of scholars which held the set of disparate texts from different times and points of view into an image of a single coherent contemporary culture, able to produce a set of rich implicit meanings. Then a series of commentaries fixed the interpretations that would count, the meanings that justified (mostly in terms of traditional Confucian morality) the social importance claimed for these texts.

We will illustrate what is at stake in this process by looking at the classic novel *Romance of the Three Kingdoms*, whose central figure is Guan Yu (see Louie [forthcoming] for a fuller discussion). As we have said, this novel was written by a Confucian scholar attempting to rework historical and legendary materials into a work that could do justice to the popular status of its hero within an overall framework of Confucian morality, constructing Guan Yu as a Confucian saint. The Confucian morality deployed in the writing was then reinforced by a series of commentaries, still in the Confucian tradition, which continued the process of policing the meanings of this text. In this way the novel, now constructed as the authenticating source of later versions of the story, including comics and religious practices, can serve to control the meanings or authority of these other forms where they departed from this tradition.

In this situation our aim in a deconstructive reading of the *Three Kingdoms* text is not to uncover and restore a hidden or repressed 'real meaning'. That would be too like a psychoanalytic form of criticism that already has problems as applied by European theorists to European texts. It would be even more contentious when applied to a Chinese work of 500 years ago. What we want to do instead is to point to certain possibilities of interpretation about its themes that have some purchase even in the classic text, as well as in other discourses that are or have been in circulation. They have, however, been systematically neutralised and negated by a tradition of criticism which is still dominant, which uses a seemingly innocent process of exegesis to enforce a normative view of Chinese social life which is implicitly puritanical, sexist and homophobic.

The basic Sinological position on issues of sexuality in classics on the *yingxiong* ('hero') figure is articulated by James Liu in his influential work *The Chinese Knight-Errant* (1967). Liu makes comparisons between Chinese works and the Western 'chivalric' tradition, but observes one major contrast: that in the Chinese tradition love and, by implication, sex, 'plays no such important part' (1967: 204). Li Xifan, famous for using Communist orthodoxy to attack established literary critics, also praised Guan Yu specifically for having only 'bright and clear feelings' and being 'unmoved by beautiful women or treasures' (1991: 408). None of these writers mentions the topic of sexuality. In contrast to this line of criticism we will argue that the sexuality of the 'hero' and the need to repress it are significant aspects of the novel itself. This sexuality is both heterosexual, resting on negative attitudes to women, and homosexual. An understanding of this process of repression is intrinsic to an understanding of Guan Yu's character as hero.

The world of the novel is mainly peopled by men, most of whom show little respect for women. In the Confucian *Analects* women are equated with the *xiaoren*, 'small men', their difference constructed as inferiority or lack (*Confucius* 1979: 148). In the novel, where a character shows excessive defer- ence for women it is constructed as a fault. One hero, Lü Bu, a huge and successful warrior full of *wu*, is killed in a siege, his mistake being that 'he listens to the words of his consorts and not to the plans devised by his generals' (Luo Guanzhong 1988: 177). Cao Cao, the most powerful and polit- ically successful figure in the Three Kingdoms period, is cast as a villain in the novel. A later commentator accused him of being an immoral human being (*bailun renwu*) because, on his death bed and in front of his sons and grand- sons, he wept and left property to his various consorts. Weeping was not the problem: unlike the stoical American Western hero, the heroes of *Three Kingdoms* weep often. His sin against masculinity lay in his public concern for his women on this formal occasion.

But these heroes are not chaste or asexual. On the contrary, they are expected to have a number of women, their 'consorts', who are unproblem- atic sexual partners, or so it is usually assumed though the novel never goes into detail on such matters. Guan Yu's chastity is an exception to the rule for heroes, though it is intrinsic to his status as the exemplary hero. The famous incident that demonstrated it is the one we have already described: when Cao Cao tempts his virtue by assigning him and the consorts or 'wives' of Liu Bei to a single dwelling. In the story Guan Yu spends night after night outside their room, reading the *Spring and Autumn Annals* by candlelight.

It is clear from the novel that Cao Cao expected Guan Yu to have more intimate contact with or to sleep with (have sex with) these women. Only his extraordinary virtue (his loyalty to his 'sworn brother', Liu Bei) was able to overcome this natural proclivity in him as a man. There is no mention in the novel of him having lustful thoughts about anyone, woman or man. But after this incident he is reported as having a dream in which he is gored in the leg by a wild boar and wakes up in fright. Commentators agree in reading this dream as an allusion to a story in the *Zuozhuan* (a book that was normally bound together with the *Spring and Autumn Annals*) in which Wuzhi murders his first cousin, the Duke of Qi, with the help of Qi's wife, whom he plans to marry. The dream is interpreted by Moss Roberts (1976: 303) as an allusion to fraternal betrayal through adultery. It thus suggests Guan Yu's unconscious desire to marry Liu Bei's wives (a form of incest given that Liu Bei was his 'sworn brother') and take over his kingdom, according to a Chinese tradition of dream analysis that long predates and foreshadows Freud.

In this man's world, relationships between a man and his women were expected but less important than his relations with other men. Here the crucial quality is *yi* 义, the most important bond between man and man, the 'brotherhood' that is the highest value in the world of the novel: so important that it is part of the title (*yanyi* 演义 'the acting out of *yi*'). So much of a defining quality is it that many later historical novels include this term in the title. It is a central Confucian virtue, and as such is the theme of many commentaries, all of which frame the meaning of the novel in impeccably noble terms. So a critic such as Andrew Lo interprets the title 'to mean a playing out of the various implications of moral principle' (1986: 669). In this tradition of commentary, *yi* as a mutual and reciprocal bond between equals is often contrasted to *zhong* 忠, the vertical bond between superior and inferior.

Guan Yu is the supreme exemplar of this virtue, especially shown in the relationship between the 'three sworn brothers of the peach orchard', Guan Yu, Liu Bei and Zhang Fei. This aspect of Guan Yu is so important that it is the other main theme in his cult, and effigies commemorating it circulate widely. Its appeal even goes beyond the Chinese community:

> Japanese business men have a high esteem for the Three Sworn Brothers in Peach Orchard. On festivals leaders of a company go to the temple of Guan Yu to burn incense sticks and remind their subordinates not to forget the spirit of the Three Sworn Brothers.
>
> (Zhu Zhengming 1996: 11)

We can note here the slippage between vertical and horizontal bonds, *yi* and *zhong*, but in the ideological uses of *yi* differences of power are often elided like this. And even in the original story one equal brother is more equal than the others: Liu Bei is the dominant, and has many more privileges than the others, who are effectively his subordinates.

But the novel also makes it clear that the *yi* bond has an intense affectual dimension. To use modern terms, it underpins forms of male homoeroticism. It is necessary to be careful with such ideologically laden terms since, as Halperin (1991) argues, these terms and practices have been constructed very differently though never precisely at different times in different societies. In the Chinese case there is a long history of representations of homosexuality in literature and art. However there has also been a strong thread of homophobia among Confucian intellectuals, especially prominent in the Qing period, when Guan Yu was particularly invoked as a god against the evils of homosexuality.

It was an interesting choice of gods. Even the site of the famous Peach

Orchard oath (why mention it, one could ask) has connotations of homo-sexuality: peaches were associated with male homosexuality and 'sharing the peach' referred to homosexual behaviour (Eberhard 1990: 227–8 and Chou 1973: 21–3). The phrase *Qin ze tong chuang, en ruo xiong di*, 'sleeping together in the same bed, loving each other like brothers' is used very frequently to describe the love of the three 'brothers'. *Tongta*, 'to share the same bed', is used a number of times in the novel, of Liu Bei and other heroes. It has always been common for people in China to sleep in the same bed, (mostly with people sleeping head to toe), and doing so does not automatic-ally mean that they are having sex. However *tongta* has had consistent sexual connotations for centuries. Long before Freud, popular traditions have taken sexuality for granted as a major human motive underlying discourses of morality.

There are no descriptions in the novel of homosexual behaviours, or of sexuality in general, but it leaves traces in the narrative, in the behaviours of various characters before and after a 'sharing of beds' has occurred. Liu Bei especially 'shares his bed' with many subordinates, especially young literati advisers. Some of these relationships are portrayed as extremely intense, especially for example with the talented Xu Shu. His relationship with Zhuge Liang is particularly problematic for the other 'sworn brothers', who regu-larly sulk and behave uncooperatively after Liu has 'shared his bed' with Zhuge Liang. These relationships are all the more unequal than his relation-ship with the 'sworn brothers', but even there a power difference exists as we have said. This method of bonding between superiors and subordinates is common in the rest of the novel. Sun Ce and Zhou Yu, for instance, are a devoted couple. There is no explicit suggestion of a sexual relationship between these two men in the novel, but Yuan Mei's *What Confucius Censored* includes a popular story about the two men which takes for granted that they have an active homosexual relationship (and defends their right to have it against a homophobic magistrate) (see 'Double Blossom Temple' in Louie and Edwards 1996: 206–8).

In the world of the novel, then, the most powerful bonds are those between men, taking the form of a more or less sublimated homo-eroticism that both underwrites and complicates the primary ethical principle of *yi*. In this respect the closest comparison in the Western literary tradition is the world of the Greek heroes, a culture with similar attitudes to women and homosexuality. The Trojan War, for instance, is fought over Helen of Troy, but the action of Homer's *Iliad* is driven by the homosexual relationship between Achilles, the supreme macho hero of the epic, and his lover Patroclus.

The apparent exception to this generalisation in the novel is Guan Yu. He not only keeps his distance from desirable and forbidden women but is never described as 'sharing the same bed' with anyone else, man or women. He may not be chaste but at least he is monogamous (he has a wife who stays safely out of the novel). His intense self-control makes him especially suitable to be the exemplar for a morality that emphasises self-denial. Again, classical Greece provides a comparison. Foucault writes:

> Thus Xenephon's Agesilaus not only 'kept at arm's length those whose intimacy he did not desire', but kept from embracing even the boy he did love; and he was careful to lodge only in temples or in a place where 'all men's eyes became witness to his rectitude'.
>
> (Foucault 1987: 20)

As Foucault remarks, such a display of abstinence 'was the visible mark of the mastery they brought to bear on themselves and hence of the power they were worthy of exercising over others'. Guan Yu's performance of asceticism outside the room of his 'sisters-in-law' is just such a display, and it is central to his contemporary status as a Confucian saint. However, in the novel the really powerful and high-status men – Cao Cao and Liu Bei particularly – do not need to display asceticism to claim power. It is the vague, euphemistic style of the Confucian writer which achieves the equivalent of a display of asceticism on their behalf by simply 'not talking about' their sexuality while implicitly taking for granted its existence.

Our point in this discussion of *Three Kingdoms* is not to offer a new psychoanalytic interpretation of this classic text, to show that its real theme is sexuality. Our target is the taken-for-grantedness of the 'truths' produced by the powerful Confucian tradition, which has appropriated and worked over some discrepant themes and experiences, while 'not speaking of', or censoring, a range of human motives, behaviours and values which do not fit in. This tradition, guardian and gateway to Chinese history and culture, stitches together a normative version of Chinese culture which is the basis for a prescriptive and sanitised account of the 'Chinese mind' and the Chinese psyche. It has been effective, too effective, as a discursive machine for drawing lessons from the past for the present, so that paradoxically it has served to cut off the full heterogeneity of the past from being available to Chinese in the present. The themes of sexuality and masculinity show especially clearly the unfortunate consequences of this discursive system. These issues are urgently in need of thorough discussion and debate, and they are too complex to be viewed only through the lenses of Confucian ethics, Confucian history or Confucian readings of the Confucian literary canon.

7 Breaking the square

Film and representations of China

In this final chapter we will try to draw some of the threads together, in a tentative way that looks forward rather than back. New definitions of China are coming on to the agenda, and new possibilities for China are jostling one another in this particularly open moment in its long history. This process of redefinition involves new ways of seeing and contesting the traditional boundaries around China, and the experiences of the overseas Chinese of the diaspora are playing a crucial role in this process. In place of the old concern with purity and Chineseness, there is an increasing interest in various forms of hybridity and in an increasingly free use of elements of the tradition. We will focus mainly on film texts, because film is itself a hybrid form which has proved remarkably flexible as a means of exploring these issues.

The new Sinologism and the problem of change

China is changing, very fast, and everyone knows it, however they try to understand it or predict what will happen next. The death of Deng Xiaoping in February 1997 aroused a paroxysm of efforts in the West to define the 'New China' which everyone was sure would replace the present one, the scene of the Chinese economic miracle which Deng was credited with initiating. *Time* magazine, in a special report on China after the death of Deng, claimed hyperbolically: 'The seismic changes Deng set in motion were daring, thrusting one-fifth of mankind in a Great Leap Outward from the crushing, dogmatic isolation of Maoism into a quasi-capitalist economic miracle' (McGeary 1977). Deng's China, the spectacular success story that *Time* was celebrating, is understood here as an ideological reversal of socialist China: apolitical, maniacally and euphorically pursuing money at all costs. The *Time* article gave its own topical instance of this myth, reporting one Beijing reaction: 'Observed a 30-year-old taxi driver named Ding, in an entirely appropriate elegy: "Everybody is too busy making money to be sad"' (p. 26).

It is true that there are many indicators that China is on the move. Beijing in the late 1990s, for instance, has a spirit of confidence, and there are displays of opulence in the shop windows of new department stores such as the Beijing Lufthansa Center that would have been unthinkable a decade earlier.

It seems easy to take the words of Ding the taxi-driver at their face value, and to accept the myth that *Time* is constructing here: China has rejected Mao and socialism, and is embracing capitalism with single-minded, simple-minded enthusiasm. But it is as well to recognise how convenient, how reassuring this myth is to the West, to readers of *Time*. To have the Chinese so eager to renounce Communism proves that 'we' in the West were right all along. And to have them do so with so little grace, such euphoric amnesia about the one to whom they owed it all, is reassuring from another point of view. Where the old Sinologism constructed the Chinese as indecipherably inscrutable, the new Sinologism constructs them as shallow and one-dimensional, not complex after all, and therefore no longer a threat. They are no longer political, and have abandoned all their traditional values, the rich culture that made them Chinese, as well as their Communist ideals. And of course, they are still not full-blown capitalists either, only 'quasi-capitalists', eager mimics of the real (our) thing.

But this picture is still a form of Sinologism, an inverted image created out of the same tactics of interpretation that Sinologism used in the past. Ding's one-liner, for instance, is taken here at its face value, as though Ding (and the Chinese generally) are unable to see the irony, the paradox, in his statement, incapable of making the obvious judgement that a *Time* reader would naturally make on this pathologically amoral response. It gives the impression that it's only we, sophisticated readers of *Time*, who can see the joke and make the judgement. But Ding is the one who made the joke, the judgement, on his fellow citizens, and the fact that he is able to make it shows that a critical perspective is alive and well in contemporary China.

What the *Time* team are doing is to take the words of one group of Chinese people and use them as evidence against the rest, at the same time as they elide the fact that this is a Chinese judgement, which expresses precisely the values that the words seem to reject. Ding's irony comes from a traditional perspective, which critiques the superficiality that he sees in his fellow citizens, perhaps even mocking it in himself. But this quotation signifies a complex and sophisticated ironic stance, with a double perspective on tradition and wealth, not the superficial lust for wealth on its own. So a prudent China-watcher of today would be ill-advised to suppose that traditional values are now obsolete in contemporary China. On the contrary, they are rapidly evolving new forms that co-exist in complex ways alongside and inside the many features of postmodern China that are also undoubtedly present in cities on the mainland, as in various parts of the diaspora.

Change is not a new thing for China, and the Chinese tradition includes many ways of understanding change and valuing creativity. Forms of calligraphy, for instance, are a classic site for reinforcing a highly conservative set of values, as we saw in the story *The Idiot* by Ah Cheng, which we discussed in Chapter 2. But there are also highly valued forms of writing that signify their creativity by 'breaking the square', allowing the energy of the line to go outside the square that traditionally framed all characters, especially for young people learning to write. In Ah Cheng's story, Lao Li the calligrapher spoke with respect of the creativity of the energetic and florid Wang style of the Jin dynasty, but he reserved his highest praise for the kind of creativity that had more 'inner strength', the Yan style which remained within the square, within the confines of tradition.

Ah Cheng, through the calligrapher Lao Li, is setting up a basic Chinese typology of kinds of creativity, kinds of relationship to tradition and, by implication, to Chineseness. On the one hand there is the approach that emphasises respect for tradition, for remaining within the basic set of resources it offers, and this is seen by conservatives as more traditional, more Chinese. But the other approach, which assimilates and transforms traditional forms, is equally Chinese, and Ah Cheng's story implies that he values this approach even more. And this indeed is what the writer did in his personal life, moving outside mainland China, living in the USA and attempting to adapt to life 'outside the square'.

It is significant in this respect that Mao, associated by *Time* with 'crushing dogmatism' and isolationism, was famous for a style of calligraphy which signified the opposite qualities: energy, freedom, creativity, 'breaking the square'. Mao in his time was as much a revolutionary as the later Deng. Decades before he engineered the 'Great Leap Forward' of the late 1950s which was such an economic and social disaster, he had welded together a revolutionary ideology which was in its own way a kind of 'Great Leap Outward', drawing on the non-Chinese body of political theory of Western Marxism. But where Mao decisively differed from the key ideologues of Communism in the 1920s was in his non-dogmatic approach to Marxist-Leninist doctrines, which he freely adapted to what he understood as the Chinese situation. The same contrast as *Time* makes between Deng and Mao could be made between the early and the later Mao.

This contrast works because these are two long-standing alternative broad approaches within Chinese culture to the problem of tradition and innovation, which different people have drawn on at different times, and as the case of Mao shows, even the same person has drawn on at different times in his career. To illustrate the second approach we draw on an exercise that the Western guru of creative thinking, Edward de Bono, has used to illustrate what he calls 'lateral thinking' (1972). This comes from a game known in Latin America as *la linea de Diablo*, 'the Devil's Line'. In it a person is given a square formed of nine dots, and asked to draw a continuous set of four straight lines which connect all the dots without the pencil leaving the page (see Figure 7.1a).

The trick is that this cannot be done with only four lines unless the pencil goes outside the square and returns, something that as de Bono points out, most people take some time to realise and do (see Figure 7.1b).

This figure, like Mao's calligraphy, literally 'breaks the square' with its first move, carrying the line beyond the square. But the next line returns to the original square, passing through it at an oblique angle before going beyond it.

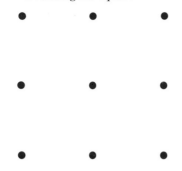

Figure 7.1a The nine dots in de Bono's puzzle

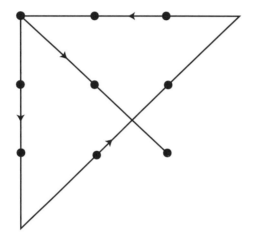

Figure 7.1b The Devil's Line in de Bono's puzzle

The next line then goes along one side of the square, to reach the starting point, before turning again and at last passing directly through the centre of the square along the diagonal. It covers the points of the square yet the figure it produces is not a square but an arrow head, not a solid bounded figure but a dynamic one, formed out of voids and lines as well as spaces.

In the rest of this chapter we will use this figure as a way of thinking about the set of options that have been used to think about the complex and evolving relationships between past and present, tradition and innovation, inside and outside, by various groups or individuals. It helps to make sense of the problematic and contradictory facts that need to be understood in order to come to terms with contemporary China, the contemporary Chinas. These are the problems of a 'tradition' that is omnipresent yet highly unstable and in a state of flux as it is renegotiated in various ways in different sites. It also helps to negotiate the problematic boundaries that constitute Chinese identity, constructing oppositions between 'inside' and 'outside', between 'China' and its others, the various overseas Chinese communities, and between

'China' in one sense or another and the rest of the world, including the 'West'.

We can use this model to map Mao's own shifts of position, so crucial for understanding contested versions of where the present situation has come from, as well as where it might go. The pivotal event here is the Cultural Revolution, the policies of the decade from 1966 which is now taken to stand for Maoism, unequivocal proof of the total failure of socialism and all its ideals, and the failure of idealism itself. But the Cultural Revolution needs to be understood in the first place as a response to the real failure of Mao's 'Great Leap Forward', which was an economic and social disaster that is believed to have had a death count of millions, far more than died during the Cultural Revolution purges. The Cultural Revolution was an ideological counter-offensive that shifted the blame by shifting the problem, reframing the issue in terms of the question: 'What was wrong with the consciousness (values, motives) of the people who did not carry out the policies of the Great Leap Forward successfully?' This was much less dangerous than the question: 'What was seriously wrong with the policies themselves?'

Since the Cultural Revolution was assigned the task of defending the indefensible, it was always going to produce ideological distortions, and as one of the most thoroughgoing ideological offensives that has ever been conducted it is an exemplary object for the study of ideology itself. The task that its ideologues were set was nothing less than a definitive solution to the relationship between tradition and modernity, specifically how to draw on as many of the values and ideological forms of the past as possible while not perpetuating the inequalities and inefficiencies of the tradition. It was basically the same task as China faces in the twenty-first century.

As discussed in earlier chapters, in recent decades there were two main methods employed in this act of renovation of the whole of the previous tradition. One was Feng Youlan's method of 'inheriting abstract tradition'. This approach attempted to pick and choose across the whole tradition, taking it however in a general sense so that the difference between new and old would become blurred to the point of invisibility. In terms of the nine-dot square, this line of argument attempted to create a new square within the square, blurring and bending the lines so that everything would still fit, solving the problem by being loose about the terms of an acceptable solution. This enterprise, balanced and inclusive, is an S-ideology form.

Increasingly, however, the ideologues of the Cultural Revolution favoured a harsh P-ideology which interrogated the tradition as it interrogated individuals, with a severe binary logic. The various schools of Chinese thought were examined and found wanting: Confucianism, Daoism, Buddhism, Mohism and the rest. Only one set of doctrines was regarded as acceptable: the Legalist School which had a kind of ruthless pragmatism that the current leadership found congenial. In terms of solving the problem of the square this method worked in exactly the opposite direction from the solution of the 'devil's line'; it constituted a reductive implosion instead of

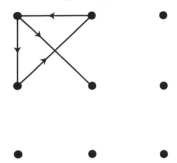

Figure 7.2 Solving de Bono's puzzle by reductive implosion

a creative leap. Instead of covering the nine dots, the majority of them were abandoned. Four lines linked four dots in a simple geometry, and the rest were abandoned, or sent off to the countryside for rectification (Figure 7.2).

In important respects, then, the 'Cultural Revolution' was not so much a revolution as an attempt at stasis, a movement inwards to compensate for a movement outwards that seemed to have gone too far. The movement inwards has been characteristic of China throughout its history, long periods of isolation when Chinese attention was confined within the square of China, the 'middle kingdom'. Neighbouring countries were seen as inferior or tributary states, Westerners were literally 'foreign devils', and the ideas and commodities and cultures they brought were greeted with deep suspicion. But it is also the case over this long history that the periods of greatest creativity in China have been those times when there was a vigorous cast outwards, an openness to foreign influences which were then brought back into the square.

In the sixth century, for instance, when the native traditions of Confucianism and Daoism had lost their energy, Buddhism infiltrated from India to play a major role, not only in its adapted form but also as a catalyst for change within the dominant religions. The splendour of the Tang dynasty was due largely to this influence. The New Culture movement early this century was also the result of contact with foreign countries. Young Chinese went abroad and brought back innovative ideas which changed the whole way of thinking throughout the country. Major changes in Europe have followed a similar pattern. The Renaissance, for instance, owed much to the rich Islamic tradition in the East, which had preserved and built on ideas and texts of the ancient Greek and Egyptian centres of civilisation, and was sustained by the flow of gold from the plundered Americas.

The Devil's Line is a useful general model for understanding the generic processes followed in major cultural and social transformations, and is helpful in thinking about the contemporary Chinese situation. It is a common lament, in China as in the West, that the changes happening in China now are simply the loss of a great tradition, the vulgarisation of a once noble people by a debased spirit of greed. We believe that this completely misses the point and the possibilities of what is happening now. China is not disappearing, about to be replaced by a gross parody, an inferior imitation of European capitalism. Both within the borders of the People's Republic and throughout the broader Chinese sphere a transformation is underway that is as momentous as any in its history, with an outcome as unpredictable. In order to begin to understand it, we need to know everything the Western tradition of Sinology can tell us. But it is equally important to be able to go beyond Sinology and its limited and limiting model, and recognise the constitutive importance of much that is not specifically Chinese in the making of the new China.

Imploding the square: Farewell my Concubine, Welcome Chinese Sinologism

In the rest of this chapter we will mainly develop our argument through a discussion of a selection of recent Chinese films. Film is one of the useful kinds of data that a cultural studies approach makes available for non-Chinese people who wish to understand Chinese culture. It has many advantages for this purpose. Film communicates through visual images which bypass the demands of verbal language, using narratives that are designed to speak across cultural differences. A single film, like important literary works, conveys the specific meanings of only a small number of people, writers, directors and so on, but if it is highly successful or popular then the meanings in play have a representative status, a reach that goes beyond the individual texts or its immediate producers. Films also circulate in other contexts, such as television and the booming video industry.

However, films are not as simple or transparent as they might seem as cultural data. They are not samples of reality to be seen but texts to be read, which draw on a complex set of codes, positioned in different ways against bodies of cultural knowledge which may not be evenly distributed across the whole of its audience, or the society as a whole. Film itself is a kind of language which arose in the West, in Europe and the USA, and all Chinese film-makers have a background and training in European traditions, more or less mediated. But Chinese films are also Chinese cultural products, all of them produced to some extent by film-makers who have 'broken the square' in both directions, departing from the square of traditional Chinese forms of representation to reach the vantage point of the European cinema tradition, while also 'breaking the square' of film production within the institutions of European cinema. All the films we look at are cultural hybrids, different mixes of Chinese and non-Chinese systems of meaning. But such difficulties are far from being a disadvantage in reading them as cultural texts. On the contrary, what we are most interested in is the different ways they negotiate meanings of Chineseness and tradition from their varying perspectives, genres and locations, in mainland China and in Hong Kong and Taiwan, in art films or popular products. Each finds its own 'devil's line', its own decentring trajectory across and beyond any notional solid and stable idea of 'China' or tradition.

Farewell My Concubine is one of the most acclaimed Chinese films of recent years. In 1993 it won the coveted Palme d'Or at the Cannes Film Festival. Its director, Chen Kaige, is one of the leading directors of the 'Fifth Generation' School of film-makers in mainland China, amongst other directors such as Zhang Yimou and Tian Zhuangzhuang. Chen Kaige has made a number of famous films such as *Yellow Earth* and *King of the Children*. Other well-known films from the Fifth Generation group include *Red Sorghum, Horse Thief, Ju Dou* and *Raise the Red Lantern* (see Chow 1995 for discussion of some of these films). The works of this group tend to be emotionally powerful depictions of a suffering China, full of characters from traditional backgrounds whose primary function is to demonstrate a capacity to endure, in a world whose bleak poverty and continuing injustice push them to their limits and beyond. These are spectacles of suffering, melodramas that celebrate an almost inexhaustible capacity of the Chinese, especially women, to be victims.

These works have proved more popular and successful in the West, in European high culture, than they have in China itself. *Farewell My Concubine*, for instance, won prizes in Europe and the USA but was twice banned in the People's Republic. This fact is treated as a selling point for the film for Western audiences. It makes the work seem a heroic act of truth-saying, presenting Chen Kaige as a courageous Chinese film-maker revealing secrets about Chinese realities that the Chinese government is trying to suppress. The film in fact was entered as a Hong Kong film at the Cannes festival, not sponsored by the government of China. There was indeed a considerable Hong Kong element in the film, in spite of its strongly mainland feel. It was based on a story by Lily Li, a Hong Kong writer (Li Bihua 1992), its star was Leslie Leung, a Hong Kong actor, and Hong Kong money helped to finance it. But all this only adds to the impression of Chen's massive integrity, showing his flexibility and ingenuity to get his risky message outside China across to the West. It is like his version of breaking the square: leaving the People's Republic to find a place from which to launch his Devil's Line into the heart of the Chinese Truth.

But there is something worth closer scrutiny in the avidness that Western audiences and readers show for representations of Chinese as suffering victims. Jung Chang's *Wild Swans* is another case in point, a best-seller written by a Chinese woman living in the United Kingdom but drawing on the recollections of her mother to build up an unrelieved picture of suffering, in which the traditional China of her grandmother is no better and no worse than the privations endured by her parents in Mao's China. It is a similar scenario to the massively popular *Good Earth* by Pearl Buck of 1931, a highly acclaimed work from the period when Sinologism reigned supreme in the West. Buck's work was written from outside China for a Western audience by one who had the authority of having been there, and it was successful because its image of China was so compatible with the core assumptions of Sinologism.

This kind of work freezes Chinese history into a museum of horrors, so unimaginably yet definitionally quaint that it seems impossible to change anything. Since both works draw on sources and models from China we can talk of Chinese Sinologism: an image of China which has its roots in a particular tradition of Chinese culture, but which is equally strongly a product of Western sensibilities and the perverse desires of a Western audience, who are happy at the end to close such books and think: 'Yes! West is best!' As early as 1925, Lu Xun had already warned of these 'foreign archaeologists' who want 'to help us preserve our past. Some foreigners are very eager that China should remain one great antique for them to enjoy for ever' (Lu Xun 1957b: 139). His judgements still have relevance today.

But it is also the case that the West was badly misled by another literary tradition, that of Maoist sympathisers like Han Suyin who gave glowing reports on Mao's China during a time we now know was a period of incredible hardship. During the Cultural Revolution, Han Suyin reported that she met no one who was unhappy, no one who was dissatisfied with Mao and his regime, and many visitors to China came back with similar comments. But as Simon Leys pointed out in *Chinese Shadows* (1977) and elsewhere, these people encountered a carefully stage-managed China, in which the same people were 'happy' in the same way in the same factories for the benefit of successive busloads of tourists. These glowing images of a happy, united China under Mao were a half-truth, one which misled a whole generation of left-wing thinkers in the West. How could we have been so wrong? they ask. The unremitting gloom of 'scarred' writers in China in the 1970s and 80s, and those outside such as Jung Chang and Cao Guanlong (Cao Guanlong 1996) and the 'Fifth Generation' film-makers, seems a guarantee of truth, or at least that they will not make the same mistake twice. But of course, a picture of unrelieved misery is not necessarily any less ideological than the naive euphoria of Han Suyin; it is only a different ideology.

Farewell My Concubine tells the story of two actors trained in the Beijing Opera, set against the background of events in China over most of the twentieth century. The action begins in 1924, when the central character, a boy who is to take on the stage name Cheng Dieyi and will become famous as an actor of female parts, begins his training. It ends in 1977, with the suicide of the actor playing the character for which he was most famous, the 'concubine' Yu in the opera *Farewell My Concubine*, rehearsing again the final scene in which the concubine herself commits suicide, expressing her devotion unto death towards the King of Chu. The king is the main male protagonist, played by the character Duan Xiaolou, who in the story has been Dieyi's closest companion since they were boys together in the actors' training school over fifty years before.

Art and life, which interweaves dangerously throughout the film, finally fuse in an ending that is as melodramatic as a Beijing opera in its savage

judgement on contemporary Chinese life. The opening words of the film
make the connection, in a scene which cuts to 1977 and introduces the two
aged actors before their story is told. They meet in a vast, deserted performance space, and exchange enquiries about each other: 'It's due to the Cultural
Revolution,' says Xiaolou. 'Isn't everything?' replies Dieyi, with weary cyni-
cism about the latest official set of excuses for the disaster that in his view is
China. The film that follows is fierce in its critique of the Cultural Revolution,
but it presents no golden age to look back to either, nor paradise to come.
'Everything's fine now,' Dieyi adds, the empty optimism of the words waiting
to be undercut by his imminent suicide.

The film sets the personal story of these two actors against an epic background, a sweep of history from 1924 to 1977. Events on the national scene,
such as the invasion by the Japanese in 1937, the capture of Beijing by the
Nationalist forces of Chiang Kai-shek, the triumph of the Communists and
the Cultural Revolution all impinge directly on the lives of the characters, as
a series of otherwise meaningless political acts, in which the various ideologies are barely distinguishable, the different regimes and their policies equally
disastrous. China as viewed through this lens is politically, culturally and
economically a hopeless case, quite incapable of any 'Great Leap Outward',
not a likely site for the 'economic miracle' that *Time* so confidently prophesies
in the late 1990s.

In the film, the traditional opera is used consistently to make political
points about the present. Throughout, various snatches of the opera are
performed with obvious reference to what is happening in the contemporary
world. When the Communists enter Beijing, for instance, we hear the plangent voices sing: 'The Han King is about to enter the city'. This explicitly
casts the Communists as the Han, 'our' side, the ultimately successful conquerors of China. But the emotional centre of the opera is with the defeated
Chu and Xiang Yu, their heroic king, and with the futile and irrational feudal
loyalty shown by his 'concubine', his wife. The Han (Communists) are
successful, the connection implies, but the values of the Chu are superior in
spite of the fact that they are no longer viable in the dirty world that now
dominates the present, as it has dominated the whole of Chinese history
since those times.

Chen Kaige uses a complex double strategy in relation to the past here.
On the one hand 'tradition' is represented by the cultural tradition, in this
case the Beijing Opera, a form which flourished in imperial China, but whose
canonical form for the twentieth century was a Qing dynasty creation,
crystallised only in the nineteenth century. This aesthetic tradition is explicitly
at stake in the film, defended with single-minded fanaticism by the two
main characters, especially by Dieyi who plays the concubine. The Opera's
high moments are recreated with loving fidelity by the film-maker. Its
aesthetic principles are incorporated powerfully into his own cinematic
style, where at key moments the main characters strike static, melodramatic
poses in carefully choreographed tableaux, against minimalist settings lit

monochromatically. Passionate red, sensuous yellow and melancholy blue intensify the dominant mood, heightened by key phrases from the plangent songs, which are as appropriate to the real world of China throughout the twentieth century as to their original context in the opera itself. In terms of de Bono's square, Chen Kaige's cinematography follows a strong 'Devil's Line', drawing powerfully on European models to create an effect that feels intensely, claustrophobically 'traditional' and quintessentially Chinese.

The film does not glamorise the tradition in human terms. The film goes into loving detail about the brutalising discipline involved in the training of a 'star' of the opera, the continual beatings administered to the young boys with routine savagery and excess, and the sadism of the 'Master'. The venality of the connoisseurs of the opera is epitomised in the film by 'Master Yuan', a wealthy and highly cultivated aristocrat who seduces Dieyi. He is obsessed with young men and old operas but indifferent to the egalitarian ideals of the socialist revolution. But all this is not so much a critique of these traditions as a perverse celebration of their perversity. Their stylised excess makes them worthy exhibits in the Chamber of Horrors that Chen Kaige assembles as his picture of the Eternal Essence of China.

His use of the traditional materials has a similar ambiguity. His strategy is to pare everything down, striving to reach some abstract universal essence of Chineseness. So the essence of the tradition is contained through references to a single opera, and the essence of that opera is contained in the relation of just two characters, the King of Chu and his concubine, or the concubine and her King. This relationship is made significant by a small set of sung phrases that are repeated in different contexts, and in this minimalist form they are free to refer to a multiplicity of times and situations. As we saw in Chapter 5, this kind of reductionism has been a major strategy in Chinese culture for allowing a many-layered form of ambiguity, one which allows contradictory political and ideological positions to coexist, whose resolution is commonly managed by a dominant 'common sense'.

The play within the play, the opera within the film as it is in this case, has a complex relationship to the concept of tradition, specifically the Chinese imperial tradition. The events it commemorates occurred just prior to the foundation of the Han dynasty in 206 BC. Although the Qin dynasty (221–207 BC) which came before is usually credited with being the first to unify China as an empire, it was brief and based on Legalist rather than Confucian principles, so that it has always been depicted as lacking in humanity. The Han is considered the first really great dynasty in China, the foundation of the Chinese empire itself, to the extent that the dominant ethnic group in China still call themselves Han.

The opera has as its main male protagonist Xiang Yu, titled Ba Wang, King of the Chu people, whose conquest paved the way for the rule of Liu Bang, the first Han emperor. Ba Wang is portrayed in the opera as an exemplary military leader, overcome only by the guile of his enemy: 'Heaven's will, not lack of skill, has lost the kingdom of Chu,' as one of the songs in the film says. Liu Bang's trick was to demoralise the army of the Chu by teaching his own soldiers songs from the Chu. When they sang these, Ba Wang's troops believed that the rest of their army had deserted, so they deserted too, leaving their leader alone without having received a single blow. A common four-character expression referring to this is sung in the film: 'The songs of the Chu can be heard on all sides' (*si mian Chu ge*). It refers to the demoralising state of not knowing who your enemies are, and what can be trusted.

In Chen Kaige's film the Chinese people are in a state of permanent confusion over whether Beijing Opera is a sign of Chineseness. First the Japanese and then the Nationalists admire this traditional form. As the Nationalists and later the Communists enter Beijing to liberate it, and again in the final episode as the post-Cultural Revolution regime of Deng comes into power, we hear another famous line from the opera: 'The armies of the Han enter the city'. The implication is that the Nationalists and the Communists under Mao and under Deng indistinguishably represent the Han, successful conquerors, founders of the Chinese state, masters of a tradition of duplicity employing a propaganda so cunning that it destroys its enemies without a shot being fired.

In contrast, Ba Wang, King of the Chu, is the carrier of a tradition that precedes the imperial tradition, a period when qualities like loyalty and duty were all that mattered. Like Guan Yu, Ba Wang is a *wu* personality, lacking the intellectual *wen* powers possessed by the Han king Liu Bang, who was destined to rule all of China. The actual title of the opera and the film is *Ba Wang Bie Ji*, literally 'Ba Wang farewells (his) concubine'. 'Ba Wang' can be translated as 'tyrant king', but it means something more like 'king by right of force'. *Ji,* translated as 'concubine' in the English version of the film, was something more respectable than the monogamous English language can easily translate. The Chinese character 姬 is made up of the two components 'woman' and 'official'. It connotes a woman who is the embodiment of the feudal relationship that bound men and women in this ideology, in its idealised form. This is the sort of woman who lives only for her lord and master, and would willingly die for him, as this concubine does in the climax of the opera – and as the actor Dieyi does, for less obvious reasons, at the end of the film.

What Chen Kaige is doing here, in his use of this story, finds parallels in other Chinese writers in the 'seeking roots' movement of the mid-1980s (see Louie 1989). Searching for alternatives within the Chinese tradition itself in order to escape that tradition, some of these writers such as Han Shaogong came to be interested in the Chu, the road not taken at the beginning of the Chinese nation, whose barbaric virtues did not survive the cunning of the Han but which nonetheless remained morally superior. This is a kind of route that others tried to take in the period of the Cultural Revolution, where some ideologues tried to resolve the problem of 'inheriting the tradition' by taking up the cause of the unpopular tradition of the Legalists, a minority radical tradition that on the face of it seemed close to the revolutionary elitism and activism of the Leninist notion of the vanguard. In both cases, the stratagem can be seen as a form of deep implosion, going into the core of the square and beyond it, behind it, in search of an ancient indigenous basis for radically new policies in the present. In both cases, this move did not win popular support.

Chen Kaige's film implies a sexual politics as well as a national politics; again, a politics that has a double face. The film seems progressive in its representations of sexuality, seeming to find a place for homosexuality in many places within the old tradition. The central character in the play, the concubine, is played by a man, as tradition dictates: transvestitism enforced by tradition itself. But the men who played the parts of women were often treated as sexual partners by patrons of the Opera, and this institutionalisation of male prostitution is not in itself progressive. As we saw in the last chapter, homosexuality had an ambiguous place in the tradition, accepted but not often referred to. In the film, forms of homosexuality are made a central issue.

The boy Xiao Douzi (the infant name of Cheng Dieyi) is surrounded by pressures on him to be homosexual, but in a central scene he makes a powerful protest. Required in his role as a female to sing the famous line: 'By nature I am a girl, not a boy,' he makes the 'mistake' of singing: 'By nature I am a boy, not a girl'. In spite of savage beatings he clings desperately to his sexual identity as male, repeating his 'mistake' time and again. As a female impersonator and star of the Opera in female roles he comes eventually to accept the role, and sing this line correctly He suffers homosexual rape by a former eunuch, and seduction by the wealthy aristocrat Master Yuan, represented in the film in powerful scenes that present this homosexuality as a violation of his essential nature. Yet his most powerful emotional bond is clearly with his friend Duan, who plays the king to his concubine, whose heterosexual relationships and finally his marriage to a former prostitute cause Dieyi intense distress.

So homosexuality is treated in a highly ambivalent way by the film. On the one hand its existence is taken for granted in the world of the film, as an integral part of the revered artistic tradition. But on the other hand Dieyi's homosexuality is represented as the complex product of a series of violations, part of his adult sexual identity only because he has been deformed and debauched by the unnatural way of life of a performer in traditional opera. Just before his suicide he makes his 'mistake' once again, and sings: 'By nature I am a boy, not a girl'. It is as though his real tragedy is not the political calamity of China but his personal crisis of sexual identity, a crisis which by implication is at the heart of the problems of modern China. As Said observed of Orientalism, China has been feminised, and has lost its masculine heart.

This is the meaning of the male protagonist of the opera, Ba Wang. Ba Wang has a similar meaning to the god of war Guan Yu, and in practice is sometimes assimilated with that figure, representing a model of hyper-masculinity which in the dominant Confucian tradition was always bound and controlled by the terms of *wen–wu* doctrine. 'I am so strong I can uproot mountains. My courage is renowned,' sings the King in the opera, and the line is repeated several times in the film. This masculine virtue is negated by the cunning of the Han enemy, but it remains central to the values encoded in the operatic text. It is because the King of the Chu is a 'real man' that his faithful horse refuses to leave him, and his faithful woman prefers death to a life without him. The Han (the Qing, the Nationalists, the Japanese, the Gang of Four, Deng's reformers as successive incarnations) may seem to have con-quered the world at the time, but it is an empty triumph if the values of Ba Wang and his woman – loyalty and devotion, feudal and patriarchal relation-ships at every level of the nation – have no place.

This is the secret text at the heart of Chen Kaige's film. Its flickering shapes have their shadowy existence at the end of a Great Leap Backwards, to a space before the problems of the square had come into being. These sim-plistic values are surrounded and complicated by some opposing tendencies, by an angry nostalgia that wants the pathos of a violated past, not its resur-rected presence, by undercurrents of sexuality that would be seen as perverse by these old values. It projects an impossible past that produces an unthink-able future, a despairing, nihilistic vision of the utter pointlessness of making links between present and past, tradition and modernity.

It is interesting that it is a vision like this which is seen by many in the West as a kind of 'truth' about modern China that other works are too compromised or too superficial to recognise. It is in this respect that we call it a form of Sinologism, a modern Chinese instance that nonetheless feeds Western preconceptions, and which is sustained in material ways by Western recognition and support. The quality that in our view makes this kind of work of a piece with the Sinologist enterprise is its relationship to the square of tradition. In all its forms Sinologism rests on the assumption of the intrinsic Otherness of China and the Chinese, whose essence is to be found in its greatest purity in the past. All explanations go into the square, never outside it, to what is most exotic, most distinctively and purely 'Chinese'. Outside the square there exists only the ever-present threat of the foreign and the contemporary that can only ever compromise this vulnerable essence of Sinicity.

Chen Kaige and others like him have their own reasons to produce a complementary version of Chinese culture from within China. Sinologism cannot be called a purely Western invention, imposed from outside by cultural imperialists. But even though Chen Kaige and his group are highly literate in European forms of thought, familiar with European technologies and operating in a network of European connections, the vision they espouse paradoxically makes it unthinkable that creativity for China can follow the leap outwards to a point from which to return along the Devil's Line.

This is our major contention: that the future of China cannot be understood within an analysis that tries to stay within what is uniquely Chinese, which does not track the interplay of influences from outside China, including influences from overseas Chinese communities as well as from the rest of the globe. That does not in the least imply that the specificities of China, or more precisely the nested set of Chinas and their linguistic, cultural and political forms cease to be of interest and importance. On the contrary, the point of 'breaking the square' in the Devil's Line, as in Chinese ideas of creativity, is to be able to understand the square better, more elegantly, more comprehensively.

'Everything's a laugh': Jackie Chan and the Hong Kong perspective

Life is never easy for the China watcher who seeks to predict what is going to happen in any part of China, but it has never seemed as hard as now for us, writing in mid-1997, in the last weeks of Hong Kong as a British Crown colony. When our book is published in 1998, Hong Kong will have been under Chinese administration for a year, with consequences that we can only predict will be unpredictable. Whether Hong Kong people will continue to consider themselves 'diasporic' in the future (for a discussion of this dilemma, see Chow 1993: 22–6), Hong Kong is too interesting a phenomenon for us to pass by, to put in the 'too-hard' basket (which already contains most of the interesting issues about China for the next millennium). Hong Kong has been the site of distinctive and important developments in the invention of China, influential beyond its size, revealing important potentialities of Chineseness in spite of the uniqueness of its situation and history.

Hong Kong, extracted from China proper by an act of blatant nineteenth-century European imperialism, became a major experiment in the possibilities of the Devil's Line, as one of the earliest 'economic miracles' that are transforming the nature of China. The shift that took place over the last five years of British rule, under the controversial direction of Governor Chris Patten, was itself a fascinating seismic shift, as the people of Hong Kong positioned themselves for the uncertain moment when the solid square of the mainland regime reabsorbed this particular Devil's Line: a Great Leap Inwards, an uncomfortable test of the Devil's Line as political move, not artistic flourish.

But though the levels of uncertainty may be higher now than in previous decades, there has been a tendency to hype Hong Kong's situation into something unique, postmodernism taken to a pathological extreme of anomie and angst. The Hong Kong Arts Festival commissioned a work from the German avant-garde choreographer, Pina Bausch, for instance, whose surreal effects were reviewed in *Time* in terms which connect them with the 'anomie that the uncertainty of Hong Kong's future inspires in some of its residents' (Hajari 1997: 119). But at the end of the review,

Bausch herself is questioned about the meaning of the piece: 'Famously tight-lipped about her work, when pressed she recalls only the contrast between abysmal poverty and immeasurable wealth that struck her in Hong Kong. The sorrow evoked by those disparities is, she avows, best expressed through wit and humour.'

Hong Kong's problems go much deeper than the present change of government. As the cover headlines of a recent issue of *Far Eastern Economic Review* declare, 'Hong Kong's 1997 Threat: It's Not What You Think' (15 May 1997). The cover story argues that Hong Kong became fabulously wealthy partly as a result of cheap labour in China, but that this labour force is now not as cheap as it used to be. Coupled with this, America's trade policies which benefit North American nations will mean that countries like Mexico will pose a challenge to Hong Kong's trade, particularly in textiles. Thus, 'it's capitalistic competition, not the imminent communist takeover . . . that is causing day-to-day heartburn in boardrooms' (Silverman 1997: 80).

Hong Kong business thus seems to look towards the 'take-over' with an air of near optimism. Besides, the people of Hong Kong have had over a century to learn tactics of survival upon which to draw in the new regime. One of these is the tactic of invisibility: getting on in business with as little complication as possible, not defying authorities but not taking them too seriously either. It is a sceptical stance that can be described negatively as cynical, indifferent to all values, but which may also be a strategy for surviving the ideological manipulation that is as endemic in British as it is in Chinese political rhetoric. The other tactic is similar in effect: the famous 'Hong Kong humour', an attitude to life that seems relentlessly superficial, refusing to take anything seriously, much to the annoyance of moralists and other serious people. 'Everything's a laugh,' to quote the theme song of the popular *Lucky Stars* action-comedy film series, which did seriously good business at the box office.

Hong Kong film is an interesting phenomenon as a site of texts for us to use to understand this whole situation. As a successful major industry it has participated in the 'economic miracle' in the past, and is now exposed like other industries to the uncertainties of capitalist life within the People's Republic. By some measures Hong Kong cinema reached a peak of popular success in 1988, when 66 million tickets were sold. By 1993 only 44 million tickets were sold, a drop of catastrophic proportions whose impact was disguised on balance sheets by a small growth in box-office takings due to much higher ticket prices (Li Cheuk-to 1994). But film is also a major medium for entertainment, where film-makers use all their professional skills to 'read' the shifting moods, the desires and fears of their potential audience, the meanings and values which underlie the production and consumption of cinema. Films which succeed in this way become valuable, if still enigmatic, texts from which we can try to gain a sense of what is going on in the 'Hong Kong mind', so long as we set our readings in the broader context of the strategies and practices of their diverse audiences.

The dominant characteristic of contemporary Hong Kong cinema is its love of farce, the widespread tendency to take serious genres and relentlessly play games with them. Many critics disapprove of this tendency. For instance Li Cheuk-to claimed that by 1993 Hong Kong's frenetic postmodern laughter had lost conviction: 'It is not surprising to see the post-modern trend coming to a dead end. Given Hong Kong cinema has little "modernity" or "traditions" to speak of, and coupled with a mercenary attitude, the post-modern trend not only did not stand a chance for healthy development, it very quickly became an excuse for mo-lay-tau and vulgarity' (1994: 98). For Li, mo-lay-tau ('nonsense slapsticks') is only the symptom of a desperate condition, not in itself a positive or creative response to any situation: 'The rise of mo-lay-tau took place in the early nineties, in the aftermath of June 4th, when the people of Hong Kong people [*sic*] needed some kind of therapy to overcome the shock and the trauma. So they ran away from reality and vented their frustration in senseless laughter' (1994: 99).

Jackie Chan's combination of violent martial arts action and slapstick is both the epitome of the 'Hong Kong' style and its most successful commercial product. Jackie Chan, whose Chinese name Cheng Long means 'Constructing the Dragon', has been making extremely popular films which have been box-office hits throughout the Chinese diaspora for nearly twenty years. While commercially successful, the films have been mostly scorned by the kind of critic, in the West as in Asia, who admired films like *Farewell My Concubine*. Jackie Chan is not holding his breath on the outcome of the next Cannes festival. But as so often in the history of film, the opposition between art and popular film is not necessarily any guide to the quality of a film or an artist. Jackie Chan has been compared to Charlie Chaplin, and the meanings that he constructs in and around his films are complex and important, however much he seems to undercut and undervalue them in a self-effacing style that is itself very Hong Kong. As Leo Ou-fan Lee observes, Jackie Chan 'is both serious and comic, often at the same time, and his double-layered acting matches perfectly the content of the story' (Leo Ou-fan Lee 1994: 203).

In 1996, with much fanfare, Jackie Chan made his own Great Leap Outward, his 'escape from reality'. *Rumble in the Bronx* was designed expressly to crack the US market. The film makes this journey explicit in its opening sequence, where we see a jet flying from right to left of screen (east to west, even though, by the shortest route, New York is east of Hong Kong), passing the Statue of Liberty to assimilate Jackie Chan's entry to America into the classic (European) immigrant experience. The Jackie Chan character, Keong, is taken by his uncle rapidly past the Great Metropolis to where the uncle lives and works: under the shadow of the network of super-highways, in the violent and dangerous underworld of the Bronx. The Jackie Chan character is a naive and cute fighting machine, quickly out of his depth in this urban jungle; but Jackie Chan the director rapidly sketches out a world divided more deeply around class than ethnicity, in which the law is relatively benign but corrupt and ineffective against the coordinated violence of organised crime. This is essentially the same world as provides the backdrop to his Hong Kong films, transposed to New York as if to show that there is no easy escape route for would-be emigrants from Hong Kong.

This combination, a schematic background and spectacular action stunts, invites a judgement that the film is superficial. An Australian reviewer, for instance, praised it in somewhat patronising terms as a film which primarily exists to give its audience 'boom, biff, bang and a dozen or so kapows. The stunts get more and more outlandish, the villains more and more desperate and the speed of his arms and legs (seemingly) more whiplike. There is a story but let's not dawdle on that too much, not when you can admire the gymnastics' (Zuel 1997: 7).

The gymnastics are indeed impressive, but the story also carries complex and subtle implications. In the first half, the film focuses on issues of ethnicity. Keong's reason for visiting the USA is to attend his uncle's wedding. The bride is a big black woman whose contribution to the wedding ceremony, conducted as a traditional Chinese marriage, is to belt out a song called 'Desire' and dance Rogers and Astaire-like with the groom, dressed in a black tux. Keong's face shows bewilderment and shock. This image of the famous American 'melting pot' is so over-the-top that it comes across as parody, implying that this is a kind of madness that no respectable Hong Kong Chinese would dream of copying. Keong's polite discomfort expresses the covert racism of his Hong Kong audience at this promiscuity between black and white, but the sequence is also open to an anti-racist reading, for a Western audience that endorses its exuberance as a celebration of racial hybridity.

The action itself involves a conflict between Keong and a large gang of motorbike hoods from various ethnic backgrounds. They are mainly European, but one prominent member of the gang is Chinese, and the girlfriend of the gang leader is also Chinese. The violence between the gang and Keong gets increasingly ugly, sliding disconcertingly between comic mayhem in which many people are knocked down but no one gets hurt, and more serious action in which everything that Keong does is more than matched by the gang. Finally he finishes up badly beaten and close to death, in a scene that is vivid and dramatic and not particularly funny.

The turning point in the film comes after a mob of serious criminals enters into the action. The plot device is conventional in this genre: the criminals lose the diamonds they have stolen, a member of the gang picks up the diamonds, the gang member then implicates Keong by concealing the diamonds in the wheelchair cushion of Keong's young companion. This young boy is also the brother of Nancy, the gang leader's girlfriend, as well as being one of Keong's love interests. The serious criminals, led by a middle-aged Anglo (Anglo-American) nicknamed 'White Tiger', are large white men in suits who use machine guns. They are in a different league and play by very different rules from Keong and the gang of bikers.

Keong sees this, and in a crucial scene risks an encounter with the gang on their own turf. He fights and defeats the gang leader in one-to-one combat as well as creating havoc fighting the whole gang, and then he turns away. As he goes, he says: 'I don't know what you're thinking. You can spend the rest of your life beating up people . . . Why lower yourself? Don't you know you're the scum of society?' And then, in Chinese: 'I hope next time when we meet, we won't be fighting each other. Instead we will be drinking tea together [English subtitles].' The Chinese hood translates this for the gang, and is asked: 'Does he mean it?' 'Yes he does,' the Chinese hood assures them, and the gang believe him. For the rest of the film they cooperate with Keong against the new enemy. The message is clear: necessary alliances in the class war override racial conflicts in this underclass. The physical violence among the gangs is real – people, including Keong himself, can get badly hurt, or even killed – and ethnicity and race remain unresolved issues. As an appeal for cooperation between Chinese and others it is muted, pragmatic and realist, an alliance that does not try to go very far or to deny difference. The one hard barrier is based on class: between the men in suits and the rest of society, who are all capable of decency as well as violence. In this film, the heavy criminals are all Anglos. In Hong Kong films they are Chinese or Anglos, with suits as the most consistent marker of their difference.

This is an action film, and most of the characters are males whose masculinity is not problematised. But though women play minor and conventional roles, the two main women characters play active roles. Elaine is elegant and middle class, wealthy enough to buy Keong's uncle's supermarket in her own right. Nancy by contrast is more working class, more 'assimilated', riding a motorbike as well as anyone in the gang, dancing in a nightclub alongside a caged tiger (Keong: 'Aren't you afraid of the tiger?' Nancy: 'We've been friends for a while.') but she also claims to go to night school. Keong is equally drawn to them both, and by the end of the film still hasn't chosen between the dynamic middle-class Chinese woman and the spunky lower-class one.

This choice, left unresolved, unobtrusively signifies a move away from the traditional gender values of Chinese culture, in which the *wen* man typically seduces the woman and leaves her. The *wu* man, as we have indicated in the previous chapter, overcomes her allure by shunning or killing her. The two women are not central in the film but they are treated with respect for the choices they make. In spite of the apparently progressive gender politics of *Farewell My Concubine* there is only one woman of any importance in it, the prostitute turned wife, who is as selflessly devoted to her husband as Ba Wang's concubine herself, and proves it by committing suicide. The women in Jackie Chan are both strong, and Keong/Chan is unthreatened by their strength.

This film is aimed at the English-speaking market and has some features not typical of Jackie Chan films. An easy judgement on it would be to suppose that its Hong Kongness has been watered down, that the film is full of compromises for the American market. It is certainly the case that Jackie Chan has made many changes in his style for this film, but these represent no betrayal of his major Chinese-speaking audience. We can see this clearly in a curious game he plays with the theme of English. The film was shot primarily in Chinese for the local market and then dubbed into English – largely by the same actors. Jackie Chan had spent some time in Australia, and his mother still lives in Australia. He speaks good English with a slight accent, and the other main actors all speak adequate English. Notwithstanding these Australian connections, the Australian reviewer Zuel commented disparagingly on the dubbing: '. . . this made-for-America film (with dubbing so bad you just know the money wasn't wasted there but saved for the stunts)' (Zuel 1997: 7). In fact this is a self-conscious trick on the English-speaking audience. In almost the first line of dialogue in the film, the uncle tells Keong: 'The more you speak English, the better you get at it, you're in the USA now,' in lines that the actor himself has dubbed. This was spoken in response to Keong's comment, again in his own voice and not dubbed: ' My English is good enough to say simple things' – which it is.

For most of the film Chan dubs himself, having demonstrated that that is what he is doing. Only occasionally, as in the central scene in the film where he confronts the gang, does he speak English directly: 'Don't you know you're the scum of society?' Then he speaks his only lines in Chinese, his promise to the gang to meet them in friendship for a cup of tea, which is first translated into English in subtitles, then translated by the Chinese hood to the rest of the gang. At this key point in the film, where the issue is precisely the problem of communication and tolerance across ethnic differences, the situation for Chinese speakers watching the Chinese language version of the film is exactly reversed. For them, Jackie Chan first speaks his defiant abuse of the hoods in fluent English, with subtitles in Chinese, then makes his offer of reconciliation in Chinese, which has to be translated by a Chinese-American hood to the Americans.

The process looks in two directions. For an English-speaking audience, as Zuel's review shows, it's an example of 'bad dubbing' to feel superior about, but for a Chinese-speaking audience who are in the know, this is a subtle and complex play on languages. Jackie Chan's triumph is only the more complete in Hong Kong eyes if he is taken by an English-speaking American public to be incapable of such sophistication, pulling a trick that is more successful if it is not even seen as a trick.

In this and other ways Chan unobtrusively signals that this film offers more than it promises, and it succeeds simultaneously on a number of levels. It closes, for instance, with a series of out-takes as the credits roll, mainly showing Chan in stunts that didn't quite come off. Like *Farewell My Concubine* this device deals with the theme of art versus reality, in the case of *Rumble* connecting outwards to the 'reality' of the process by which the film was constructed, whereas *Farewell* makes the connection inwards, suggesting that 'reality' makes sense only as refracted through (classical) art.

But the 'reality' shown in this coda to *Rumble* is artfully managed, making a series of rapid points to construct Jackie Chan for this new audience while reassuring his old audience that this is still the familiar Jackie Chan. Seeing stunts that don't work is funny in the familiar 'bloopers' tradition, but these are also signifiers of the hard and dangerous work that Chan, the working man's hero actually does in his job as a comedy action hero. Part of the publicity for Jackie Chan is the claim that he has broken every bone in his body doing his own stunts (unlike the American action heroes like Stallone, Willis or Schwarzenegger, a Hong Kong fan might note). In these out-takes he is shown really hurting himself, breaking a leg again and having to perform stunts in a cast. The final image in the film is not Keong but 'cheeky Jackie Chan' himself, smiling cockily at the audience and giving them the thumbs up, engaging his English-speaking audience but connecting in particular with his faithful Chinese audience. He is both serious and funny, writer, director and actor, able to make the cross-over from East to West, from Hong Kong to America: the Great Survivor doing it the Hong Kong way.

Because of this skilful and subtle evasiveness, Hong Kong humour is likely to be misunderstood and undervalued. Certainly, not all Hong Kong humour is as subtle and complex as Jackie Chan's, and Li Cheuk-to's irritation with mo-lay-tau as a staple ingredient in Hong Kong cinema is often justified. But humour has often been a richly productive form of 'Devil's Line' in the history of culture. It isn't always mere escapism into frivolity because reality is too dreadful to contemplate, as in 'gallows humour' or in the defiant gesture of the Roman phrase: 'Eat, drink and be merry, for tomorrow we die'. Hong Kong humour is not a single thing, but a complex set of responses to a complex situation. On the mainland, the popular writer Wang Shuo in the late 1980s also described life as something which is not to be taken seriously (Barmé 1992: 23–64), but this had different connotations and implications, reflecting the different situation and possibilities within China, within the square itself.

Bausch, brief visitor to Hong Kong, like so many Sinologists before her, followed her own European Devil's Line as it passed through Hong Kong and returned as quickly as it came. Perhaps she nonetheless saw the basic structure of Hong Kong humour pretty well: as a healthy response to the stresses of a class-divided society which long predated the prospects of a move back under the mainland Chinese government, not as a pathological inability to cope with a nightmare. Democrats like Martin Lee and Emily Lau have good reason to be concerned about civil rights under the new regime, but Hong Kong's future is perhaps only a nightmare of existential angst to those Western thinkers for whom China is still as mysterious and dangerous as for early Sinologists. As Jackie Chan shows in his films and in his film-making, there are many options still open to the citizens of Hong Kong. For all its problems and uncertainties, reunification does not look like the worst thing that has ever happened to Hong Kong, although only time can tell how many options will stay open, or how many new ones might come into being.

Triple happiness: Taiwan and the third of two options

Taiwan is next in line for reunification in the People's Republic's 'One China' policy; and the Chinese navy's show of force in 1996 at the time of the Taiwanese elections showed, if proof were needed, that reunification by force is still on the agenda. But Taiwan is also a key extraterritorial site for the contemporary reinvention of China, where different versions of Devil's Lines loop and return and cross over, complicating and expanding the possible forms that 'Greater China' might take. Like Hong Kong, Taiwan was forcibly removed from the Chinese square. In 1895 the Japanese took over the island, and held on to it until the end of the Second World War. But then the Taiwanese, mainly Southern Chinese Hokkein-speakers, were 'liberated' by Chiang Kai-shek's Nationalists, in a new 'Devil's Line'.

The Nationalists clung to dreams of 'One China' under their rule and called their state ROC (Republic of China), although now it is the People's Republic of China (PRC) which has the one seat for China on the United Nations' security council. But influence still flows both ways. For visitors to Beijing nowadays, the clearest symbol of the transformation currently underway is the springing up of huge department stores which look disconcertingly like fragments of Taipei inserted into the drab Soviet-style streetscapes of Beijing.

Since the end of the war, Taiwan has been the site of a productive set of contradictions between tradition and modernity, 'China' and 'the West', that are generating the new shape of postmodern China. Even more than Hong Kong, the Taiwanese regime militantly preserved traditional Chinese culture, rejecting language reforms and maintaining other traditional practices that were under threat on the mainland, especially during the Cultural Revolution. At the same time it became one of the most successful of the 'Tiger economies', a capitalist nation with close political and economic ties with Japan and the West, especially the USA. English, or American (*Meiyu*) as it is known in Taiwan, is the first 'foreign' language taught in schools, and most younger intellectuals have received American training of some sort. But Mandarin, the official language and the medium of instruction in schools, is in important ways itself a foreign language for the native Taiwanese, who remain 84 per cent of the population. The democratic movement on the island is pushing strongly in the direction of Taiwanese self-rule, at exactly the same time as the mainland government is pushing towards reunification, seeking to reabsorb Taiwan into the Chinese square (for a discussion of the language situation in Taiwan, see Chen 1996).

In this section, which in part deals with the relationship between Taiwan, the mainland and the West, we will base our discussion primarily on one film, *The Wedding Banquet* by Ang Lee, a Taiwanese film-maker. This film received considerable acclaim, both artistic (Berlin Golden Bear 1993, Academy Award nomination for best foreign film 1994) and commercial (*Variety* named it the most profitable film for 1993, ahead even of *Jurassic Park*). Set in New York, its central character, Wai-Tung, unlike Jackie Chan's Keong, is a successful businessman who has made it in the United States, and the son of an important Taiwanese figure, the recently retired General Gao. The relationship between Chinese and American culture seems totally unproblematic for Wai-Tung. His problem derives from the fact that he is gay, and living in a stable relationship with Simon, an Anglo-American, but his parents expect him to marry and give them grandchildren. To stop their constant and misguided attempts at matchmaking Wai-Tung arranges to marry for 'convenience'. His bride is Wei-Wei, an artist from mainland China who is faced with deportation from the USA since she has outstayed her visa. The marriage was intended to be convenient for both parties – Wai-Tung would be relieved of pressure from his parents and Wei-Wei would be relieved of pressure from the immigration authorities.

Their plans for an uncomplicated ceremony are rudely disrupted when Wai-Tung's ecstatic parents immediately catch a plane to attend the ceremony and meet their new daughter. Wai-Tung and Wei-Wei are forced to maintain not only the charade of a formal marriage ceremony but also the charade of marital harmony after the wedding while the parents remain in America. Forced to drink to excess during the ceremony, Wai-Tung is seduced by Wei-Wei once they are alone in the honeymoon suite of the hotel (she jokingly refers to the promised sex as his 'liberation' [from homosexuality]). This encounter leaves Wei-Wei pregnant, much to her consternation; Simon is disgusted by his partner's infidelity and careless abandonment of their mutually agreed 'safe sex' rules.

The value of this film for someone wanting to understand contemporary China is not that it claims to be reportage or prediction. Nor is it a Taiwanese perspective on China, although its highly intelligent contribution to debates on the redefinition of China carries traces of its Taiwanese origins. It combines a polemic on behalf of the Gay Liberation movement in Taiwan with social satire, examining processes by which Chinese political and gender identities are currently being negotiated and reinvented in different sites, particularly in the West and in Taiwan. The film develops new subjectivities, new forms of consciousness which are part of the problem and which are inevitably bound up in any possible solution.

Like Ah Cheng's stories, Ang Lee's films are based on sharp and insightful observation of conventions and contradictions in Chinese social and discursive practices, productively focused on moments and sites where tradition and modernity collide, where pressure from new problems and situations forces tradition to reveal its duplicity and creativity. From this point of view it is a special advantage of the film that it was produced collaboratively, its text built up by a sequence of movements to and fro along its own Devil's Line. In this case, the original script was co-written by Ang

Lee and Neal Peng (Li Ang and Feng Guangyuan 1993) and then rewritten, in a complex inter-linguistic process, with the American James Schamus (1994). Schamus, in the Introduction to the English publication of the script, described something of the paradoxical nature of this process in ways that carry a more general point about cultural production in the hybrid spaces of postmodernity. Some of his rewrites, he reports, were rejected by Ang Lee as getting the Chinese psychology wrong. He tried the classic Sinologist solution, 'to study even harder . . . Chinese poems, stories, and histories' but to no avail. However, when he abandoned his earnest Sinologism and wrote the scenes 'as "Jewish" as I could make them', Lee would say: 'Ah ha! Very Chinese' (Lee 1994: xi).

The low-budget film seemingly has a straightforward narrative style, but one device it uses is a form of the Devil's Line: a set-up in which the crucial action happens outside the frame, while the camera records something that is meaningless or irrelevant – the empty corridor of the hotel while Wai is impregnating Wei-Wei, the empty street as Wai turns the car when Wei-Wei is deciding not to have an abortion, or a formal occasion (a meal, a wedding) which is equally empty of meaning in a different way. The opening also uses this device: a black screen as background to the voice of Mrs Gao, Wai-Tung's mother, speaking from Taiwan into a cassette, she explains, because her 'shoulder is acting up'. Then we see Wai-Tung's face. He is wearing headphones as he exercises on a stairmaster machine in a New York gym, the perfect yuppie and the dutiful Chinese son, two halves held together by a piece of communications technology that may have been made in Taiwan.

In this film the theme of homosexuality is used to explore another fundamental issue in Chinese discursive and social life, the role of secrets. In Ah Cheng's 'The Idiot' the calligrapher's secret was his idiot son. Li Jian's career was destroyed because he failed to realise that the secret of the Cultural Revolution was no longer meant to be concealed. In private as well as in public life, some of the most important pieces of knowledge have to be both known and not known, or at least not acknowledged explicitly. They are denied and repressed from speech but not from consciousness.

Sometimes this suppression seems harmless, a normal condition of life. 'You're right, it's kind of stupid, all these lies. But I'm used to it,' Wai-Tung says to Simon at one point (Lee 1994: 130). But lies aren't only necessary when concealing gayness. Miss Mao, the mail-order bride the Gaos find for their son, explains how it is that she has come to America in this way: 'My mom did it for me. Just like you, I have a white boyfriend. And I don't have the guts to tell my parents either' (Lee 1994: 136). Simon is scathing about Wai-Tung's motives: 'No, really, Wai. Look at yourself – your parents send you a form in the mail and you practically pee in your pants. You know, you are an adult – as a matter of fact, you're practically middle-aged.' To which Wai responds: 'Fuck you!' (Lee: 129).

The film interrogates the general role of secrets in the family. When Wai finally confesses to his mother that he is gay, for most of the conversation she 'misunderstands' him, claiming to think that his 'secret' is Wei-Wei's pregnancy, and in a family crisis she expresses gratitude towards Simon ('It's a good thing that Simon was there'), as though unaware that Simon is what the confession is about. The irony generates humour for the audience, because Mrs Gao says more than she knows, but this subtle device by Ang Lee makes the audience, non-Chinese as well as Chinese, complicit in Chinese practices of secrecy. Whether or not Mrs Gao 'really' knew about Wai and Simon is not made clear, but it is certain that she is complicit in the process of secrecy, indicating unmistakably to Wai that she does not want to hear this confession, that 'truth' is no bond between a Chinese mother and her son.

When Mrs Gao is finally forced to recognise what her son has to say she still insists that the father not be told. 'It'll kill him,' she says, sobbing quietly (Lee 1994: 195). It is true that the father has had a series of strokes, but this concern for his health (like Wai's concern for his mother's inability to take the truth) masks the systemic role of secrecy as a bond in a patriarchal structure of authority. For the patriarch to know or show that he knows about things that are inconvenient or worse, things which cast doubt on the reality of his power, would threaten his authority. The greater his power, the greater the prohibition on any challenge to it. In public life, this comes out as a blanket prohibition on news which reflects badly on the leadership. In private life, the bond between father and son is cemented by this refusal to challenge the limits of the father's knowledge and power. Within this sort of family, the mother is attributed with much of the power of the patriarch, so she too cannot be told much, but it is easier to tell her than to tell the father, the general.

But the general himself has his own secret. Just before the Gaos depart he gives Simon a birthday present, a munificent gift, an envelope full of money. In the process Gao reveals to Simon that he actually speaks English, and has known about his son's relationship for a long time. 'I watch, I hear, I learn. Wai-Tung is my son – so you're my son also' (Lee 1994: 205). Simon laughs: 'Why you old –.' But Gao expressly forbids Simon to reveal this to anyone else: not Wai-Tung, not his mother, not Wei-Wei. 'Our secret,' he tells Simon. 'But why?' 'For the family,' he says enigmatically. Then he adds, in Chinese (which excludes Simon from this further level of entry into the structure of secrecy): 'If I didn't let everyone lie to me, I'd never have gotten my grandchild!'

The old general here reveals (though not to Simon) the cunning that was a necessary part of the tradition for those who had to work within its terms to survive, a cunning that, to serve the interests of the powerful, could conceal an unexpected measure of flexibility and open-mindedness co-existing within the traditional framework. Simon is bewildered at the switch in languages: 'I don't understand'. 'No – *I* don't understand,' says the general, smiling, the secret half revealed, and complicity established with this man, American and gay, whom he has incorporated into a place within the traditional structure so that it can survive and (literally) reproduce itself.

It is this kind of understated insight that gives such credibility to the film's attempts to construct a plausible image of reconciliation and harmony. Ang Lee is heir to the rich tradition of S-ideological forms and practices within the Chinese tradition, and with *The Wedding Banquet* he adds to the stock at the same time as satirising the whole process. He uses the traditional motif of the wedding, that classic site for representing the partnership of man and woman as a model for a harmonious, mutually beneficial relationship, as in the philosophy of *yin* and *yang*. The general takes the opportunity to make a speech about the significance of this union: 'Wai-Tung, Wei-Wei, you two grew up differently. But fate unites the two of you here so far from home. It's something you should treasure. If differences arise . . . opinions . . . habits . . . you must work to resolve them. Always be thoughtful of each other. That's the key to a successful marriage' (Lee 1994: 169).

In its comic context this comes across as an inappropriate platitude (Wei-Wei breaks into tears before he finishes it) but it is also sound advice in this complicated situation. The general is not a buffoon repeating obsolete wisdom. The film constructs him as an exemplar of *wen–wu* virtues, as good a tactician in the miasma of family dynamics as he was on the field of battle, a successful and respected military man who is also a fine calligrapher. In a scene that speaks more eloquently to a traditionally educated Chinese audience than to a Western one, Wei-Wei praises his calligraphy as a fine example of the Wang style. In Ah Cheng's 'The Idiot' the traditionalist calligrapher was disparaging about the flamboyant Wang style, with its vigour that breaks the square, but this is what Gao has done, both in his life – leaving mainland China for Taiwan – and now, in his observation that to be 'so far from home' offers new opportunities.

This union, between a Taiwanese man and a mainland woman, between a businessman and capitalist and an artist from a socialist background, is indeed something that would be more difficult in either the People's Republic or Taiwan. The movement of the Devil's Line which each followed to New York offers the chance of a different kind of rapprochement between the mainland and Taiwan, not the PRC's brutal takeover policy or the ROC's unrealistic dream of unity on their own terms. Options become thinkable, far from home, like Keong's uncle marrying a black woman, or Simon and Wai's cross-cultural relationship, or even some vaguer notion of a greater China which goes beyond existing borders and categories. But the reconciliation symbolised by this marriage only goes so far. It is between two people of a high level of education, a mainlander and the son of a Mandarin-speaking Taiwanese; it is not across class or linguistic barriers.

Gayness is treated with similar complexity. It is part of Wai-Tung's culture and identity, not trivial, not to be apologised for, but coexisting with other aspects of his identity. Where *Farewell My Concubine* represents homosexuality as the product of a brutalising social system, *The Wedding Banquet*'s position on homosexuality shows greater tolerance and acceptance. Wai-Tung's sexuality is accepted without question by himself and his friends, even by Wei-Wei, who wishes it were otherwise. In the final image of the film, Wai-Tung, Simon and Wei-Wei carrying her unborn child stand together arm in arm, waving goodbye as the parents board the plane for Taiwan. The performance – of the parents as well as the happy triple – signifies that each is able to accept differences in ideology and lifestyle, and live easily with the contradictions in themselves that are necessary for such reconciliation to work convincingly in human terms.

In this respect the film is a comedy of reconciliation, an allegory in which all oppositions – gay and straight, male and female, China and America, tradition and modernity, Taiwan and the mainland – are resolved with humour and grace. But the rest of the film has exposed the reality behind the other façades these characters are so skilled at constructing. We have been shown the tensions in the triple, and the anguish and sense of loss of the parents. In the original Chinese script there is a line by Wei-Wei, arguing with Simon: 'No, yours is a big, big mistake to begin with, have you heard of *Yin* and *Yang*, the way the world is supposed to be?' To which Simon replies: 'Don't push, little girl . . . just don't push.' (Li and Feng 1993: 206). The classic ideal of *yin* and *yang* is both restated, in the new balance between the three, and also critiqued. For Ang Lee, tradition provides seductive models of harmony and reconciliation and also a set of standards that distort and falsify the new kind of life that people must lead.

The cover of the Chinese-language version of the film captures this contradiction in a single image. The picture shows the three main characters formally posed in a wedding picture, dressed in traditional European clothes. 'Tradition' as a concept is legible between China and the West, even if some of its forms are culture specific. But there are three people in this picture: the bride and groom, together but at a different level, with Simon above them, holding Wai's hand, integrating the group. It looks predictable, conventional, stable, but is subtly and profoundly different, assimilating the complex relationships of this very postmodern triangle into the generic forms of the traditional wedding photograph. It is an ideological masterpiece, simultaneously a new model of relationships and a work of art. Meanwhile outside the frame, after the occasion, life goes on with all its complications.

The cover includes the title, *Xi Yan*, 'The Wedding Banquet'. But the written characters that make up this title are themselves a significant and innovative performance. *Xi* here is represented by three elements (see Figure 7.3) which in fact repeat a character which can stand on its own to mean 'happiness', and is used so often at weddings that it comes to mean 'wedding'. In practice what is normally found at weddings is the double happiness character, written on red paper, a popular innovation that is often not mentioned in dictionaries but is nonetheless universally understood. What Ang Lee has done here is simply to follow the same principle as the folk tradition, and add another 'happiness' to form a 'triple happiness' character, 'breaking the square' by adding another character on top. This character is completely new, not in any dictionary, yet it is immediately comprehensible. It is as though the tradition has been waiting with the resources to create an appropriate symbol for this new and highly non-traditional relationship, welcoming the creative ingenuity of an Ang Lee. Although so simple in form – just an extra radical added on top – it is complex and ambiguous in its effect. Does it just mean 'very, very happy'? Or does it refer to the happiness of a bisexual triangle, in a joke which suggests that a triangle like this is even happier than a heterosexual or homosexual union of two people?

In this film Ang Lee explores and creates new forms for recognising and resolving contradictions and oppositions which constitute China and Chineseness. He provides means for thinking a new postmodern China which could only come into existence if it becomes thinkable, but which will not of itself cancel the mechanisms of power, the dangerous play of antagonistic forces in political and social reality which also need to be understood. His vision of a reconciliation that takes place outside the square in order to return to it is not 'truer' than Chen Kaige's nightmare of punishment. Nor is a comedy of manners artistically better or worse than claustrophobic melodrama, or all-action farce such as Jackie Chan's film. Ang Lee's contribution to the polyphony of voices trying to define China is marked by his creative use of a traditional feeling for harmony and balance. His appeal for tolerance and understanding is topical but not yet official policy in Taipei or Beijing. Its 'truth' rests not on the accuracy or likelihood of its images of reconciliation, but on its insight into the social processes and discursive habits through which problems and solutions alike must be lived and negotiated.

We have finished this book with a discussion of three films, because this is a medium which reaches out, crossing enough of the boundaries of language and culture to speak to people outside China. Films are not simple messages, and there is not a single universal language of film. On the contrary, films are constructed out of a multiplicity of languages, verbal and visual, with multiple coding systems that are more or less culturally specific, producing meanings which are open and polysemic, not a single fixed 'content' that everyone who understands the film will agree on. But reading a film is in its own way an exemplary form of the 'Devil's Line', a model of the kind of encounter with China and Chineseness that we have been advocating in this book. We (teachers, students, tourists, business people, English-speaking, Chinese-speaking) occupy specific positions in the square of our home culture, fixed in received assumptions about ourselves and the culture of the 'other'. Watching films is one salutary kind of experience that invites us to go out of the square, to go as deep as we dare into the experience of the film and engage in fruitful if imperfect dialogue with its makers. That's why films like the ones we have discussed are worth a thousand books.

It is a set of messages, not glimpses of reality, that we receive, with films, with videos, with a long tour or a brief trip into a local Chinatown, with

Figure 7.3 Triple Happiness, cover design for the filmscript of *The Wedding Banquet*

casual interactions or deep friendships, with every interaction across the boundaries of our square. Sinologism in its time was also an attempt to enter the square of the Other. We criticised the limitations of Sinologism as a practice for today, not because it made this attempt, but rather for the ways with which Sinologists have continued to try and mystify China so that understanding between different groups of people has been unnecessarily made more difficult. General Gao's words, which seemed so platitudinous at the fake wedding of Wai-Tung and Wei-Wei, are not ironised away by the complex demands of a postmodern, multicultural world. 'If differences arise ... opinions ... habits ... you must work to resolve them. Always be thoughtful of each other.'

Bibliography

Ah Cheng (1984) '*Shazi*' (The Idiot), *Wenhui yuekan* (*Literature Monthly*), 10: 38–41.
—— (1985) 'The Chess Master', trans. W.J.F. Jenner, *Chinese Literature*, Summer, pp. 84–131.
—— (1990) *Three Kings: Three Stories from Today's China*, trans. Bonnie S. McDougall, London: Collins Harvill.
Bailey, Charles-James N. (1982) *On the Yin and Yang Nature of Language*, Ann Arbor: Karoma Publishers.
Barmé, Geremie (1992) 'Wang Shuo and *Liumang* Culture', *Australian Journal of Chinese Affairs*, 28: 23–64.
Barrett, T.H. (1989) *Singular Listlessness: A Short History of Chinese Books and British Scholars*, London: Wellsweep.
Bettelheim, Bruno (1976) *The Uses of Enchantment*, Harmondsworth: Penguin.
Bloom, Alfred (1981) *The Linguistic Shaping of Thought: A Study in the Impact of Language on Thinking in China and the West*, Hillsdale: Lawrence Erlbaum Associates.
Bono, Edward de (1972) *Po: Beyond Yes and No*, Harmondsworth: Penguin.
Bourdieu, P. (1984) *Distinction: A Social Critique of the Judgement of Taste*, Cambridge, MA: Harvard University Press.
Bourke, Barbara (1997) 'Maximising Efficiency in the Kanji Learning Task', unpublished PhD dissertation, University of Queensland.
Bucher, Urs (1986) *Vocabulary of Modern Chinese*, Felsberg: Tobun.
Buck, Pearl (1931) *The Good Earth*, New York: Random House.
Bucknell, Rod and Stuart-Fox, Martin (1986) *The Twilight Language*, London: Curzon Press.
Cao Guanlong (1996) *The Attic: Memoir of a Chinese Landlord's Son*, Los Angeles: University of California Press.
Cao Xueqin (c. 1760) *Hong lou meng* (Dream of Red Chambers), translated as *The Story of the Stone* (1973–1986), 5 volumes, Harmondsworth: Penguin. The first three volumes translated by David Hawke, the last two by John Minford.
Chan Wing-tsit (ed.) (1963) *A Source Book in Chinese Philosophy*, Princeton: Princeton University Press.
Chang, Jung (1991) *Wild Swans*, London: HarperCollins.
Chao Yuen Ren (1968) *A Grammar of Spoken Chinese*, Berkeley: University of California Press.
Chen Ping (1996) 'Modern Written Chinese, Dialects, and Regional Identity', *Language Problems and Language Planning*, 3 (3): 223–43.

Chinese–English Dictionary (1978) Beijing: Shangwu yinshuguan.

Chou, Eric (1973) *The Dragon and the Phoenix*, London: Corgi Books.

Chow, Rey (1993) *Writing Diaspora: Tactics of Intervention in Contemporary Cultural Studies*, Bloomington: Indiana University Press.

—— (1995) *Primitive Passions: Visuality, Sexuality, Ethnography, and Contemporary Chinese Cinema*, New York: Columbia University Press.

Chun, Allen (1996) 'Fuck Chineseness: On the Ambiguities of Ethnicity as Culture as Identity', *Boundary* 2, 23 (2): 111–38.

Confucius (1979) *The Analects*, trans. D.C. Lau, Harmondsworth: Penguin.

Connell, R.W. (1995) *Masculinities*, Sydney: Allen & Unwin.

DeFrancis, John (1950) *Nationalism and Language Reform in China*, Princeton: Princeton University Press.

—— (1976) *Beginning Chinese* (second edition), New Haven: Yale University Press.

—— (1984) *The Chinese Language: Fact and Fantasy*, Honolulu: University of Hawaii Press.

—— (1985) 'China's Literary Renaissance: A Reassessment', *Bulletin of Concerned Asian Scholars*, 17 (4): 52–63.

Dong Yuequan and Song Jun (1987) '*Hanzi de xuexi he kua wenhua yanjiu*' ('The Study of the Chinese Characters and Research Across Cultures'), *Yuwen jianshe* (*Language Construction*), 2: 13–17.

Duke, Michael S. (1985) *Blooming and Contending: Chinese Literature in the Post-Mao Era*, Bloomington: Indiana University Press.

Eberhard, Wolfram (1990) *Dictionary of Chinese Symbols*, Singapore: Federal Publications.

Eco, V. (1977) *A Theory of Semiotics*, London: Macmillan.

Edwards, Louise (1994) *Men and Women in Qing China: Gender in The Red Chamber Dream*, Leiden: E.J. Brill.

—— (1995) 'Late Twentieth-Century Orientalism and Discourses of Selection', *Renditions*, 44: 1–11.

Foucault, Michel (1972) *The Archaeology of Knowledge*, trans. A.M.S. Smith, London: Tavistock Publications.

—— (1976) *Archaeology of Knowledge*, trans. Alan Sheridan Smith, New York: Colophon Books.

—— (1977) *Discipline and Punish*, trans. Alan Sheridan Smith, Harmondsworth: Penguin.

—— (1979) *History of Sexuality I: An Introduction*, trans. R. Hurley, Harmondsworth: Penguin.

—— (1980) *Power/Knowledge,* trans. Colin Gordon, Brighton: Harvester.

—— (1986) *History of Sexuality 3: Care of the Self*, trans. R. Hurley, Harmondsworth: Penguin.

Fredlein, Shumang and Fredlein, Paul (1995) *Ni Hao*, Brisbane: ChinaSoft.

Gilmartin, C.K. *et al.* (1994) *Engendering China: Women, Culture, and the State*, Cambridge, MA: Harvard University Press.

Goffman, E. (1959) *The Presentation of Self in Everyday Life*, Harmondsworth: Penguin.

—— (1967) *Interaction Rituals*, Harmondsworth: Penguin.

Gramsci, Antonio (1971) *Prison Notebooks*, London: Lawrence and Wishart.

Hägerdal, Hans (1996) 'China and Orientalism', *IIAS Newsletter*, 10: 31–2.

Hajari, Nisid (1997) 'Picture of a City in Motion', *Time*, 17 March, p. 119.

Halperin, David M. (1991) 'Sex Before Sexuality: Pederasty, Politics, and Power in Classical Athens', in Martin Bauml Duberman *et al.* (eds), *Hidden from History: Reclaiming the Gay and Lesbian Past*, Harmondsworth: Penguin.

Hanyu da zidian bianji weiyuanhui (ed.) (1993) *Hanyu da zidian* (The Chinese Character Dictionary), Chengdu: Sichuan cishu chubanshe.

Higgins, Andrew (1993) 'Language Loopholes Bring a Buzz to Beijing', *Sydney Morning Herald*, 3 June. Reprinted from the *Guardian*.

Hinsch, Bret (1990) *Passions of the Cut Sleeve: The Homosexual Tradition in China*, Berkeley: University of California Press.

Hodge, R. (1986) 'Cliché and Reality-Control: The Modality of Duckspeak', *Sociolinguistics*, 16 (2): 35–44.

Hodge R. and Kress, G. (1988) *Social Semiotics*, Oxford: Polity Press.

—— (1993) *Language as Ideology* (second edition), London: Routledge.

Hua Ming (1981) '*Ping "Zui ru hua cong"*' ('A Critique of "Drunk amongst Flowers"'), *Zhongguo qingnian* (*China Youth*), 19: 4–5.

Huang Kuangzhong (1980) *Nan Song junzheng yu wenxian tansui* (An Investigation into the Military Administration and Texts of the Southern Song), Taipei: Xinwen Feng Chubanshe.

Jenner, W.J.F. (ed.) (1983) *Fragrant Weeds: Chinese Short Stories Once Labelled as 'Poisonous Weeds'*, trans. Geremie Barmé and Bennett Lee, Hong Kong: Joint Publishing Co.

—— (1992) *The Tyranny of History: The Roots of China's Crisis*, London: Allen Lane.

Kraus, Richard Curt (1991) *Brushes with Power: Modern Politics and the Chinese Art of Calligraphy*, Berkeley: University of California Press.

Kristeva, Julia (1977) *About Chinese Women*, trans. Anita Barrows, New York: Urizen Books.

Leach, Edmund (1976) *Culture and Communication*, Cambridge: Cambridge University Press.

Lee, Ang (1994) *Two Films*, New York: Overlook Press.

Lee, Gregory B. (1996) *Troubadours, Trumpeters, Troubled Makers: Lyricism, Nationalism, and Hybridity in China and Its Others*, London: Hurst & Co.

Lee, Ou-fan Leo (1994) 'Two Films from Hong Kong: Parody and Allegory', in Nick Browne *et al.* (eds) *New Chinese Cinemas: Forms, Identities, Politics*, Cambridge: Cambridge University Press.

Lévi-Strauss, Claude (1963) *Structural Anthropology*, trans. C. Jacobson and B.G. Schoepf, New York: Basic Books.

—— (1966) *Savage Mind*, Chicago: Chicago University Press.

Leys, Simon (1977) *Chinese Shadows*, New York: Viking Press.

Li Ang and Feng Guangyuan (1993) *Xi yan* (The Wedding Banquet), Taipei: Shibao wenhua.

Li Bihua (1992) *Ba wang bie ji* (The Tyrant Farewells His Concubine), Hong Kong: Tiandi tuchu.

Li Charles N. and Thompson, Sandra A. (1981) *Modern Chinese: A Functional Reference Grammar*, Berkeley: University of California Press.

Li Cheuk-to (1994) 'The Postmodern Turn in Hong Kong Cinema', *The 18th Hong Kong International Film Festival*, Hong Kong: Hong Kong Urban Council.

Li Dejin and Cheng Meizhen (1988) *A Practical Chinese Grammar for Foreigners*, Beijing: Sinolingua.

Li Jian (1979) '*"Ge de" yu "que de"*' ('"Praising Virtue" and "Lacking Virtue"'), *Hebei wenyi* (*Hebei Literature*), 6 (June): 5–6.

—— (1981a) '*Shui niang de kujiu*' ('Who Fermented the Bitter Wine'), *Wenhui yuekan* (*Wenhui Monthly*), 8 (August): 54–7.

—— (1981b) '*Zui ru hua cong*' ('Drunk amongst Flowers'), *Zhanjiang wenyi* (*Zhanjiang Literature*), 6 (June): 29–37.

Li Jikai (1981) '*Ping Li Jian de jipian xiaoshuo*' ('A Critique of Several Stories by Li Jian'), *Wenhui yuekan* (*Wenhui Monthly*), 8 (August): 52.

Li Peiyuan *et al.* (1980) *Elementary Chinese Readers*, Book 1, Beijing: Foreign Languages Press.

Liang Shuming (1922) *Dongxi wenhua ji qi zhexue* (Eastern and Western Cultures and Their Philosophies), Shanghai: Shangwu yinshuguan.

Link, Perry (ed.) (1983) *Stubborn Weeds: Popular and Controversial Chinese Literature after the Cultural Revoluition*, Bloomington: Indiana University Press.

—— (1984) *Roses and Thorns: The Second Blooming of the Hundred Flowers in Chinese Fiction, 1979–80*, Berkeley: University of California Press.

—— (1987) 'The Limits of Cultural Reform in Deng Xiaoping's China', *Modern China*, 13 (2): 115–76.

Lui, James J.Y. (1967) *The Chinese Knight-Errant*, London: Routledge & Kegan Paul.

Liu Xun *et al.* (1981) *Practical Chinese Reader*, Book 1, Beijing: Commercial Press.

Lo, Andrew (1986) '*San-kuo-chih yen-i*', in William H. Nienhauser (ed.) *The Indiana Companion to Traditional Chinese Literature*, Bloomington: Indiana.

Louie, Kam (1980) *Critiques of Confucius in Contemporary China*, Hong Kong: Chinese University Press.

—— (1983) 'Between Paradise and Hell: Literary Double-think in Post-Mao China', *Australian Journal of Chinese Affairs*, 10 (July): 1–15.

—— (1986) *Inheriting Tradition: Interpretations of the Classical Philosophers in Communist China 1949–1966*, New York: Oxford University Press.

—— (1989) *Between Fact and Fiction: Essays on Post-Mao Chinese Literature and Society*, Sydney: Wild Peony Press.

—— (1991) 'The Macho Eunuch: The Politics of Masculinity in Jia Pingwa's "Human Extremities"', *Modern China*, 17 (2): 163–87.

—— (1992) 'Masculinities and Minorities: Alienation in "Strange Tales from Strange Lands"', *China Quarterly*, 132: 1119–35.

—— (forthcoming) 'Sexuality, Masculinity and Politics in the *Yingxiong*: The Case of the Sanguo Hero Guan Yu', *Modern Asian Studies*.

Louie, Kam and Edwards, Louise (1994) 'Chinese Masculinity: Theorising "Wen" and "Wu"', *East Asian History*, 8: 135–48.

Louie, Kam and Edwards, Louise (eds and trans.) (1996) *Censored by Confucius: Ghost Stories by Yuan Mei*, Armonk: M.E. Sharpe.

Lu Xun (1957a) 'The True Story of Ah Q', *Selected Works: Volume 1*, trans. Yang Xianyi and Gladys Yang, Beijing: Foreign Languages Press.

—— (1957b) 'Sudden Notions (6)', *Selected Works: Volume 2*, trans. Yang Xianyi and Gladys Yang, Beijing: Foreign Languages Press.

Luo Guanzhong (*c.* 1522; reprinted 1988), *Sanguo yanyi* (Romance of the Three Kingdoms), Volume 1, Taipei: Guiguan tushu.

McDougall, Bonnie S. (1990) Introduction in Ah Cheng, *Three Kings: Three Stories from Today's China*, trans. Bonnie S. McDougall, London: Collins Harvill.

McGeary, Johanna (1997) 'The Next China', *Time*, 3 March, pp. 26–34.

Minh-ha Trinh (1989) *Woman Native Other*, Bloomington: Indiana University Press.

Morton, Tom (1997) *Altered Mates: The Man Question*, Sydney: Allen & Unwin.

Palmer, Martin (ed. and trans.) (1986) *T'ung Shu: The Ancient Chinese Almanac*, London: Rider & Company.

Renmin jiaoyu chubanshe yuwen yishi (ed.) (1984–7), *Yuwen* (Language) 12 volumes, Beijing: Renmin jiaoyu chubanshe.

Roberts, Moss *(*1976) *Three Kingdoms: China's Epic Drama by Lo Kuan-chung*, New York: Pantheon Books.

Ru Zhijuan (1958; reprinted 1985), 'Lilies', trans. Gladys Yang, in *Lilies and Other Stories, Chinese Literature*, pp. 7–18.

Rubin, K. (1987) 'Keeper of the Flame: Wang Ruowang as Moral Critic of the State', in Merle Goldman *et al.* (eds), *China's Intellectuals and the State: In Search of a New Relationship*, Cambridge, MA: Harvard University Press.

Said, Edward (1979) *Orientalism*, Harmondsworth: Penguin.

Sampson, Geoffrey (1985) *Writing Systems: A Linguistic Introduction*, London: Hutchinson.

Schamus, James (1994) Introduction in Ang Lee, *Two Films*, New York: Overlook Press.

Schein, Louisa (1997) 'Gender and Internal Orientalism in China', *Modern China*, 23 (1): 69–98.

Schulz, Muriel (1975) 'The Semantic Derogation of Women', in Barrie Thorne and Nancy Henley (eds), *Language and Sex. Difference and Dominance*, Rowley: Newbury House.

Seagrave, Sterling (1995) *Lords of the Rim*, London: Corgi.

Shi Nai'an (*c.* 1350) and Luo Guanzhong (1980) *Shuihu zhuan* (Water Margin), trans. Sidney Shapiro as *Outlaws of the Marsh*, 3 volumes, Beijing: Foreign Languages Press.

Short, R. (1996) Report on speech by John Howard, *Australian*, 12 June.

Silverman, G. (1997) 'Hong Kong's 1997 Threat: It's Not What You Think', *Far Eastern Economic Review*, 15 May, pp. 80–82.

Spence, Jonathan (1982) *The Gate of Heavenly Peace: The Chinese and their Revolution, 1895 1980*, London· Faber and Faber.

Spender, Dale (1980) *Man Made Language*, London: Routledge & Kegan Paul.

Spivak, Gayatri (1990) *In Other Worlds: Essays in Cultural Politics,* New York: Routledge.

Sun Longji (1983) *Zhongguo wenhua de 'shenceng jiegou'* (The 'Deep Structure' of Chinese Culture), Hong Kong: Jixianshe.

Tan Huay Peng (1980–3) *Fun with Chinese Characters*, Singapore: Federal Publications, 3 volumes.

Tang Xiaobing (1993) 'The Function of New Theory: What Does It Mean to Talk about Postmodernism in China?', in Tang Xiaobing and Liu Kang (eds), *Politics, Ideology and Literary Discourse in Modern China*, Durham: Duke University Press.

Thompson, John (1986) *Studies in the Theory of Ideology,* Oxford: Polity Press.

Van Gulik, R.H. (1974) *Sexual Life in Ancient China*, Leiden: E.J. Brill

Wang Meng (1984) '*Qieshuo "qi wan"*' ('About "Chess King"'), *Wenyi bao* (*Literature and Arts Journal*), 10: 45.

Wang Ruowang (1979) '*Chuntian li de yigu lengfeng*' ('A Cold Wind in Springtime'), *Guangming ribao* (*Guangming Daily*), 20 July.

Wang Shucun (ed.) (1996) *Guan gong bai tu* (A Hundred Illustrations of Duke Guan), Guangzhou: Lingnan meishu chubanshe.

Wang Tian (1988) '*Hanzi jianhua baobian tan*' ('On the Merits and Demerits of the Simplification of Chinese Characters'), in Yuan Xiaoyuan (ed.), *Chongxin renshi hanyu hanzi* (Taking Another Look at Spoken and Written Chinese), Beijing: Guangming ribao chubanshe.

Whorf, Benjamin (1956) *Language, Thought and Reality,* Cambridge, MA: MIT Press.

Williams, R. (1986) *Keywords,* London: Fontana.

Wittgenstein, Ludwig (1971) *Tractatus Logico-Philosophicus,* London: Routledge & Kegan Paul.

Wu Naitao (1987) 'Intellectuals and Bourgeois Liberalization', *Beijing Review*, 30 (15): 21–2.

Xu Shen (1981 edn) *Shuowen jiezi* (*Characters Explained*), Shanghai: Shanghai guji chubanshe.

Zhang Xianliang (1989) *Half of Man Is Woman*, trans. Martha Avery. London: Penguin.

Zhonghua renmin gongheguo guojia jiaoyu weiyuanhui (1986) *Yuwen jiaoxue dagang* (Language Syllabus for Both Middle Schools and Primary Schools), Beijing: Renmin jiaoyu chubanshe.

Zhu Hong (ed.) (1991) *The Chinese Western: Short Fiction from Today's China*, New York: Ballantine Books.

Zhu Zhengming (1996) *Legends about Guan Yu of China*, Beijing: China Today Press.

Zuel, Bernard (1997) 'Rumble in the Bronx', *Sydney Morning Herald, The Guide*, 3–9 February, p. 2.

Index